US FIGURES

ARETH

P9-BJC-106

ORICAL JESUS FIGURES
4th Century A.D.)

SATAN: ANTI-JESUS FIGURE

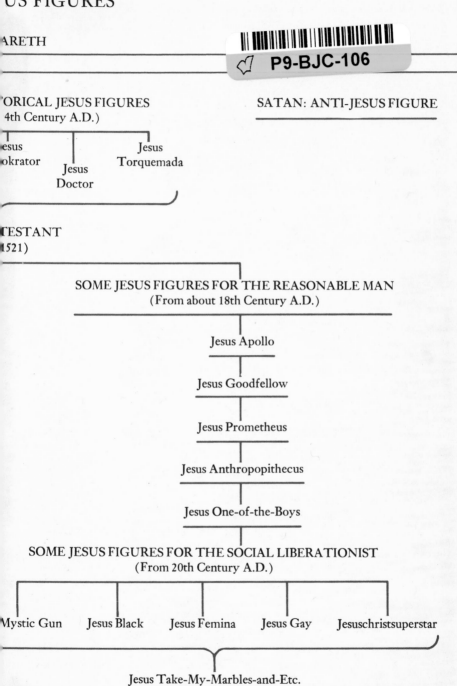

esus
okrator

Jesus
Doctor

Jesus
Torquemada

ESTANT
521)

SOME JESUS FIGURES FOR THE REASONABLE MAN
(From about 18th Century A.D.)

Jesus Apollo

Jesus Goodfellow

Jesus Prometheus

Jesus Anthropopithecus

Jesus One-of-the-Boys

SOME JESUS FIGURES FOR THE SOCIAL LIBERATIONIST
(From 20th Century A.D.)

Mystic Gun   Jesus Black   Jesus Femina   Jesus Gay   Jesuschristsuperstar

Jesus Take-My-Marbles-and-Etc.

JESUS NOW

Books by Malachi Martin

The Scribal Character of the Dead Sea Scrolls

The Pilgrim (under the pseudonym, Michael Serafian)

The Encounter

Three Popes and the Cardinal

Jesus Now

MALACHI MARTIN

JESUS NOW

232
M364

112502

LIBRARY ST. MARY'S COLLEGE

WITHDRAWN

E. P. DUTTON & CO. INC. | NEW YORK | 1973

Copyright © 1973 by Malachi Martin
All rights reserved. Printed in the U.S.A.
First Edition

No part of this publication may be reproduced or transmitted in any form or
by any means, electronic or mechanical, including photocopy, recording, or
any information storage and retrieval system now known or to be invented,
without permission in writing from the publisher, except by a reviewer who
wishes to quote brief passages in connection with a review written for inclu-
sion in a magazine, newspaper or broadcast.

Published simultaneously in Canada by
Clarke, Irwin & Company Limited, Toronto and Vancouver
ISBN: 0-525-13675-4
Library of Congress Catalog Card Number: 73-8272

Contents

Contents   vii

Preface

The men and women of America in the 1970's are no longer human in the way people were fifty years ago. Among them there is a new condition. They have no way of thinking about it; and they cannot put it into words. But they are increasingly aware that this new condition is rapidly making the past and all in it newly alien and unaccountably distant. We of the present generation will be the last ones capable of perceiving the difference between the old and the new. Shortly, there will be millions of Americans who will never have known the difference. As yet, even we notice and comment only on one of its side-effects: the constantly recurring dislocation of order, our malaise at surprise events. It is in the nature of America, due to its importance, to draw the rest of the Western world in its wake. Already the change has gone beyond American shores.

There is at work in the world of men and women a will of irresistible power creating a new circumstance in our society. It is the fulfillment of many men's dreams, but by unheard-of processes. Many, despairingly, read what is happening today as the action of some doomsday machine bringing beauty, happiness, culture, and all humanness to an end. Many more, unbelievingly, read it as an iron-clad natural process none of us can resist. Some, fear-filled, even see it as the plot of a summarily evil intelligence. But, in fact, it is the victory of gentle and transforming love which is being prepared, not the working out of some ungovernable whimsy of nature or, worse, the victory of some irreversible mechanism or diabolical hate that wishes most men and women to misery and chaos in this life and to the cold of eternal death once life ebbs from their bodies.

Love it certainly is, at work within the processes of the spirit; but love neither as a vaguely nice feeling nor as an abstract principle expressed in dreamy inaction, mental ooze, or steamy words. Nor is it a summons to febrile activism in search of relevance and identity. It is love as subsisting in the intelligence and the will of Jesus, while he works within the sequence of human events.

For this prime reason, at first sight most unreasonable, there is no longer any place in our society for the worship of any "figure" of Jesus as a source of unique salvation for all men and women nor for churches and groups that proclaim such a worship. Ever since Jesus was born and died over nineteen hundred years ago, there has been a long series of such figures, from Jesus Messiah in the 1st and 2nd centuries, Jesus Caesar in the 4th and 5th centuries, down to Jesuschristsuperstar in 1970. Romans, Greeks, Russians, Celts, Latins, Nordics, all imaged Jesus to their like. Jews formed their figure of Jesus; so did Muslims. Every new Protestant sect and church from the 16th century onward created its own Jesus figure. So did the professional atheists and convinced agnostics of the 19th and 20th centuries, as did the Jesus People and the ecumenicists of the 1960's and 1970's.

Today the most striking aspect in the matter of Jesus is that all these figures are being fragmented and, one by one, dissipated into nothingness. Every familiar landmark in the personal lives, and in the society around men and women is going up in smoke, disappearing from one year to the next, leaving no grace but intense longing.

This decline in the commanding power of the figures of Jesus is all the more arresting since, once upon a time, many men were convinced not only that they knew him, that through the prisms of these figures they could glimpse the radiant light, Jesus himself, but that he loved them and they him; and that he was an ever-living savior. In his name, millions regulated their daily lives as well as their private thoughts and their personal actions. And, hoping in him, they died. Millions more were put to violent death, either because they believed in him, or because they refused to believe in him, or because they attacked those who believed in him. Cities were built. Oceans were crossed. Empires were founded. Great art was born. Immemorial sculptures were fashioned. Imperishable literature was produced. All in his name. And, today, all that is seemingly ended. At first, not abruptly. Nor, as it were, by a sudden, crashing, vertical collapse into an unexpected abyss. But, imperceptibly, in a slow decline, a gradual decay.

Doubtless, for some diminishing millions of men, women, and children, a figure of Jesus is still granted a vaguely honorific position in their memories, and it enters automatically into their periodic praying. A Jesus figure is present sometimes in certain men's hopes, but not effectively in their ideals, rarely if ever in their lives as citizens, and still less often in the assertion and vindication of their dignity as individuals. At the crux of very big decisions and at the very important moments of death, life, and love, a Jesus figure is involved only sporadically, usually ritualistically, and quite often merely provisorily. "Dear Jesus, I am writing this to you just in case . . ." were Lucille's words in Frederick Buechner's recent novel *Open Heart.*

Jesus of Nazareth as he was and is is not given any practical importance or prime symbolism for human beings. In the Bernstein "Mass," the Chalice and the Cross—the prime symbols of Jesus—are smashed: nobody has really objected. And some time ago, Jesus not only ceased to be publicly acknowledged as important for the individual self each of us claims to be; rather, he now provides some extra food for our masochism. "This is my body. Take it. Eat it . . ." has been used at least three times in recent theater. Each time it referred to fellatio.

For the first time in many centuries, the death and not the life of Jesus is the salient factor about Jesus. And this death is not sudden or recent. Jesus of Nazareth, we know, died. His death was and still is an accomplished fact. The marked change in the attitude to Jesus today is the accepted note of human finality abroad, like an audience reluctantly acknowledging that dead silence has just swallowed the last haunting echoes of a beloved symphony, and that there is nothing more now than the cold and the immobility of a corpse. As with all dead and honored corpses, an ever-growing silence and the soft mercy of human forgetfulness envelops his image, his principles, his actions, and his memory.

In the hands of historians, the only stature conceded to Jesus —rather grudgingly—is meager and mind-shriveling. A man who lived at one time in one place. About whom we know a few sparse, insignificant facts. Of whom we have no flesh-and-blood picture appreciable to us moderns, as we conceive reality, beyond his name—and even that can sometimes now be given a mere orgasmic touch: "How come they called you Jesus?" wrote Lucille. "Jeeezzus sounds like it had vaseline on it to make it slip in easy." As a person of "unusual human significance," there are still some facts to discover and tabulate about Jesus, some more to sift and test, much more to puzzle us indefinitely, and still much more to discard daily and yearly. There thus seems to be a common conclusion at which large numbers of men and women have arrived surreptitiously. And the situation is precisely as if they had trekked to his tomb in the Garden and found that he was, indeed, dead; that, after all, his death had persisted; and that all their image-making of him as alive and triumphant had been empty figure-making. In earlier times, however distorted the Jesus figures were or became, through them men perceived a reality. But by now, the figures have become opaque; only the distortions look upon men who still seek reality and truth. Small wonder that there is little concern as the figures fragment.

But the fragmentation is of Jesus figures and is directly the action of Jesus. For he intends that his love and his creation of happiness be accessible to all men without distinction of color, of region, of culture, of economic status, or of the moment in time when a man or woman is born and lives. The figures are useless for this purpose. Most of them were chosen in view of a Second Coming of Jesus: Jesus had "gone away" and was going to "come back" on some final day. This was and still is plain myth; and the Jesus figures—refined violations of the First Commandment forbidding false gods—turned out to be the idols of that myth. Jesus is not going to return, because he never went away. Besides, all the figures, however fine some were in their beginnings, have ended up as mere distortions of Jesus' salvation which should have nothing elitist about it but which has been elitist from the start of Jesus-figuring.

As a multipurpose figure, Jesus became all things to all men: for white Western believers, a symbol of their superiority and a justification of their excesses; for Jews, a repellent figure replete with Christian hate; for Muslims, a supreme prophet, born of a virgin, second only to Mohammed; for Africans and Asians, a symbol of Western colonialism and power. What Jesus achieved and achieves became visibly identified with "Christianity." And this "Christianity" became synonymous and practically coterminous with white culture and Western civilization. All that had to end.

Like broken instruments, the various Jesus figures are now tossed aside as more than useless. And this has profoundly affected the mentalities that spawned them, the structures that would still fatten on them, and the men who are still mesmerized by them: all of the nostalgic ones with memories redolent of the incense, the Latin, and the triumphalism of past days; all those bent on making Jesus relevant by means of febrile engagement in social issues and political questions; the charismatics who would make the spirit of Jesus come in their day and in their way; those who seek a "democratic" solution to Church problems, as well as the Jesus revolutionaries who take it that—in the Maoist phrase —the spirit comes out of the muzzle of a gun; those who insist that Jesus is definitively dead and gone, as well as those who live in the shadow of his imminent "return." All are faced with the inevitable uselessness of any mere figure of Jesus they have chosen.

The process of fragmentation has gone quite far. Indeed, if in our human universe there were only the irreversible flow of time, then both those who mourned it and those who hoped for it would surely see the day when the figures of Jesus jostled with those of Moses, Buddha, Confucius, Mohammed, and Aurobindo for notice and place in the Hall of Great Men.

The most poignant and puzzling casualty in this situation is the individual, the human self, each one of us claims to be. The human self was always seen as a burning consciousness moving along an ever-hurrying and one-way line of time in space. It had a beginning in time and space: birth. And at death, the burning light of consciousness flickered and went out; the line went dead for ever. While living, the self was in bondage to its fractional line of existence together with the pains it involved, the failures it brought, the impotence it imposed, and the final negation it assured each man was his inescapable lot. And this is human bondage.

Along its line of existence, the self sought two kinds of knowledge: factual information and meaning. While facts were useful and necessary for living, meaning meant more than merely living. It was a signification, not only in facts themselves, but in the whole ongoing process of the self from the beginning of the line to its end and beyond that end. By means of that sought-after signification, the self hoped to obtain deliverance from the human bondage. And this is human salvation.

In this search for signification, there was born the moral basis for human actions: the human self would, should, act in this way and not in that way, if deliverance and salvation were to be attained. There were many models and archetypes for the moral basis: the Buddha Self, the Jewish Self, the Roman Self, the Muslim Self, to mention a few. For white Western civilization, it was the Christian Self. Over a long period that Self was figured in multiple ways, and always as an imaged archetype embodying the moral basis for all human actions and all human hopes. In that proliferation of Jesus figures, there were three principal Jesus Partners: churches and sects, who claim Jesus; the white nations of the West, whose civilization and way of life were originally based in a belief about Jesus; and the Jewish people, whose conditions of existence were, for a very long time, defined and worked out in terms of opposition to any and all figures of Jesus.

In the present terminal stage of the Jesus figures, we are witnessing a situation among men and women within countries and among individual countries and races, in which power of all kinds —corporate, economic, military, monetary, political, educational —is increasing gargantuanly, but without any moral basis either operative or even acknowledged. Any moral basis for human living and human action in the West was formerly gridded on the archetypal figures of Jesus. These figures are now proven inept; and the moral basis of power and of living they facilitated is eroded. Men cannot any longer agree even as to what the word "moral" means. In the practical politics of living today, the question is never: "Is this good or bad?" It is: "Does this increase or decrease my power, your power, our power, their power?" The figures of Jesus, the worship they inspired, and the moral basis they authorized have lost applicability in ordinary human lives.

At the same time, that individual self we each are seems to be more and more panic-stricken about one frightening possibility: that this self is nothing, has no destiny, is a mere process; that its only motto may truly be: "I function; therefore, I am"; and that corrosive forces are tinkering even with this process, forcing it inexorably to a repulsive extinction we know not how or where or when. Our ego panic drives us to look at everything, politics, sexuality, painting, sculpture, music, literature, clothes, food, outer space, as in a mirror. We become actors in a theater of longing, as we seek a reassurance that we are, we really are. Each one seeks for some suggestion or sign that he is himself and that he can be sure of his destiny tomorrow. At the maniac tip of this panic, we can even identify ourselves with some Jesus figure of our desperate fantasies: "I am Jesus Christ," sobbed Lazlo Toth, as he shattered the nose of Michelangelo's *Pietà*. "If you kill me, I will only go to Heaven."

In this morality vacuum, the most facile illusion becomes the most widespread and, in the United States, the most tempting for the individual. If that illusion had a voice, it would state: The very structure of your society and life in that society is baleful; all your science, every new technological advance, all your modernization hastens your end; corporate power, governmental control, urban living, and the homogenization of education, of goods and services, in the hands of an unseen, powerful, immune, and impersonal bureaucracy—all this is a vast, inescapable quicksand into which you, the individual, are sinking daily and irretrievably. Ah! to be in Nepal, Kabul, or Connemara, in Mallorca, Scotland, or the Samoa Islands, where an individual can still be an individual, where windows give on to man's true heaven, the skies smile down on real life, and magic casements still yawn invitingly on to wide plans and untrafficked seas! Each time your "progress" and your technology invade a still virgin human situation, each time merely marks another step in your corruption.

That is the illusion; but the truth is other. Nowhere is the individual more free than in the United States. And nowhere can he find the same opportunities for human living. Everywhere, not merely in the West, the human configurations of morality are fading, not because of science and technology, but because that which guided the use of science and technology, making them and everything else human, seems to be disappearing with the rest of our landmarks.

The source of this illusion is unmistakable. With the fragmentation and disappearance of the Jesus figures, the Jesus Self has no longer any convenient vehicles for our minds. Words, therefore, fail us. Faith is papered over with shibboleths. There are no referent images or figures valid for us, by which our ideal could be known mentally and verbally as living. Images have become things; figures are objects; they are no longer transparencies through which we see deep within us the truth that is imaged for our minds. Something substantive, it seems to us, has been withdrawn, some common persuasion that love stands behind all human things, that man is somehow in God's image. Without a living ideal, the human self feels lost.

Yet, within the optic of the Jesus Self, nothing more merciful could have happened to that former individual self and its self-made, brittle ideal. For that provided men with many reasons for wanting to die but no major and universally felt reason for living. The old ideal itself is skeletal, desiccated, fading, as impressive as bare bones clanking in the passing winds of time. And desperate minds in revolt have already picked away at any substance clinging to it.

The Jesus Self, however, is spirit, the height, the depth, the breadth of love itself, adhering to man and to his human universe. A strange, unusual concept for our modern minds, which often confuse love with benevolence and spirit with what is called the a-rational. Here is love, not merely a loving person; spirit, not simply a spirit. And the Jesus Self is not a straw thrown to a drowning man, not something tacked on to a miserable fate in order to make it bearable. It is personal and constitutional to each one of us. It infuses the history and the society of humans. It tells us that we never really wished to die, to be nothing. Maybe to be at rest. But not to die. And, after that, to know how all our going and coming could take place in spirit and in love. Not in view merely of our past, and burdened with the totality simply of our human experience.

This book is a journey through the quagmire of distortions, deformations, and illusions piled around our view of Jesus. It is a journey that continues through a society drawn in painful and constricted lines; where in reaction to the sham and the grossness accumulated in Jesus' name, men and women attempt a vision of themselves and their society that excludes Jesus of Nazareth and so excludes the Jesus Self each of us inexorably is. If that were the end of our journey, we would merely have arrived at the Land of Nowhere, a Planet of Banality. But the end is to arrive at the Word. The Jesus Self. Jesus. He who did not come in order to depart, and need not come again because he never went away. Jesus past. Jesus future. Jesus now.

DEFORMATIONS
AND
FALSE SEARCHES

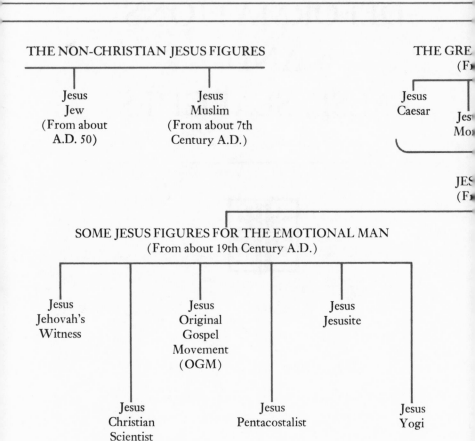

SCHEMA OF TH

JESUS

THE NON-CHRISTIAN JESUS FIGURES

Jesus
Jew
(From about
A.D. 50)

Jesus
Muslim
(From about 7th
Century A.D.)

THE GRE
(F

Jesus
Caesar

Jes
Mo

JES
(F

SOME JESUS FIGURES FOR THE EMOTIONAL MAN
(From about 19th Century A.D.)

Jesus
Jehovah's
Witness

Jesus
Christian
Scientist

Jesus
Original
Gospel
Movement
(OGM)

Jesus
Pentacostalist

Jesus
Jesusite

Jesus
Yogi

[JE]SUS FIGURES

[NA]ZARETH

[HI]STORICAL JESUS FIGURES
[abo]ut 4th Century A.D.)

SATAN: ANTI-JESUS FIGURE

Jesus
[Pa]ntokrator

Jesus
Doctor

Jesus
Torquemada

[PR]OTESTANT
[A.D.] 1521)

SOME JESUS FIGURES FOR THE REASONABLE MAN
(From about 18th Century A.D.)

Jesus Apollo

Jesus Goodfellow

Jesus Prometheus

Jesus Anthropopithecus

Jesus One-of-the-Boys

SOME JESUS FIGURES FOR THE SOCIAL LIBERATIONIST
(From 20th Century A.D.)

[Jes]us Mystic Gun   Jesus Black   Jesus Femina   Jesus Gay   Jesuschristsuperstar

Jesus Take-My-Marbles-and-Etc.

PART I
DEFORMATIONS:
THE JESUS FIGURES

1. The Great Historical Jesus Figures

Jesus Caesar

If Jesus of Nazareth were to appear in, say, Rome of the 6th century, Constantinople of the 9th century, Moscow of the 17th century, the Vatican of the 20th century, or Riverside Interchurch Center of this day and year, he would have a hard time identifying himself. However, identifying himself would not be his greatest difficulty. This would be that he would find no room. Jesus Caesar is already there, occupying the executive chair, sitting at the green-topped table during the board meeting, entering the sleek, black limo to be whisked to the airport, and signing the immaculately typed orders for the government of the Jesus imperium. Men were saved by Jesus of Nazareth. But the Church of Jesus is ruled by Jesus Caesar.

Jesus Caesar was the first of the really great Jesus figures in human history. The point is: power in itself, naked power, has everything—strength, domination, endurance, confidence, independence. Except beauty. Unless you just want to talk about the beauty we associate with the mammoth weight of an elephant herd or the quick lethal beauty of the tiger, that dreadful symmetry which Blake sang of in the forests of his dreams. Power is the beauty of the beast. And no man lies down with that beauty easefully, nor does he propose with impunity to cohabit with it forever. Power in itself is never winsome.

Now the secret of Jesus Caesar is that he unites power with beauty. Or at least that was the idea. Jesus of Nazareth, after all, had a great beauty, winsome beauty. Beauty of character. Beauty of moral ideal. Beauty of compassion. Beauty of love. Beauty of the merciful gesture, the consoling word, the enlightening solution. Beauty, above all, of a promised eternal homecoming. But in our world of realists, here now, was and is, Jesus Caesar uniting that beauty of Jesus with power. Beauty and the Beast.

What, in other words, was and is the use of all that beauty in a hard, hard world where might is always (well, nearly always) right? And how could Jesus of Nazareth live on in tabernacles of churches, if there were no one to pay the mortgage to the bank, no guardsman outside to shoot down invading robbers? Really, no use—for all practical purposes—unless you back it up.

Christianity made great strides when a mailed fist held the baptismal font. We, all of us, have grown used to savagery in the sacristy and to a smell in the sanctuary; used to the incongruous idea that Jesus and his Spirit are found only where material independence and power is found. Well. The Church has to live. The Pope must be independent. The Patriarch must have panoply.

The invidious will speak, of course, about politics in religion; about politicking clergy, Byzantine priests, Jesuitical ecclesiastics; and point out that this has nothing to do with Jesus of Nazareth. Perhaps. But it has everything to do with Jesus Caesar. His Holiness, the Patriarch of Moscow, is a marvelous example of an expert on Jesus Caesar. For, unbelievably, Jesus Caesar can survive a Soviet government which denies Jesus of Nazareth any position. While that is a tour-de-force example, in lesser but quite effective ways each and every clergyman who is committed to power (political, financial, sociological, cultural) in the work of Jesus, is serving Jesus Caesar.

True, today the house of Jesus Caesar is weathering an onslaught unparalleled in its history. The timbers of its roof are creaking, and it is filled with that uneasy feeling, that queasiness in the pit of the stomach, as when the quick air of an approaching storm first filters in silently.

Any onrush of the Spirit disturbs Jesus Caesar and his followers; but then they go crazy—take to politics, oppose the government, demonstrate—anything except take to the Spirit. Turbulence is exacerbated, fed by events. All the more, men cultivate Jesus Caesar. At least, they seem to be saying, *his* securities are visible, something solid you can rely on.

By now, they say (not exactly in a tone of justification, for they haven't yet been exactly accused), the message of Jesus is tied historically and therefore inexorably to Jesus Caesar. Touch him and you touch Jesus! Oppose him and you oppose Jesus! Besides, who finally makes the Church work? Not your nun saying her beads. Not the layman and laywoman with their sins and needs. Not the holy man, the professional Christian. But the operator who can clink his glass at the diplomatic reception, haggle over a portfolio return, and stalk the palace of the local dictator.

Jesus Caesar, in fact, has a program for the glory of God. But, for the love of the same God, he implores us, give the program a chance. Let us who understand Jesus Caesar get out there and work. Stump a little! If we use jet planes, cocktail parties, bank balances, and such like, so what? Have you a quicker way of moving than the limo?

This is the situation as long as the merely human environment is in control of human destiny. For there you will find no victory over dead works and mortal necessity, no resurrection and ascension of the human spirit. Jesus Caesar is included in the grab bag of dead works and mortal necessity. Only Jesus of Nazareth and his victory has liberated man in his natural environment so that he is no longer a puppet of circumstances.

The future, to be humanly endurable, must be the product of divine compassion and human response to that compassion. It is a course to be run, not by miles of computer tape and interoffice memoranda and interpower tracts, but by the running notes of human desires tied to the North Star of God's promise, as it was heard once on the lips of one man, Jesus, and as it exists perdurably today.

As the limo sweeps by, Jesus gazes out from behind the eyes of every human being loaded with the melancholy secret of human wasting and of human griefs, closed in upon themselves, inarticulately faced with the sheen of power. He is to be heard in the tones of every humanly touched thing; a violin, a baby's cry; the protest of innocence; the plea for mercy, and the desire for brotherhood and sisterhood.

Jesus Torquemada

As things went in the early years of the Church, another Jesus figure had to come to the fore. It was not enough just to be poor and simple, just to be humble, just to wait for the Second Coming of Jesus, or just to preach the doctrine of Jesus and to celebrate his salvation. Nor enough to have a sword handy to cut down the recalcitrant. What about the health of the mystical body of Jesus? I mean, the Church? Church members are still men and women, still subject to error of judgment, and open to wild fancies in ideas and in practice. Unity suffers when people do not say yes in unison and mouth the same syllables. In the last analysis, it is the mind and the will which must be kept clean.

Thus arose Jesus Torquemada.

The process was triple. First, there were ecclesiastics: men (only) who governed the Church and told you what to think and say, so that Jesus would be pleased. Then a new version arose: ecclesiacs. These were ecclesiastics who assumed a watchdog role in the areas of land, money, political power, and doctrine. Finally, there arose Torquemada characters embodying the principles of Jesus Torquemada. The rationale of Jesus Torquemada is uncomplicated: all corruption is bad, but the corruption of the best (Christians) is the worst.

Torquemada himself died in 1498, full of years, having decreed roughly 2,000 burnings at the stake and driven about 160,000 Jews from Spain as undesirable aliens. His name, Torquemada, etymologically has some meaning in Spanish. Torquemada, ecclesially, means accuracy of doctrine, unyielding conservation of revealed truth, a devilish nose for the slightest whiff of heresy and wrongthink, and an unflinching touch for punishing. All, of course, for the glory of God in Jesus Torquemada.

Torquemada at rest looks like Rousseau's child of instinctive natural goodness. Torquemada aroused is the anti-hero of your worst tree-falling nightmare or the most vivid drama of how bad is the corruption of the best. The Torquemada drama does not resolve itself in tragedy as a death struggle between good and evil. It is all-vibrant, with a perdurable irony as a sustained struggle between the two irreconcilable selves in any one of us: the good self and the evil self. Jesus Torquemada concentrates on making that evil self suffer.

It is worse than useless, it is untruthful, to think that the Roman Catholic Church has had a monopoly on Jesus Torquemada. The near history of Protestant sects in the United States, for instance, shows that they can almost claim a modern monopoly. And surely the world has rarely seen or experienced the solid stream of lies, denigrations, false attributions, libels, slanders, untruth, hate, invective, fear, scorn, and superstitious imaginings that, until quite recently, poured from the vitals of the champions of Jesus Torquemada embodied in the Luthern Churches in Sweden and in the Reformed Churches of Germany, France, Holland. Everyone was screened and tested for any trace of Romishness. Contempt was hurled like wet gravel in the face of anyone who did not adhere to their purity of doctrine. Their civil structures, their governments, their armed forces, their high societies, their private clubs, their public life, were presided over by Jesus Torquemada. In his name, they tortured and racked stride for stride with the Roman Catholics. Someone once said that an ardent Catholic, an ardent Lutheran, an ardent Calvinist, had one thing in common: they protected their little doctrines with an equally jealous hate and an equally vitriolic ostracism.

The truth is that today the common judgment on them all is: a plague on all your houses! Begone from the human scene, for you serve no humanly good purpose, and you long ago ceased to serve a divine one. But Jesus Torquemada is not banished as easily as all that. This figure of Jesus has served too well in too many ways and ages to be easily retired from the arena of men's claims to power and their scramblings for any piece of it. This figure of Jesus is alive and only too well in the 20th century city of man's folly.

The first manifestation of the Jesus People, if you please, is Jesus Torquemada. Everybody, except them, is rotten, corrupt, contemptible, lying, hypocritical. The first thing Mary Baker Eddy did and her followers do, the first thing John Smith did and his followers do, the first and the last thing the Jehovah's

Witnesses do is to conjure up Jesus Torquemada and in his name
decry all others as erroneous, outmoded, dangerous, noxious, diseased, prejudiced.

Torquemada is the living inspiration for the Greek Orthodox
priest who denies Holy Communion to the Roman Catholic
("You cannot have my precious little private Jesus"); he lives in
the heart of an Episcopalian member of the World Council of
Churches opposing Roman Catholic participation in W.C.C. activities ("We all know what the Catholics want"); he inspires the
mind of the Soviet-sponsored Patriarch of Moscow as he pietisti-
cally sets up an autocephalous American Church—"the better
to foment the Christian doctrine," says His All-Holiness from
Moscow—a statement that must make Satan laugh all the way
to Hell and the Angels weep all the way to Calvary.

But Torquemada moves not only among those who walk with
power in religious institutions. His masquerade is more complete
and he assumes a wierder grimace still, as he parades in the ranks
of a science that begins to claim all knowledge for itself and
brands all it cannot define or encompass as the new heresy; or in
the ranks of a technology which, spurred by such a science,
claims the ability and therefore the right to control us. Literally
to make us over in its own image. And Torquemada sits in the
chairs of media editors and politicians who define their thought
and values as unbiased and, for the glory of freedom and the freedom of men, banish the rest from the public forum, branding it as
unenlightened, as "obviously sectarian."

Jesus Doctor

The most beautiful expressions ever penned in Christian literature are affixed to the start of the Fourth Gospel: "In the beginning, was the Word. And the Word was with God. And the
Word was God." The most pejorative and, by now, the most injurious and burdensome element of Christianity is to be found in
the roles and role-playing that were evolved on the basis of those
expressions. Unfortunately, this happened quite early in Christianity's history. And, when you think of it, could it have been
avoided, what with the verbose Jews and the mentalistic Greeks
and the heavily logical Latins, who together crowded the early
Church? In fact, the figure of Jesus Doctor was inevitable.

The Jews were and are the People of the Book, of sacred words. The Greeks were natural fashioners of words and actually taught two millennia of human beings how to conceptualize. And this is not yet over. The moment someone has a religious experience, into words it must go, and into concepts it must fit. The Church must be reformed? The Churches must merge? The Church must be effective today? Write it down. Hold a conference and speak. Assemble a convention and dialogue. With millions of words and miles of paper. Jesus Doctor, in fact, emerges naturally.

The Christian start of all this, of course, lay back in a time when very few could read or write, when a great man like Charlemagne could hardly scratch his name, and when it was far easier to control the masses by using arcane Latin and Greek and Slavonic and Old Syriac words than by living a mystery and embodying a grace—things which of themselves molded, taught, and directed men's lives. Polysyllabic terms, composite phrases, sacrosanct tags, holy shibboleths, technical terms, became legal tender in the divine commerce of religion and authority.

Jesus of Nazareth had taught. With peace. With authority. With dignity. With regnancy. With healing power. With unifying effect. Every priest, bishop, minor cleric, consecrated nun, theologian, philosopher, preacher, parish priest, seminarian, became, or tried to present himself as, a reproduction of Jesus the Teacher. But being human, they became doctors of doctrine and not curers of the heart, dispensers of words and not ministers of the Word.

Jesus Doctor became the sign of priesthood (forget the sacrifice and the cleansing from sins), the proof of episcopal dignity (forget the pasturing of the sheep), the test of a true Christian (forget the holiness of life), and the strength of Christianity (forget the Holy Spirit). Easily, unconsciously, with the connivance of some and the stupidity of many, that Word which became flesh and dwelt among us was encased beneath the brooding domes of Western thought. Jesus became a definable entity, known by his doctor's cap and his teacher's colors. The wonder is that the Word was not smothered completely.

Still, for all their heaviness, it is not mere words and concepts that characterize Jesus Doctor. And it is not the congealing process whereby words used in the 3rd century A.D. by an ancient man must, willy-nilly, be used today. Rather it is that by some innate trick of personality, man more readily holds to the medium rather than penetrate and live the message. Jesus Doctor whispers in the ear of every formulator of belief. He sheds, not drops of blood, but words and concepts, whereby to save men. Even someone who leaves a Church will think and speak of himself or herself as a former Lutheran, a lapsed Catholic, a converted Jew, a free-thinking Greek. Even when they call themselves atheists, agnostics, or simply inquirers, the implication of thoughts and words is clear.

Jesus Doctor is a great one for the externals and their variation. The latest and most feverish activity of Jesus Doctor is to be seen in the rash of formularies, contracts, verbal agreements, joint statements, and paper beliefs churned out by the Churches for the last ten years. Jesus Doctor even travels abroad to do this, bustling about to Moscow, to Helsinki, to Rome, to Canterbury, to Geneva, to New Delhi, as if all that bustle made him more credible.

Specific instances lie all about us, in the new version of the Bible, of the Latin Mass, of the Creed, of the "Ave Maria," and of the "Our Father." The presumption is that new words will renew. A ludicrous instance is to be found in the new "Masses" (rock, blues, guitars, colored balloons, miniskirted altar girls, and ministers in sport shirts and skin-tight jeans). The ludicrousness lies in the efforts of men who in decrying words and formularies can find their best efforts only in the placing of another layer of formularies, all dressed up to the age, on all the old, ossified layers. In the end, just another addition to the heap.

Of course, Jesus Doctor holds his time-worn and traditional place in Roman Catholicism and in the Eastern Orthodox Churches. There are the Sacred Canon, the Sacred Tomos, the Philokalia, the Dobrotulubiye, the Fathers, and the Teachers and the Doctors. But the dilemma is here: the most ancient and, in principle, the most trustworthy of the Churches, those named above, are frozen in the creeds and concepts of their origin. The key to what those creeds expressed and those concepts mirrored is, exclusively, in the hands of the doctors, the Jesus Doctors. But, if Jesus was God and if the Church is his presence, he must have ensured that more than words would live, and something more alive than concepts would stay around to maintain the life of his Church.

Only two or three churchmen in our day have shown a consciousness of this reality, a realization that the Word has been frozen by men beyond all human melting. Two of them, Pope John XXIII and Patriarch Athenagoras of Constantinople, are dead already. One, Paul VI, has come lately to this realization. In their lives, John and Athenagoras were beyond contemporary history: they lived the Word; they found out that they could not minister it; but they refused to cede and adopt new words. Athenagoras realized that Eastern Orthodoxy was frozen into warring ice caps. John saw that structurally his Church was desiccated. Paul will change nothing except protocol and ceremony; for he knows that the deeper change is being wrought by Jesus, and that all other change would serve the interests merely of Jesus Doctor.

Actually, Jesus Doctor's day is almost done. For the sun is setting on the day of the human word. A later age will preserve our words in microfilm and on tape. Later generations who rediscover the value of human words and realize that the Word of God, Jesus, cannot be entombed in words, will record that the greatest punishment for the Western mind was to let it strangle itself on words and choke its life with concepts.

Jesus Monk

To understand Jesus Monk, you have to leapfrog over several recent social systems and religious ideals, all the while reminding yourself that once upon a time virginity was not considered a blotched incapacity, celibacy was not analyzed into oedipal complexes, and chastity had not yet been decried as psychological constipation. In fact, it was a time when men and women had no difficulty in getting together. No crisis of male identity. No question as to what a woman was. No man had to learn how to "relate to a woman." No woman had "to find herself." There was such a time. About one thousand years ago, to the year, it flourished. And Jesus Monk started to walk among Christians.

The ideal was fine. This life is short. Eternity is long. The more merit you accumulate here, the higher you'll be in Heaven,

LIBRARY ST. MARY'S COLLEGE

and the greater the crick in the neck everyone will have looking up at you. Besides, Jesus of Nazareth never married. Mary his mother was a virgin always: before and during and after his birth. Jesus' favorite disciple, John, was the only virgin, we are told, among his followers. So why, in effect, not renounce the pleasures of the flesh, enter a monastery, meditate, chant God's praises, and die full of years and full of merits?

This was the origin of Jesus Monk, a figure that took some hundreds of years to develop. The fact was that inherent in the ideal of monk and nun was the idea that Jesus was just about to come back like a thunderclap to punish the wicked and reward the just, and all human life in the world would be over.

It was way past the year 1000 A.D. (People in the last decade before that year expected Jesus on the dot of 1000 A.D. They even sold all their goods and chattels and waited for the end which never came.) When it was understood that he was not coming for at least another thousand years, a new surge came into European life. But by that time the religious orders of monks and nuns had been incorporated as an essential part of the Church of Jesus. They could not diminish in importance and a whole new outlook grew up. Before, to be a monk or nun had been to be as perfectly disposed as possible for the proximately expected heavenly perfection. Now, monkhood and nunhood became states of perfection on earth. Beneath monks and nuns came priests living in the world (monks and nuns had "left the world"), and beneath them were the ordinary men and women.

These latter creatures were in a hazardous situation. Not in a state of perfection, but constantly harried by sin and lusts, they were told to direct their eyes to the religious states of perfection occupied by nuns and monks. The latter's vow of celibacy was called a vow of chastity, as if non-nuns and non-monks were automatically unchaste. In fact, the love acts of married people were considered to be sort of permitted sins; and even down as far as the 20th century, theological students studied marital morality under the general title of *De Actis Impudicitiis* (The Shameful Acts allowed married people).

In Eastern Orthodoxy, there were monks and not nuns. In the rest of Christianity, that is in all Protestant sects, monkdom was abolished in the 16th century, alas not merely because of higher motives, but in reality for double-edged and very realistic aims; on the one hand, because nuns and monks had many possessions Protestants wanted; on the other hand, because some nuns and monks themselves simply wanted to marry and be happy ever after. It was a mutually satisfactory arrangement.

All this came to a logical head in the 19th and 20th centuries, when the ideal of Jesus Monk was most rampant. Jesus Monk was the ideal of the holy man (who became a monk) and the Bridegroom of the holy woman (who became a nun, of course). Only they could teach religious doctrine. Only they could claim that all their actions, eating as well as talking, drawing a blind, blowing their noses, dressing and undressing, were so many chits of religious merit and perfection. Writers like Dom Columba Marmion celebrated the singular glories of Christ the Monk. Sophisticated society liked to have monks in their drawing rooms and to have their girl-children "educated by the nuns," preferably in France, Spain, or Italy. Besides all this, the whole system of nuns and monks and religious was a marvelous source of economical man- and woman-power for the Roman Catholic authorities. On this basis alone, it is understandable that they are in favor of the "states of perfection."

But these states of nunhood and monkhood are ridden with difficulties today. Economic difficulties; personnel difficulties; and then some peculiar inertia: some blood or juice or, perhaps, some vital grace had drained away from the whole ideal of Jesus Monk by the middle of the 20th century.

Fundamentally, it must be noted, the ideal of Jesus Monk had implied certain things. Very little beauty and no gracious living, for one thing. There was something sinful, it was held, in physical grace, and something ungodly in a living style that had exterior satisfaction. More importantly, Jesus Monk did not allow thought. All initiative was in the hands of superiors, men and women. Provided that the nun or the monk obeyed, this was all. There arose, then, the idea that the religious superior represented Jesus, was Jesus by proxy. Many reproduced his gentleness, his compassion, and his love. Many a psychological harridan beat the mental joy and self-confidence out of trusting young women by claiming the authority of the chief Bride of Jesus Monk. Many a pathological abbot and religious superior got his own back on life by discharging on idealistic young men his neuroses, his psychoses, his hates, his fears of his own weakness, in the name of Jesus Monk. Much supposed religious decorum, meekness, tranquillity, sobriety, delicacy, inculcated in men religious as the "way Jesus is," was merely a reflection of incipient or latent homosexuality in superiors. Much of the hale and hearty "uncomplicated" behavior taught to women religious as befitting the Brides of Jesus Monk, was merely an expression of Lesbianism or unadmitted female chauvinism.

At any rate, in the Church of mid-20th century, it was felt, "religious life was threatened." So a cry was set up about the invading corruption of the "world," the corrosion of the Christian ideal, and the way in which evil was undoing an essential part of the Church of Jesus Monk. Monks and nuns were equally crass. Some left the monastery and the convent for footling reasons. Others stayed; but they unionized themselves, against the bishops or the Roman authorities, demanding their rights, discussing new dresses, acquiring personal bankbooks, drinking vodka martinis at 5 P.M., and going to see X-rated films.

But the authorities who so protested and the monks and nuns who so behaved were still, each in his or her own way, trying to preserve the old flashy ideal of Jesus Monk, that very special Jesus who made them so special. The authorities wanted their bread buttered on both sides. The monks and nuns wanted their cake and to eat it, too. Neither seemed to realize that a profound change in the human dimension had taken place because of what must be called the change in human affairs wrought by Jesus; that the concept of man, woman, priest, nun, religious observance, needed total reworking. Not, as is the craze, to discover new forms of ministry. And not, as is the danger, to make an unbridgeable break with the past. But to find what Jesus wants. For he wants the ministry of men, the service of women. But in his Spirit.

Jesus Pantokrator

To show us what Jesus of Nazareth looked like, we have no portraits, no statues, no mosaics dating from his lifetime. Still, for us his visual appearance and its representation is intriguing. There is one reliably very old visual representation of the *feeling* which his physical appearance deposited in men's memories. It is not so much a feeling of the physique of Jesus of Nazareth as of the physique of a Jesus figure. Jesus Pantokrator. The visual representation of that figure dominates the ikonic art and liturgy of all Eastern Orthodoxy—Greek, Russian, Cypriot, Cretan, Yugoslav, Rumanian, Bulgar, Georgian, Syrian. And that feeling was filtered, as a light, through the purple lattices of the Greek ethos, not hewn and placed irremovably by the lapidary touch of the Hebrew mind. Jesus Pantokrator, whether in Athens of the 5th century A.D., in Peking of the 8th century, in Kiev of the 11th century, or in Seoul, Korea, of the 20th century, is Greek of the Greeks.

Today, Greek means (for the ordinary mind) one of two things. Either the lyrical light of Sophoclean choral odes and the eternal symmetry of the ideal Hellas—this latter, by the way, a quasi-invention of the Renaissance Neo-Hellenists. Or an illogical mélange encompassing fabulously rich shipowners, poor flower sellers, powerful colonels, and classic isles basking in the sun. Jesus Pantokrator is Greek in neither sense.

No history of Greek ikonography will tell you so, but the "Greekness" of Jesus Pantokrator started on a small Mediterranean island, thirteen square miles in area. It is really a sickle-shaped volcanic plinth, rocky, bare, rising to eight hundred feet above the eastern Mediterranean waters. It is the island of Patmos. Sometime in the fall of 95 A.D., sixty years or so after the death of Jesus of Nazareth, a very old Jew named John was put ashore here in exile at the order of the Emperor Domitian. As a young man, he had known Jesus of Nazareth, was the latter's special confidant, took care of Jesus' mother when Jesus passed on, and spent over sixty years of his life in sweet indenture to the finely shaped molds of innerliness made possible by Jesus. John, the living soul of a Jew, became the life-giving spirit of a Christian.

With him to Patmos came that recorded feeling of Jesus. From John and Patmos it went wherever Orthodoxy went. It was new on the human scene. It had a life-giving spirit. It was "Greek" because Greek language spoke of that feeling, Greek hands depicted it in painting and mosaics, and Greek minds conceptualized it. But originally, before Byzantine trickery and Slavonic brutishness took hold of it, the humanly clean essence of the feeling was intact and the divinization of its mortality was translucent through the features, like sunshine through crystalline waves. John, within a grotto somewhere in that plinth shape, wrote the Apocalypse, saw God's brightness, and died. Then the morbid mortality of his successors froze the liquefied feeling into a permanent, almost schematic, unyielding man-shape. Hence Jesus Pantokrator.

Today on Patmos, in from the harrowing blue and light of the Aegean sky and its dazzling slavemaster, the Mediterranean sun, you are surrounded by large-eyed faces, The Forty Martyrs, St. George, St. Eudoxia, St. Makarios, St. John, and others, gazing mournfully out of the gray time clothing the walls of the grotto. Gazing not at you. Gazing through you and through the silver and gold votive lamps hanging from the ceiling, at the felt invisible presence of Jesus Pantokrator. Above, from the rounded dome there bends over the pygmied worshipers and onlookers the enormous and brooding head and shoulders of the Pantokrator, Christ the All-Dominant One. Always bearded. Always unsmiling. Always overpowering. Always Byzantine-faced. Always with upraised index finger and forefinger signaling power for the faithful and, with it, blessing; for the unfaithful an inescapable punishment.

There is a human trait noticeable in any genuine ikon of the Jesus feeling that came with St. John to Patmos. But the face is human torn awry by something more than human. It is mortality blown almost out of recognition by immortality. Always, one thinks of the reverse side of the cosmic clown. As if, by an alchemy unknown to the conscious spirit, that universal figure was, on one side, human, and, on the other side, divine. Somehow, the sadness is graveness, the magnetism is pathos. The clown's dunce hat, his awkward limbs, hooded eyes, spots, and bulges are lost in the hush of an audience who, because they cannot laugh ,for human weakness, must either weep or be silent at the majestic folly in divine love given to man.

The ikon, or representation, of this Jesus feeling was one thing. The Jesus figure as nurtured by Church authorities was and is something else. Ikons of Jesus Pantokrator took on a facile seriousness and a human pomposity sometimes outdoing, in artificially conveyed dignity, awesomeness, and power, the Pharaoh Tutankhamen, Abraham, King Sargon of Agade, Moses, Theseus, Ramakrishna, Julius Caesar, King Chandragupta, Pope Gregory the Great, Charlemagne, and Josef Stalin at the annual May Day parade in Moscow. These ikons were representations of the Jesus Pantokrator adopted by the various Orthodox Churches. Gone was the divine translucence. Gone was all compassion. Jesus Pantokrator was nationalized. For Holy Mother Russia (and all her serfs). For the glorious Byzantine Empire (and all its vassals). For the freedom-loving Cypriot people (with their assassinations and their libels). For the ancient nation of Egypt (and all the caviling of Coptic priests).

Jesus Pantokrator became the patron of powerful dynasties and the watchdog for warring princes. He told the poor to stay poor, the rich to get richer, the ungodly to get more ungodly. He sanctioned the oppression of people's minds by an ecclesiastical caste who had more pomposity than Egyptian dynasties and more moral tomfoolery than the Bourbons, the Romanoffs, and the Borgias combined. He sanctified a parochialism of teaching, a hating prejudice and a hateful xenophobia, and a myopia as crass as it was unchristian. He kept holy priests living on the naked edge of starvation, locked monks up in filth, physical decadence, cadaveric atmospheres, and humanly degrading isolation. Above all, he took political sides for the love of God, and he celebrated the mysteries of God for the love of Mammon.

He fathered a dark tradition of lying, deceit, plotting, envy, jealousies, assassination, seduction, entrapment, and human corruption such as the world has rarely seen and of which the world must finally be rid. There is no real difference between the prostitution of the Moscow Patriarchate to the Russian Politburo today and the whoredom of the Constantinopolitan Patriarchate with the Byzantine Empire in the past, or the total and freely adopted enslavement, chosen by the Anglican Church in the 16th century, to Henry VIII, to ease the latter's impotence and to satisfy its own desires for wealth. Satan must lick his chops in memory of all three. And in Christian terms, more Orthodox ecclesiastics must have died despairing and in blackness of soul than Orthodoxy would ever like to admit.

Yet, as always, this Jesus Pantokrator of the princes and the potentates has nothing but a flimsy surface to connect it with John's vision and his memory of that feeling. In little white-washed shrines on Samos, on Sifnos, on Chios, and on hundreds of other Greek islands, peasant women pray to him, and rough Greek men sail seas, work mines, dig the earth, because of what the Pantokrator promised once and guaranteed forever. When will their All-Holinesses and Sacred Metropolitanships and Eminences, Pimen of Moscow, Nikolaos of Alexandria, Elias IV of Antioch, Benedictos of Jerusalem, Ieronymos of Greece, Emilianos of the W.C.C., Iakovos of North and South America, Makarios of Cyprus, Paavali of Karelia and All Finland, and all the others, most venerable brothers, when will they stop their efforts to suck a bitter power from distorted ikons of Jesus Pantokrator and ask Jesus for light together?

2. The Non-Christian Jesus Figures

Jesus Jew

For Jews, the figure of Jesus Jew has had two interchangeable forms during the last sixteen hundred years. From about the middle of the 3rd century in the Christian era until about the end of the 19th century, the dominant form was what can be best described as Jesus-Jew-We-Fear. From that time onward, another form became more and more prevalent: Jesus-Jew-One-of-Us. Today, in the last decades of the 20th century, the latter is the most often invoked, although, when pressure is applied and fear mounts once more, the previous form appears occasionally.

Jesus-Jew-We-Fear was a formidable figure for Jews. The followers of Jesus gained immense power, and they used it unscrupulously to hound Jews in the name of Jesus; every Jew who suffered at their hands was made to feel this: "Because of Jesus you will suffer, until you have renounced your Jewishness." So threatening did this form of the Jesus figure become, and so great a symbol of destruction was Jesus as he was presented to Jews by Christians down the years, that within Judaism his name was proscribed, and a whole litany of evils, pejorative brandings, and near-salacious epithets were identified with him. All this obloquy

was directed to Jesus as specifically Jewish and as intensely dis-
liked by Jews.

The figure of Jesus-Jew-We-Fear was an object of genuine fear
on the part of Jews. "Measure my enemies' fear by the names
they call me," Talleyrand once said. By that well-used yardstick,
Jews described Jesus in great measures of fear. Jesus was Balaam
—the man without a people—because he had renounced his
people; he was an apostate, bastard son, necromancer, black magi-
cian, in league with Satan, son of a whore, the abomination of
desolation, liar, thief, traitor, blasphemer, Roman puppet, drunk-
ard, sent by evil spirits, gambler, ignorant peasant, unlettered de-
ceiver, false prophet, a Samaritan, corrupt, preacher of evil and
error, seducer of women and corrupter of men. And so on for a
long series of specifically Jewish denunciations which might seem
innocuous to the non-Jewish world, but which labeled Jesus of
Nazareth as a blight on human history, a vast error of twisted nature, and something the world could well have done without.

Of course, the entire history of this first form of Jesus Jew has
been marinated in the hate of centuries and of millions of people
on both sides. Jews hated Christians for their treatment of them.
Christians hated Jews as only Christians can hate—for the love
of Jesus. And this last was blasphemous and an act of indescrib-
able hypocrisy. It does not help now—except for those who re-
taliate revengefully for any wrong ever done—to recall that
Christian hate and persecution of Jews was originally a hate
given for a hate received, a persecution returned on former perse-
cutors. The historical record shows that the first religious hate,
persecutions, and pogroms between Christians and Jews were the
work of Jews against Christians. The Jews lost. And to the shame
of Christians and to the pain of Jews, this is the name of the
human game when compassion is stifled. But, in fact, neither
Christian nor Jew is engaged in such a purely human game.

The figure of Jesus-One-of-Us-After-All is quite different from
its predecessor. First of all, Jesus was thus reinstated—in one
sense. Actually, said New Testament scholars such as Joseph
Klausner, Jesus *was* a Jew: a simple Galilean carpenter-fisher-
man-peasant-pious-Essene-misrepresented figure. He lived obscurely, died rather peacefully, in spite of all the subsequent
brouhaha. No sooner in his grave, a band of apostates and tinker-

ing Greeks set about "projecting" his "image." There was more. Science was born in the 18th century. Between 1850 and 1960, new prophets walked abroad in the roles of Christian scholars and scientists; and the partial conclusions of some of them were taken as proving that Jesus was not divine in any sense, that he was just an ordinary Palestinian Jew of the 1st century. They further decided that all men were descended from chimpanzees, shellfish, and fluid hydrogen. Biblical scholars claimed to show the utter irreconcilability of the four Gospels, concluding a little hastily and illogically that therefore the Gospels were mere fiction. The Dead Sea Scrolls were taken as proving that Jesus was an Essenian and Christianity an Essenianism which succeeded. All became clear. Jesus was a Jew. Period. No need to fear him.

Then imaginative writers like Sholom Aleichem came along and cast a whole new role for Jesus in the setting of historical novels. Jesus Jew had the background, the sex life, the beliefs, the hangups, the accents, and the end of any Jew in any Russian *staedtl* or any Hasid bending and praying in a Polish *stiebl*. And Hugh Schonfield, master of the cryptogram gone awry, stated conclusively that Jesus was a Jew; that no one rises from the dead on the third day; and that Jesus was simply Jewish. Jews in modern Israel read Paul's letters and concluded that Paul had spoken as a Jew, a naughty one, an apostate, but, let's face it, a Jew.

The arrival of this second form of Jesus Jew was aided by other and related events which diminished Jewish fear of Jesus and of his followers. For one thing, there was a considerable turnabout in many Christians who began to feel terribly guilty. They were mindful of all the pogroms, persecutions, expulsions, killings, Good Friday whippings of Jews, and a long, blighting history which testified, not to love, but to a nourished hate and a taught contempt. There was Adolf Hitler and the German people—basically a Christian people in the Christian West. Many Christians felt that Hitler could never have gone as far as he did in his Final Solution were it not for the past anti-Semitism of Christians. Christian churchmen and Christians in Germany connived—at least by silence—at Hitler's persecution of Jews, until their own time came. Then it was too late. Pope Pius XII did quite a lot; no one questions that. But he did not do what he should have done; and that in hindsight is what counts. In fairness, let it be said that what he failed to do was, also, what many informed American Jews failed to do, as they sat in New York, Miami, and Los Angeles through the thirties, eating tref food and drinking tref drinks, assimilated to the Gentile world and quite happily so assimilated, until Gentiles like the stubborn British, expatriate Italians, and suffering Greeks started screaming murder. But, also in fairness, let it be said that there is only one Pope, and he claims to be the vicar of Jesus and to exercise a mandate of universal care for all men and women.

Then, again, after World War II, Christian ecumenism started with great impetus. This was a conscious and concerted Christian effort at least to reduce the tension, remove the pressure. And all were invited to participate. "Let's forget the differences. And let's do things together," said many Christians. A man called Pope John XXIII made sure that his Church issued an official statement (for differing reasons, many Christians and many Jews opposed it) to the effect that anti-Semitism is unchristian and that the Jewish race can in no way be called accursed by God. Catholics went to Seders. The Mass was said in Hebrew by some hardy spirits. Some Jews grouped together proclaiming Jesus to have been the Messiah (but not God, of course). Joint Christian-Jewish conferences and committees were formed, always to eradicate anti-Semitic elements from the official texts of Christianity such as catechisms, theological treatises, and so on.

To top all this, contemporaneous Protestantism, under the steady doctoring of Paul Tillich, Reinhold Niebuhr, Karl Barth, Rudolf Bultmann, and others, had reverted to a new emphasis on some Judaic elements of Christianity. Images and myths, for example, were said not to matter any longer to Christianity, as they had not mattered to Judaism. They were harmful and primitive. All religions were essentially the same, had great lawgivers like Jesus and Moses. The Sacrifice of the Mass became the *Abendmahl*, a lovely brotherhood supper, where you all feel good because it's good to feel good, because you are good, because we are good, because they are good, because God is good, and we're all good, good, good, good, good. "With anguish and concern," added Tillich apologetically, just like the prophet Jeremiah. "With your conscience as your only guide," chorused Barth and

Niebuhr, as good Old Testament scholars. "With a mind purified of images and myths," said Bultmann like a latter-day Moses announcing the first of his own Ten Commandments. "Within the secular city," reminded Harvey Cox, "and don't forget it's all holy, all of it." "For the liberation of the Third World," added the clergymen from the developing countries.

Furthermore, the problem of religion, as Martin Buber so convincingly put across on an impoverished Protestantism and a parched Catholicism, became the problem of the "I-and-Thou" relationship, how to get them together. For obviously the "I" belonged to the "Thou" and vice versa. It was a tailor-made problem for some modern minds and some minds in search of relevancy and modernity, who had been lovestruck by the personalism and ego-search of the age. Abraham J. Heschel suggested, in refinement of this idea, that the "I" (man) was not really looking for the "Thou" (God). On the contrary, the "Thou" was desperately in need of the "I." Now, God was at our mercy. And the emphasis was off Jesus.

In sum, a series of particular developments—Christian guilt and Christian ecumenism, scientific treatment and reduction of the story of Jesus, rediscovery of the historical Jewishness at Christianity's beginnings, the decay of Christian theology— coalesced in force to produce in Jews the second form of Jesus Jew. For the fearful aspect was removed from the Jesus figure; Jewish and human elements were reread into it.

The calming of fear in the Jewish mind was also achieved by the undoubtable and proven durability of the state of Israel. It had emerged, at the end of the sixties, militarily supreme in the Middle East, economically ebullient—if dependent—and enjoying a special status with the number-one superpower in the world, the United States. On the Jewish horizon, there was and is to date no threat from a civilization or culture built on the ideals of Jesus of Nazareth.

Whether it is Jesus-Jew-We-Fear or Jesus-One-of-Us-After-All, the deficiencies inherent in this way of thinking about Jesus are obvious. While it claims to be built on facts, it does not show the reality; and, although it purports to reveal the truth, it leaves no room for compassion. For, just as Jesus-Jew-We-Fear was a creature of hate, Jesus-One-of-Us-After-All is a figment of compromise. It leaves a gap in the mind where understanding should have flowed, and an ache in the spirit where love should have liquefied. It attempts an easy ending of the Jesus chapter in human life and Jewish history. And it decides all too quickly what Jews are in relation to Christians. It does all this on the ground of history and on the sociological bases of Christian-Jewish relations. It says: the facts are in; so calm down everyone.

At best, people do calm down. A certain quantum of hate has been extinguished. What remains is summarily unsatisfactory. It is that neither form of Jesus Jew permits Christian and Jews to see the face of the Jewish people, the face of the Jew, or the face of Jesus. All is lost in an awry montage—now taken as the sole facts making sense of the Jewish odyssey in history—of faces and grimaces which crowd in tumultuous anger, in regret, and in yearning around the Jew since the day he became the constant underdog of Christian Europe, down to and including the granite resolve of the modern Israeli citizen, soldier, statesman, politicians, and the new buoyancy of the American Jew. For, thus, the face of the Jew comes to us all, Jews and others, swathed in the sustained pain of centuries and of exile, in the still felt fear of total annihilation which Hitler inculcated, in the calculated drumming up of martial attitudes and a siege mentality, the acceptance of territorial expansionism as an alternative to submersion by hostile neighbors, and in the parade of competing symbols which promise security but never bring peace: a resourceful Moshe Dayan, a stubborn Golda Meir, an abrasively brilliant Abba Eban, an ever-victorious Israeli army which cannot afford one defeat, an ever-efficient Jewish lobby in Washington, a generous and ever-alerted American Jewry, and the position of power and influence which Jews enjoy within the American commonwealth.

But, clearly, there is within this montage a double artificiality, an *ad hoc* situation on two levels: on the level of Jewishness and on the level of Jesus. And both artificialities are intimately related.

On the level of Jewishness, no one will rationally claim that present attitudes can be frozen into a permanent character. No people can exist in permanent contention with their immediate neighbors; no nation can hope to make friends and achieve brotherhood with those it deprived of land, houses, and wealth; nor can one ethnic minority permanently influence the foreign policy of a modern world superpower; nor will human beings accept forever the status of guilty ones because of their forebears, and permit the descendants of those who suffered under those fore-bears a form of self-willed behavior which in any other circum-stance would be immediately labeled as rank arrogance. All these are obviously *ad hoc* circumstances, transient conditions. Until they pass, neither Jews nor Christians will be able to see the face of the Jew, hear his voice, or be enriched by his spirit. All three are, as yet, hidden behind that awry montage.

For behind it, and shielded temporarily by the iron grillework of defensiveness stained with the memory of pain, there is a voice of the Jew whose wisdom has been stilled for nearly two thou-sand years; and there is a face of the Jew whose beauty the world has not seen for all that time; and there is a perdurable spirit of the Jew which is surely the breath of God's lips and an inextin-guishable treasure for all men in this world who no longer need saving but merely a loving of each other in a savior already come.

On the level of Jesus, clearly, neither Jesus as a fearful person nor Jesus as "just like one of us" will finally do. But they will persist as exclusive alternatives for the Jewish mind, until all the stimuli of fear are muted, all the defiant gestures of victorious sur-vival are stilled, all the deep pain alleviated and melted in forget-fulness, all the surrogate arrogance mitigated to legitimate pride, and the desire for revenge is translated into human understand-ing. In the meantime, neither Jesus-Jew-We-Fear nor Jesus-Jew-One-of-Us-After-All corresponds as a figure to the reality of Jesus, the Jew from Nazareth: for Christians—savior, healer, compassionate God; for Jews—the strongest and ever-returning claimant to be the embodiment of Messiah and, at the very least, the most outstanding man they have ever given to us others in the scarred and soaring history of mankind. "Salvation is to be had among the Jews," remarked the hard-nosed Paul. He knew.

Jesus Muslim

In the world of today, Jesus Muslim is the most significant of the figures of Jesus, not because of the details in his profile, but because his birth and formation tell us by concrete example and most accurately about the history of love and spirit in Western Christianity.

There is, however, one very facile description of Jesus Muslim. It has been abroad for a very long time; it is the one which occurs most frequently to the non-Muslim, in particular to the non-Christian mind. According to it, Jesus Muslim is a simple adaptation from the Christian Gospel. The Prophet, Mohammed, evolved his doctrine in comparison with Christianity and Judaism, taking various elements from the Jewish and Christian Bibles. One of these elements was Jesus of Nazareth. But since the central piece of Islam was God's (Allah's) uniqueness, Mohammed could not conceive of Jesus as being God (Allah). Jesus, therefore, in this Muslim context had to be taken as a just man, as a prophet, and as a messenger sent by Allah, but not as Allah himself.

In this view, then, Islam is reduced to being an imitation of Christianity as of Judaism. And Mohammed is seen more as a firm and intelligent plagiarist than as an originally inspired religious thinker. Within this optic, and restricting ourselves to this view of Islam and its origins, only the above-mentioned interpretation of Jesus Muslim is possible. It is not a pleasant one for Christians or a consoling one for Muslims. It presumes that the origins of Islam as a faith and a religion were other than divine, and that Islam—as well as any other religious belief—can be explained on the basis of sociological developments and cultural interminglings between different people. Ruled out is any real possibility that the origin of living religious belief can or could be divine. In fact, it is presumed that the divine can be ruled out as a factor. And all this on the basis of scientific inquiry, historiography, and the cultural interpretations of men. But any accurate treatment of this figure cannot proceed on the usual present-day assumptions about religious origins and the "a-rational" character of man's religious faith.

The difficulty is further compounded by the historical developments of Islam and Christianity. Christians decided from the start that Mohammed had erred. The Jews took the same view. Both regarded Islam as an aberration. Conversely, it was a central point of Islam that Christians and Jews had both erred: Allah had sent Mohammed precisely because his two previous attempts to communicate his truth, love, and spirit to all men and women (the roles of Moses and Jesus) had been foiled by the corruption of those men and women. It was from this mutual presumption of error in the gravest of matters—God and his revelation to men—that there sprang into being the firmly opposed and exclusionary mentalities we find reigning officially in the three religions from the 10th century onward. Since then in history, the politics of Europe and the Middle East have provided all three religions with cultural accretions, personal attitudes, and dogmatic opinions which did little to bring understanding but did much to widen the gap between them. But there is a difference. Christians and Jews have been locked together one way or another since Christianity was first born; both have attempted to lock Islam into isolation.

Yet at this late hour in their development, Christians would do well to rethink the birth of Islam, its fundamental tenets, and the nature of religious belief they as Christians claim to possess. Christians need, then, to take one further step forward and have the courage to abandon once and for all the deepest of their negative persuasions. But this would be a momentous step. It concerns, not the essence of Christianity, of the message of Jesus and the quality of his achievement, but their (Christians') *understanding* of that essence, that message, and that achievement. That understanding has been encased, as spring water in a rock-bound cavern beneath the solid earth, in the thought and terminology of one cultural phase and age of man which started about the end of the 5th century A.D. and reached its culmination just prior to the European Renaissance, its peak expression being Scholastic philosophy, its visible symbol the temporal power of the papacy, its language Church Latin, and its interpreters the citizens and children of Western Europe. Even with the disappearance of many external trappings, that understanding is still so encased and so hidden. For Christians, willy-nilly, have had up to this point no means of talking about and no means of thinking about the original message of Jesus except in terms and thoughts provided by that one cultural age.

Reigning, therefore, between Muslim and Christian there has been hitherto a mystery of mutual misunderstanding, an inability to communicate to each other, not in the arena of mutually exclusive viewpoints and reasoned oppositions (*there* they have communicated), but in the free atmosphere of the sons of one god whose love for that god makes them recipients of that god's spirit. For the barriers between Christians and Muslims are all in the spirit. Somehow, for some reason, it has not been given them to start from love in the spirit and proceed to gain the spirit's light. The figure of Jesus Muslim is a distortion born of Muslim inability to compromise: they recognized that the Christian Jesus figures were distortions; but their failure lay in their inability to see the Christian spirit striving toward Jesus through these figures. The Christians, in a failure of Christian love, saw only the Muslim rejection.

This double contradiction in terms of spirit and love is at the heart of all religious difficulties today. We may, of course quite logically, stress how important the free choice of the individual may be in religious belief; we may lay down many provisos for the evil in man. But in strict observance of the law of love Christians professed and in accordance with their professed dependence on the power of the spirit, Jesus Muslim could not have arisen if Christians had relied only on love and only on the spirit—before Mohammed's time and after Islam became a living thing, from the first moment of their contact with Islam and before a confrontation froze both Muslims and Christians into warring camps. Mohammed was correct in saying that Christians had corrupted the way of the spirit and the love of God.

If, by the year 621 A.D., when Mohammed began his campaigns to establish Islam, Christians could not speak to him (and they could not) except in a language and with a thought which was intelligible only to Western minds, then the way had been corrupted. Mohammed set out, in the middle of a culture riddled with polytheism and containing isolated centers of Christianity and Judaism, to establish the worship of one god. Neither he nor his contemporaries were able to assimilate the Greek concepts of regnant Christianity, much less adapt themselves to the language and the domination of Greek Byzance—both constituted the price of entry into Christianity. Both were alien, and actually neither had anything to do with the truth of Jesus.

On the face value of what Christians said about Jesus and his divinity and his salvation, Muslims could not accept Jesus; already, that divinity came clothed in the raiment and regalia of more than one Jesus figure and, for the Arabian mind, lacked any authentic trappings of divinity. But Muslims could not reject Jesus or, for that matter, his mother, Mary the Virgin, or his divine mission. For those were integral parts of the spiritual experience of Mohammed. And so Jesus Muslim arose. Later theological and philosophical developments within Islam froze the Jesus Muslim figure. And the behavior of Christians only confirmed that stance.

The immediate tendency both of the modern mind in general and of the modern Christian "ecumenical" mind in particular, is to veer toward the idea of a plurality of diverse beliefs united in mutual permissiveness, a democratic "live and let live" path, a Christian polytheism, an acceptable and rather anodyne system of thought in which Abraham, Moses, Jesus, Buddha, and the other religiously inspired leaders constitute merely "several moments in man's quest for his destiny"—to quote one modern thinker. It is that, or a shadowy concept of universalizing all religions including Christianity and Islam into a new rationally based system. But the former has been tried with continuingly disastrous effects and an increasing decay of Christianity within the World Council of Churches; and the latter was attempted by a religious near-genius called Mirza Husain Ali (known to his followers as Bahaullah or "Splendor of God"), a 19th century Persian and founder of the Baha'i faith. Baha'i is a moribund organization. The World Council of Churches is a weakling sociopolitical organization. Neither has given birth to spirit and love.

Basically, there can be no solution of religious differences until Christians for their part come to their knees in the truth of humility, acknowledging that they do not know the truth, praying: "Lord, teach us, because we do not know and we do not understand. Give us your spirit of understanding." This is not an understanding that "we are wrong, they are right," much less "we are right, you are wrong, and here's how." It is an understanding of what Jesus was and is, and the power to communicate this, and a corresponding power of understanding in all who listen —including Muslims with their Jesus Muslim figure. But this power of understanding, in the spirit, the effective working of Jesus in humankind, does not mean an evacuation of Islam, a conversion of Muslims to Christianity. It means what Jesus signifies and it grasps what Jesus achieves.

3. Jesus Protestant, and the Dawn of the Great Age of Jesus-Figuring

Of course, with the stage set for proliferation of Jesus figures, the inevitable took place. In hindsight, it was to be expected. When you put Jesus Caesar in conjunction with Jesus Torquemada, with Jesus Doctor and Jesus Monk prancing around the wings, and Jesus Pantokrator gazing gloomily from above, the role in center stage is bound to be affected. When Jesus of Nazareth is fitted out with those figures successively, in combination, and in a stop-and-go rhythm, undoubtedly a severe dysfunction sets in throughout the whole drama. A deep inner sense of distortion and dissatisfaction arises in the players. And some of the actors in minor roles begin improvising. They feel they have to do something. I mean, to keep the show going. In time, Jesus is transformed again.

Now, this is approximately how Jesus Protestant was born. By the circumstances of his birth a changeling, Jesus Protestant is the one great historical Jesus figure which was born to shed other Jesus figures as a bitch drops a litter. Virtually every later figure was devised and developed on the basis of credentials stamped and sealed with the imprimatur of Jesus Protestant.

The Protestant Reformation of the 16th century has been generally represented as an idealistic revolt of the mass of the people against the corruption and authoritarianism of Rome. Jesus Protestant, therefore, is held up as a brave and heroic figure striking out for purity in doctrine, morals, politics, and religion. The practical reality of Jesus Protestant was not so simple. It was Jesus Caesar all over again; men in Germany, France, Holland, England, and Switzerland wanted to wield the power of Jesus Caesar and to enjoy the golden privilege that power entailed. But, without fidelity to traditional Church structure and authority, it took on tantalizingly chameleonlike possibilities.

Right from the very start (and throughout the whole charade up to quite recently), Jesus Protestant was two definite things. He was, first, anti-Pope and anti-Roman. Second, he was the special salesman and charter representative for a remarkable brand of personal freedom.

Whatever else he became (and he became many things), Jesus Protestant hated the "Red Lady of the Mediterranean." This hate was, when all was said and done, a very practical thing. It conferred on this Jesus figure an *envergure* which had never existed before. It was the apogee of the theater of Jesus figures, with thanks to a few master playwrights: Henry the Impotent VIII of England; the Virgin Queen Elizabeth I ("No more a virgin than you or me," sniffed the Irish pastor contemptuously); Martin Luther; John Pain-in-the-Soul Calvin; Philipp Goldlover Melanchthon; Huldreich Zwingli; a marvelous trio of fakes called the Zwickau Prophets. With that momentum as a base, it cannot be surprising that a whole new brood, a fast new generation, was quickly spawned, including Anabaptists, Socinians, Hugenots, Messianists, Hussites, Knoxites, Nicodemites, Remonstrants, Wesleyanites, Moravians, *et al*.

These quickly gained yet a new supportive cast of noble thugs, royal bastards, princely pimps, pure and impure Puritans (with a lust for the Crown), half-baked monks, nuns, priests (with feet firmly planted in this world), and ignorant burgers and peasantry (with empty bellies). In England and Germany and Holland, men wanted more. All wanted more. More money. More land, More power. More women. More. More. More. But, note! All for the love of Jesus and his Church. To purify the Church, no less.

They were, they said, testifying (-testant) only for (pro-) Jesus!

And for the purity of his doctrine. And they all had a rare old time writing the *Confessio Belgica* and the *Confessio Hafnensis* and all the other *Confessios*, tracts, denunciations, pamphlets, screeds, books, tomes, translations, disputations, philosophical cockfights, and what not: with burnings, counter-burnings, cursings, denunciations, excommunications, counter-excommunications, hatings, foul language, and booty and wine and women and song thrown in, for good measure, together with all those rich lands and real estate. Jesus Protestant was the goods! One can understand with a wry smile how right (and how righteous) Archbishop Ramsey of Canterbury was in his retort to the Romish question: "Where were you people [Protestants] before the 16th century?" His Grace, succinctly: "where was your face before you washed it?" He spat that one out like an offending fishbone from between his Anglican molars. That was a washing! And the net result: Jesus Protestant.

Second, as the special salesman and charter representative for personal freedom, Jesus Protestant urged: follow your own bent; your own conscience and mind are the only criteria you need follow. Everyone, in fact, could even have his own little dutiful Jesus figure who echoed his personal wishes, thoughts, and aberrations. The changeling character of Jesus Protestant, the very aspect which jammed open the floodgates of Jesus figures, began to emerge with considerable effect at this stage, although its full efflorescence was reserved for shortly later. Jesus Luther, with wide-eyed innocence, blessed Martin Luther's marriage with Katherine von Bora (herself an ex-nun), just as he loved the cannibalism in Pomerania during the Thirty Years' War; Jesus Luther, in fact, said to all: "Sin strongly! Believe more strongly!" Jesus Calvin had his eyes shaded into narrow slits: "Doesn't really matter what you do, poor devils," said Calvin's Jesus. "You're damned already or saved already." Jesus Zwingli told Zwingli to cut out all that nonsense about fasting, celibacy, and the Real Presence in the Sacrament: "A nice bit of bread," said Zwingli, "but spare yourselves the rest of the hocus-pocus." So it went.

As Jesus Protestant strode such easy and varied paths, he wore, at the same time, a special and specific mask: this Jesus, the Reformers said, was the original Jesus—before the Mediterrraneans corrupted him. Jesus Protestant was gleaned only from one

source. The Bible. He depended only on the Bible for authorita-
tive teaching. He was, therefore, naturally pure, noble, free of
evil machinations or sadistic cruelty or Romish superstitions. He
respected individual liberty. Holiness was his alone. But again the
practical reality was not so simple; for Jesus Protestant was heavily based on all the dogmatism and prejudice of Jesus Doctor—
minus any guarantee that he was not talking arrant nonsense.
He had the cruelty and inhumanity of Jesus Torquemada but
denied the victim Last Rites, Absolution, or after-death prayers.
They had thrown all that, or most of it, out the window.

First of all, the trinity of three persons in God caused trouble.
Things that are equal to the same thing are equal to one another.
The three persons are equal to "God"; therefore, they are equal
to one another. Therefore, they are identical. So you could be a
Unitarian and drop the trinity. Anyway, the trinity was a Greek
and Roman fantasy, they said.

Then the divinity of Jesus became troublesome, a hindrance to
pure faith. The Jews had not needed a mediator or savior—or
so they said; so why should we Christians? In fact, as a Protestant, you could and can believe that Jesus (1) was just a simple
man, (2) was just a very outstanding man, (3) was just a specially
chosen man, (4) was just a hallucinating man, (5) was just a
clever propagandist, (6) was just a son of God in a general sense
(we are all sons of God in a general sense), (7) was just an imaginary personage, or (8) was just God himself walking around on
two legs. It is a simple matter of multiple choice. And just as you
feel. No difference to your Protestantism in its purity, really.
After all, this is the liberty of the sons of God that permits it all
and all at once. Behold: the amorphous Jesus Protestant.

As you might expect, once the changeling character of Jesus
Protestant started to jell properly, the air sizzled for the next
three hundred years with a dazzling chorus of the must un-
dreamt-of figures. Like every good fireworks display, the thing
started off popping in what seemed a pretty lively manner,
though in reality it was moving only moderately by comparison
with what was coming. In addition to the variations introduced by
Luther *et al.*, there was a whole gaggle of others: Methodists,
Unitarians, Presbyterians, Covenanters, Shakers, Quakers, Holy
Rollers, Hussites, Dippers, Hutterites, Mennonites, Old Order

Amish, Pentecostalists. But it was more or less in the 19th century that the activity and excitement reached its first real pitch. There was one almost continuous effusion culminating in a New Thing.

Merely to mention the highlights will give some idea of the profusion. In 1830: Jesus Mormon. In 1831: Jesus Millerite. The world, William Miller said Jesus said, would end on March 21, 1843, then on March 21, 1844, then on October 22, 1844; when it didn't, the Millerite Adventists split into Seventh-day Adventists, Advent Christian Church, Church of Abrahamic Faith, and Life and Advent Union. In 1872: Jesus Jehovah's Witness. In 1875: Jesus Christian Scientist. In 1924: Jesus Foursquare Gospeller. In the 1950's: Jesus Pentecostalist. In the 1960's and 1970's: Jesus Shining Beauty (Kaguya Hime).

Of course, the next development one might have expected was something like an assembly where all the little Jesuses, old and new, could discuss matters like reasonable men. And, indeed, it was born. The World Council of Churches, mind you, is not there to replace Rome or Canterbury or Moscow or Constantinople or Jerusalem. It is a forum where all the members can come to proclaim deepest faith, to lambast their home governments with grandiose statements of principle, and to feel that they are getting together more in that way. Nobody loses a thing, really. Most interestingly, however, and changelingly, these church representatives as a group are transformed willy-nilly by this totally political process (after all, it could not be a church process, until after a vote to decide *which* church): the ayes have it. And if Jesus were not to like it, it would be clear that he was politically conservative and wrong to ignore the justice of the method. The cardinal rule is: nobody is wrong; nobody is right; we're all okay, brothers.

With democracy to replace the Word and the vote to replace the Spirit, several clear main figures are at last free to do battle —if not to lighten the souls of men; and each main figure, as in the heat of the fight, has thrown off its own series of figurelets. Such was the effectiveness of the appeal to personal fulfillment, such was the ease of change introduced with Jesus Protestant, that no total survey of the spectrum of changeling figures from this time forward is possible or necessary. The cameos that follow in succeeding chapters here and the family tree of Jesus figures are illustrative; and they do represent, if not exhaustively, the principal stereotypes, and graphically demonstrate the organic logic in the progression of succeeding "generations" of figures. Each serves less and less to bring man to Jesus, and more and more to fashion and refashion "Jesus" in order to fit the shibboleth of the day, to serve the showy, blowy banner of whatever special movement or passing quasi-philosophy might capture any segment of public fancy. Finally, not only is Jesus God absent from the succession of Jesus figures thrust upon him in his own name, but even man is absent from the ultimate paltry, gray figures. There are left only interchangeably wispy, dry concepts and causes. And that is the end, the final shattering, of all effective Jesus-figuring.

Chronologically, the first main group to spin off, once Jesus Protestant stepped forward and opened the floodgates of Jesus-figuring, was one which offered figures of a marvelous emotional effusion, figures fashioned for the needs and predilections of the man in whom emotionalism totally overrides the demands of reasoned progression; an emotionalism whose satisfaction is all the truth he needs or seeks. The figures chosen to represent this group, and to reproduce fairly the spectrum of its attributes, are: Jesus Jehovah's Witness, Jesus Christian Scientist, Jesus Original Gospel Movement (OGM), Jesus Pentecostalist, Jesus Jesusite, and Jesus Yogi.

As a parallel, but in no way overlapping the figures of the emotional man, there appeared a veritable string, or, aptly speaking, a bridge, formed of figures for the intellectual man (if one is not careful about the use of the term "intellectual"). These figures do not gather to themselves identifiable sects or groups of religionists of one particular stripe or another; rather these figures serve as intellectual rallying points for those who would deny Jesus altogether but cannot squarely face so crude an intention. Confusion between the requirements of faith and the great desire to fulfill the modern mania for scientific proof of everything brings us to the Jesus figures for the man who would fashion God after binary logic and bring Jesus better into line with what rational men "know" to be reasonably defensible. This is the bridge of fatal compromise.

Its first plank is most aptly called Jesus Apollo: Jesus emptied of whatever is divine and filled with nature, Beautiful Nature, with harmony and symmetry and comeliness. Jesus Apollo does not strain credulity, is sympathetic, and fills the senses with tangible beauty. It is then only a step to Jesus Goodfellow—the *sine qua non* figure of the Reasonable Man. He aims to please; and he will not freeze one into any mental or emotional stance which would be a strain. He's comfortable. Like old shoes. And he makes simpler the placing of the third-plank figure: Jesus Prometheus; when you have reduced God to near-human size, there is no reason not to reduce God's qualities as well, and then to appropriate them. You can figure out what to do with them as you go along. Once that is understood, Jesus Anthropopithecus finds his niche logically hewn in the string of compromises congenial to the "unfettered reason" of man; if you think that "reason" was "put together" slowly over billions of years by amino acids and chimpanzees with brain-circuitry feedback, Jesus Anthropopithecus is grotesquely heroic in its simultaneous denial of divinity and usurpation of divinity's claim to self-sufficiency. But even Jesus figures so reduced as these must serve the idealistic among us. And this is the function of Jesus One-of-the-Boys.

This figure embodies the total submersion of the divinity of Jesus, but provides us with the "if only . . ." concept of a slobbery egalitarianism projected over the whole of the world. All differences are ignored (to point them out is regarded as tantamount to name-calling, or is equated with prejudice; to be named as different is to be named inferior), but all individual liberty is preserved. "If only," this figure pleads, "If only we can find a common base which will prove that everyone is right without saying that anyone is wrong; allow for the affirmation of opposites; justify every regime; nationalize the universalities and universalize the particular; level and homogenize us all into a generality which nevertheless will neither submerge nor violate nor even offend any individual . . ." It is a United Nations concept of God, and looks toward the same fate as its more political model. But this is a concept. Purely and only a concept. There is no man who could live in so dry a desert, and no god who would shield it with the wings of his love.

Thus is completed the fatal bridge of compromise joining Jesus

Protestant and his august predecessors to the main Jesus figure of the 1960's and 1970's, together with its attendant figurelets.

Once man is clearly in the driver's seat of all creation, up pops Jesus Liberation. There is by now little or no God content in the Jesus figure. There is, however, total identification of freedom in Jesus with liberation of individual groups in purely material terms. We find in these now far-removed figures of Jesus a total justification for the actions and aims of the moment in the face of the particular injustice we are fighting. In none is there a quality specific or necessary or unique to a divine figure.

The figure that stands at the head of the line of Jesus Liberation, the heir of total rationality and the servant at the gateway of man's purely social needs (very legitimate social needs), is Jesus Bleeding Lord. Sacrifice is now symbolic only; men understand banners, seek charismatic leaders, smear blood, and devise events as rallying points; but men have been warned to strip away all messages of the transcendental as attempts to seduce their rational nature and subvert even the meager social progress already won. With transformation of divine reality into mere symbol in men's minds, and with man's modern fear of the transcendental, his hope in salvation becomes confused with his hope for fair civil treatment; and Jesus is transformed into figures that are at our beck and call, to fetch and carry whenever there is a tight situation and we can use another hand.

Following quickly on the heels of such a drastically emasculated figure is a succession of Jesus figures which bravely but sadly show us the face of sacrifice shorn of all possibility of the transcendent, of the divine, of the salvific; and exhibit for us the tortured and disgusting embodiment of mere symbol. The exemplary list of cameos drawn here to illustrate the Jesus figures who nod in deference toward Jesus Bleeding Lord as they sally forth to confront new and often achingly real social needs are: Jesus the Mystic Gun, Jesus Black, Jesus Femina, Jesus Gay, Jesuschristsuperstar, and Jesus Take-My-Marbles-and-Etc.

Finally, no family tree of Jesus figures would be complete without a nod of serious acknowledgment to the constant adversary, the offshoot of no figure, the eternal Jesus Anti-Figure, Satan. He prances in satisfied accomplishment at the end of this presentation of the stereotypes of all the roles and masks which

distort Jesus of Nazareth but are thrust upon him in his own
name. But Satan is separate from them. As intimately bound with
Jesus as they, only his bond with Jesus is totally negative, and he
alone invokes no name but his own.

Given the profusion of figures which have developed in fifteen
hundred years, one can safely suppose that, if Jesus of Nazareth
were to take part in a meeting of the World Council of
Churches, he would likely be given to understand that he is God
by vote of 89 to 70 with some abstentions, and that there is no
cause for him to be so authoritarian and highhanded as to send
messages through friends and apostles (and beware: the vote on
them comes later!) to the effect that we are right if we are with
him, wrong if we aren't. Voting on his admission, much less his
godhead, might bog down, on the issuance of such a haughty
statement, in political argument among the men in gaiters and the
men in purple and the men with beards and the men with coni-
cal hats and the men in serge. All advantage would be protected.
"Go and come no more," as Dostoyevsky's Grand Inquisitor told
Christ. "Come not at all. Never! Never!"

4. Some Jesus Figures for the Emotional Man

Jesus Jehovah's Witness

Some few hundred years after Jesus died, a simple dark-skinned Libyan called Arius found out what a mess had been made about Jesus by the light-skinned, white racists in Greece and Rome and by some renegade Jews. People around him, Arius found, were teaching that Jesus was God. They had forgotten the truth. They had been duped by clever little Paul of Tarsus and others. Thus, no one knew the truth: Jesus, a good Galilean peasant, had received a sort of communication or infusion from God Jehovah. He became Jehovah's agent, a Jehovah's witness. Arius started to correct the error. But the racists got Arius. Hounded him from Libya to Alexandria to Constantinople to Jerusalem and so on. You know how these things go. Condemned him. Finally, he died, probably poisoned. Jesus Jehovah's Witness became unknown again.

Not for long. In 1872, Pastor Charles Taze Russell of Pittsburgh, Pennsylvania, was touched and nudged by Jesus Jehovah's Witness. Said Russell: 1874 will be the year of Jesus' return, an invisible return. It was so invisible that no one, not even the good pastor, saw Jesus. But Jesus *would* come visibly, he said. In the meantime, he had come invisibly. And Jehovah's agents would be there to witness to this coming. And Jesus Jehovah's Witness himself would be establishing the Theocracy through his agents. That, my friends, is the new reign of Jehovah over this land and over every other land. In this reign, the sinful would either be reconciled with Jehovah or perish in the Armageddon (blood, thunder, rapings, burnings, lootings, strangulation, earthquakes, fire, floods, and what not). Who are the sinful? Why, those who are not Jehovah's Witnesses—at least that is part of the answer. For, on that last terrible day, only 144,000 humans from the entire history of mankind will be saved and reign with Jehovah. There are still 10,000 places open, say the Witnesses.

Said Russell: 1914 is to be Armageddon, "the end of the times of the Gentiles." It wasn't. As far as we know. But that does not matter, because the end is near anyway. As Judge Joseph Franklin Rutherford stated piously in the 1920's: "Millions now living will never die." Millions did die, of course: 25 million in Hitler's war; 20 million building Stalin's trans-Russian canal; 30-odd million in Mao's glorious liberation of Mainland China; 2 million Armenians at the hands of the Turks in World War I; and sundry other millions in Biafra, Bangladesh, Malaysia, Cyprus, India, Palestine, Ireland, Cuba, and elsewhere. And Judge Rutherford died. And Pastor Russell himself died on a train in Pampa, Texas, on October 31, 1916.

But there are some few billions still alive; the Jesus Jehovah's Witnesses are waiting and happy in their waiting. Jesus Jehovah's Witness, meanwhile, speaks through Russell's book (16 million copies in 35 languages), and in the 2,000 newspapers which published his weekly sermons. Today, the *Watchtower* has a circulation of 4.5 million in 68 languages and *Awake* has a circulation of 4 million in 26 languages. Daily, 100,000 books and 800,000 magazines are published at the international headquarters in Brooklyn, New York. All that financial success and the knowledge that there are jobs for all JW's in the Theocracy makes the waiting and witnessing more tolerable. Day in and day out, the message of Jesus Jehovah's Witness is drummed in: near-disaster of Armageddon. In the meantime, no blood transfusion; no war; no military service; baptism by immersion (no sprinkling or dunking or pouring or etc.). And, most importantly, everybody else is wrong. Peace is only in Jesus Jehovah's Witness. Only to be found in the Kingdom Halls where the JW's pray. There alone is the answer. It is either join or perish on the near day of Armageddon when the earth will become a paradise for the lucky 144,000. That is why, also, the Witnesses have developed their communal 1700-acre farm at Newburgh, New York, with 800 head of Hereford, Angus, and Charolais cattle; producing Cheddar, Swiss, Monterrey, and Limburger cheeses; feeding the 1,400 Witnesses stationed at Brooklyn Heights, New York.

But this means that approximately 210 million Americans are in the wrong (the figure of the doomed mounts with the population growth), together with a couple of billions of other human beings throughout the world. And being in the wrong in this story of Jesus Jehovah's Witness means something terrible. It is not a question of being of the wrong opinion or in the wrong political party or in the wrong country. It is being wrong in such a way that you are going to end up roasted alive, burnt, punished, dead, and stinking in Hell forever. When Jesus Jehovah's Witness says it's wrong, it is wrong, wrong, wrong. No matter how you love God or Jesus or your country or your wife.

If Russell were to rise from the dead (we need not count the number of days he has been in his grave) to stand beside Jesus in the working of such a wonder, the radiance of love and compassionate gratuitous welcome must melt us free of such a hammer lock of choices.

Jesus Christian Scientist

A lot of Christians (and non-Christians) are not going to like this at all, but very early on after Jesus had died and was buried (the divine part loaned to him by God went back to God, of course), the truth was lost. Jesus of Nazareth was a very good man. And there is no mystery about God at all. Roman Catholics and Protestants and others produced the Mysterious God syndrome. His mother, Mary, a no-nonsense sort of a decent woman, conceived the idea of God and called her idea Jesus. Jesus had, therefore, a divine selfhood. Of course, he suffered and died on the cross at Calvary. His divine selfhood did not. Actually, there was no value in his sufferings and blood. That is just more of the syndrome. Blood, like all material things, is evil. Jesus' included. Jesus rose again, because his divine selfhood taught him the Science. Now the Holy Spirit is this Science.

Jesus had practiced this Science during his lifetime, curing the blind and epileptic and working miracles. Only the Science (and health through it) matters. All this, however, was lost until Mary Baker Eddy was inspired by God to write the new Bible, *Science and Health*, in 1875. She founded the Church of Christ, Scientist in order to "reinstate primitive Christianity and the lost element of healing." Now, healing is the whole Christianity.

As we said, her book *Science and Health* is inspired. Just like the Bible. You cannot change a word of it. Everything else is unnecessary. It contains all you need to know. The whole purpose of Jesus in life was to teach the Science of healing. Healing cannot be accomplished except by faith. Only Mrs. Eddy's Science can teach you that faith. You must have her book (hardcover or softcover).

It's very simple, the Science. There is no such thing as matter. Only Spirit. But, still, people believe that matter exists. Presto! Matter exists. Such belief and the matter it makes (that is, all matter) are evil. All is evil but Spirit (including the matter of the actual book, *Science and Health*, its paper, print, cloth, smell, weight, price); all is evil. The different material things around you are merely different forms of your carnal mind. Thus you live in a dream-sense, Mrs. Eddy said; and thus you sin. Sick and sinning man is an illusion. Of course, he sins because he believes that the table is really there, that his leg is solid, that his stomach rumbles, that the girl has beautiful legs. Jesus, through his divine selfhood, taught us to disbelieve in matter. You need not be ill, therefore. Just believe that your cancerous womb does not exist. *Finito!* That impacted wisdom tooth? Forget it! (If you are not cured, you have not had enough faith.)

Mary Baker Eddy (1821–1910) was the chosen instrument of Jesus Christian Scientist. As a young girl, she heard the Lord calling her several times, sang her father's pigs to sleep with lullabies, married three times, had one son whom she rarely saw, and throughout her life had to cope with very poor health. She decreed that all churches and beliefs between her time and the time of Jesus Christian Scientist were false. Jesus never meant us to celebrate the Last Supper, to baptize children, or to use material symbols in worship. Some people have surmised that at least some of this came from her reading of many of the German Idealist philosophers. They thought that all matter was illusional; only some sort of *Ding an sich*, a peculiar bodiless blob, existed somewhere out there. Mrs. Eddy has much in her books that at times seems to be lifted straight out of those German philosophers. But perhaps Jesus himself pointed those passages out to her in the philosophers. Better still, Jesus Christian Scientist probably gave those passages to the Germans.

Strangely enough, Mrs. Eddy did not reject sinful matter during her life. She had a beautiful house on the outskirts of Concord, New Hampshire, with handsome horses, a rose garden, a fountain full of fishes, a pond full of bullfrogs, and an old picturesque farmhouse made of evil matter which she remodeled with more evil matter, which leads one to believe that evil is relative, depending on its form and suitability. And weren't all those bullfrogs and fish, the horses, and the fountain, the warm clothes she wore in the winter, all evil? Jesus Christian Scientist will perhaps explain this to us—as well as Mrs. Eddy's use of a special train for herself to travel in. Another material problem: the very pages and covers of her book and the money she earned from the book and the buildings she put up for her church, all those must be evil, too. Why, then, did her Church lobby at Congress (successfully) to get a perpetual copyright, which they still hold and in virtue of which they receive the royalties for its sale? Excellent sales, by the way. Isn't money bad because it is material? Not if it comes from the sale of Mrs. Eddy's book, evidently.

Jesus Christian Scientist has a lot of further explaining to do. Have you seen the marvelous new building complex which the Church of Jesus Christian Scientist is putting up in Boston? Acres of it. Go see it; and marvel that evil things can be so beautiful. For the mortar, stones, bricks, cement, steel, chrome, wood, staircases, telephones, elevators, carpets, furniture, all material things in that building are intrinsically evil. But it is a marvelous building complex.

The very paper of the *Christian Science Monitor*, a journal which Mrs. Eddy herself founded and which deservedly enjoys an excellent reputation for journalism today, is evil. Why print it or sell it? And all those funds, salaries, investments, real estate holdings, Christian Science Reading Rooms, libraries, and so on: all very, very evil. In fact, to apply Mrs. Eddy's thinking stringently: they do not even exist, except in disbelieving minds.

But all that would not matter so much in the long view, because Mrs. Eddy's interpretation of the Bible is like so many other mythologizations spewed out by Christians down the ages. It will be modified and brought into line merely by the passage of time and the victory of common sense in ordinary beings. And, to be fair and just-minded about it all, the appearance of Christian Science has revived an interest in the role of faith as a means of keeping a sane balance of mind and getting over illness.

What does matter and what is put in severe jeopardy by her Science is the essential meaning of Jesus, his life and his death. His real body and his real blood and his real life were liquidated as a proof of his love and as a guarantee that we can live forever. If this is not so, if nothing of all that matter of Jesus was real, then there is no salvation and no love. In that case, all of us non-Christian Scientists are missing out on something vital; and our constant prayer should be: Please, Jesus Christian Scientist, please (or, alternatively, please, Mrs. Eddy, please), come back and tell us how to succeed in using material things so well and so successfully, without believing that material things even exist. Tell us the trick. Otherwise, we are cheated not only of the sublimest thing ever offered to man, but also of the meager that is left without it.

Jesus Original Gospel Movement (OGM)

Actually, you may never have heard of the people who gave Jesus OGM a running chance. The first genuine trickle of Jesus OGM was detectable at Amherst College, Massachusetts, when Dr. Seelye was a freshman and Colonel Clark was a mere sophomore. This was in the early 1870's. Then the original sparkle shone again at Sapporo, Japan, in 1878: the Colonel brought that heavenly nectar all the way from Massachusetts. Today, in the early 1970's, the OGM is in full flower.

In the intervening decades, of course, Jesus nudged Sister Aimee McPherson. During the 1920's, she almost made it with the Foursquare Gospel; with newly burnished wings on the Holy Spirit; with a real return to the fire and brimstone and what not for all poor sinners; and with her radio station, magazine, books, lectures, and generous followers. However, people did not believe she walked in the desert with Jesus Foursquare Gospel (or at least they felt it was in bad taste to call her boyfriend that). And did not Sister Aimee herself tell us: "Do as I say, not as I do"?

But Ikuro Teshima was the man whom Jesus OGM finally nudged. Western Christianity had already been established in Japan. There was *Kyodan* (national Christian Church grouping; really a potpourri) and the *Muk-Yokai* (the No-Church). But Ikuro Teshima introduced genuine Christianity when he started the *Genshi Fukuin* (the Original Gospel Movement, or OGM as its members often call it). Christianity, Ikuro Teshima found out, is a Hebrew religion. Further, it is only to be understood by the Hebrew-minded, as Professor Uchimura (the second to be nudged) said. "When Christianity is stripped of its Western, Gentile and cultural elements, it is *very* Jewish," wrote Arthur Katz, another very keen OGM follower and a spirit-filled Hebrew Christian. At the same time, its members and followers call OGM the Protestant Third Force. (We are left to fend for ourselves in finding the First and the Second Forces.) And the OGM motto shows its genuineness: *Ichi-nichi Issho* ("One day, one life").

Going back to the Gospel meant, for the OGM, *finding* the *real* Jesus—that is, Jesus of the Original Gospel Message. This Message tells us that the Hebrew Jesus, Jesus of Nazareth, was a man, a good man, a simple man. Now the Spirit of the Christ (*Messiah;* that's Hebrew) took hold of Jesus. Jesus' ego was gone. Henceforth only the eternal life abided in Jesus. He was only the son of man (no capital letters, please). But the *Logos* (that's Greek) is God tabernacled among men through him. And all is clear. Jesus died, of course, on the cross. The Christ Spirit immediately took off and sat down again beside the Father's knee in Heaven. It is useless, therefore, to worship Jesus or God externally. Only in spirit and in the Spirit. And that, whatever anyone else may think, is the Original Gospel Message.

Now, of course, continues the Message, only the Oriental and the Hebrew mind can grasp this. This Jesus Shining Beauty,

Jesus Kaguya Hime, Jesus OGM, the masterpiece, could issue only from the real source of wisdom: the East. Westerners are so struck in the mire of science and greed and colonialism, only Japanese are able to receive the Truth. But there are a few from the West who are acknowledged to be enlightened ones: Otto Piper of Princeton, Swiss-born Peter Schmid, American missionary W. P. Woodard, Sassoon Jacoby of the *Jerusalem Post*, Professor Simon Ritterson, and some others. But in the Message itself you find none of those nasty intricacies which characterize Western legalism and philosophy. Pure thought, in other words. In contrast, modern Western Christianity only knows Christ who died on the cross. And what use is that? It only fits into a theory of Penal Substitution; but it accommodates no actual experience of being redeemed from sin and, above all, no encounter with the Spirit.

How different it all is with *Genshi Fukuin* (OGM)! The Tabernacles (the meeting places of the OGM people) are open to the Marvelous Effusion. OGM followers are baptized directly by Nature's unadulterated water (rivers, waterfalls, and the like). They pray; and, by Buddhist techniques, they raise themselves to ecstasy. "Mountain-top experience" is what they want. Joy, love, ecstatic prayer, levitation, utter tranquillity. They cure and heal by faith. They receive the Effusion from the sky. For OGM people have seen Jesus of the Original Gospel Message, as they stand in Jigaku Plateau gazing at sacred Mount Aso from Kumamoto Castle. They pray standing naked in the freezing waters of Nippon's most sacred river, Ise-Isuzu. They walk on burning charcoal and red-hot embers, believing, believing, in ecstasy, singing the mystical and exalted *haiku* of the poet Basho: "I know not / What Flower of What Tree; / But How Sweet Is Its Smell!" For the Incarnate Logos is full of emotion, say they. Didn't Jesus jump for joy, groan in spirit, weep, get angry?

One of the most recent memorable events of Jesus OGM was in July 1966, at Miya, Japan. The OGM conference. Thousands. All humming a weird melody reminding the crass Western newsmen of Isolde's *Liebestod* chant: a single cry for surrender and mystical dissolution. The Cherubim, no less, appeared in the night sky as Flying Saucers, triangular, rectangular, elliptical, square, sausage-shaped, round, all shining. At Hakone, July

22–24, another OGM celebration. On hand to partake of it all were genuine Hebrews: Israeli General Uzi Narkiss, Yaakov Lieberman, Chairman of the Israeli Community of Japan, and M. Bartur, Israeli Ambassador to Japan. The crowd of Japanese Hebrew Christians, filled with the effusion of the Original Gospel Faith, cried "*Shalom! Shalom!*" just like Jesus. They danced the *hora*, just as Jesus must have done once upon a time.

Perhaps it is not surprising, then, that Ikuro First-to-Be-Nudged Teshima called President Gamal Abdal Nasser of the United Arab Republic "the head of Satans" in a letter to all faithful OGM's. And he ended that letter with the Blessing of Jesus OGM, the Marvelous Effusion: "May the God of Abraham, Isaac, and Jacob continue to prosper and magnify this moment throughout Japan, the East, Israel, and all the world." All the world is fortunate to be remembered, even in the last place. But in the emotional effusion of the moment, where is Jesus? Or, alternatively, where are the Gospels without him, and where is the Original Gospel Message without him?

Whether or not you get the Effusion, there is clearly a large puzzle on the OGM horizon. It is nothing so simple as what the Rabbinate in Israel may think of all this. It is something larger, something still moving, still pushing outward. Early Christianity went through severe pains in order to escape from a Jewish backwater in the 1st century, to become available to Western man. Recently, Christianity is in an unparalleled upheaval, because its adherents realize that Jesus is for all men, not simply for Westerners. How, then, could Jesus really have meant all along that his religion be contained again, be primarily intended now for the Far East and for modern Israel? To try and make that the meaning of Christianity is like trying to put the toothpaste back into the tube. You have a real mess on your hands. You cannot wipe out two thousand years of Christianity simply by bathing in a Japanese waterfall.

Jesus Pentecostalist

Funny things happen when words go free from thought. "Mana-glub-glub kee do koo-koo slipwashtingo-feenless." This is (more or less) the authentic voice of the Spirit, of Jesus Pentecos-

talist, speaking through the tongue of Gloria Stilltoe Widdles on
the 5th of May 1971, in the middle of all the Sistern and Brethern
screaming hot lava out from souls and spirits, out along the ether
waves and waving, weaving, moving, moaning with the rhythm
of their tactile selves, their olfactory selves, their hearing selves,
their whole selves, just out, out, and free. And Brother Walter
Strathan Kehoe screams antiphonously: "Jesus C! Jeek u polsti
elkio ridpak ekegekgon parats umfo peeweeting gusa gua gura
kinch!" "No doubt about it," comments the Episcopalian bishop
to the reporters who asked his reaction, "the Spirit of Pentecost is
once again stirring Christians with the rapture of charismatic
gifts."

The point is: fifty days after Jesus "ascended into Heaven"
("fifty" is *pentecosta* in Greek), the Spirit descended on the disciples and apostles in the form of tongues of fire and they started to
talk "in different tongues about the wonderful works of God."
Glossolalia, they call it: speaking with tongues. But then came
the word-weavers: grubby little wordsmiths, thoughtsmiths, logic-
fashioners, hammerers of commas and colons and periods.
Locked out the Spirit. Froze our glossolalia. No more swooning,
eyes closed, zipping thrills. And, chiefly, no speaking "in different tongues about the wonderful works of God."

Then along came John XXIII, Pentecostalists point out. Jesus
Pentecostalist told him: "Heely foretodildy." Meaning: "Let my
people go, man." So John opened the windows of the Church.
And in flew the Spirit like a housebroken Picasso dove looking
for the toilet mat. And here we are. Glossolalia all over. Christians talking marvelously. Got right away from nasty logic, clear
enunciations, knowledge of the facts, all such bourgeois values.
The Church was a bourgeois buggery box, say the Pentecostalists. But now suddenly it's great. For years, the Church has been
unable to speak to the "kids" (aged anything from seven to seventy-
seven) and to the dollar-coddled suburbanites. And now: here
are the "kids" screaming blue bloody love in the language of
Jesus Pentecostalist and here are your suburbanites fixed in
frenzy.

Not only among the kids or merely in suburbia. Jesus Pentecostalist is all over. Wherever words are newly unintelligible. We
expect everything to be unintelligible nowadays. Pure and whole-

some passion (Mick Jagger) is the new grail, the goal, of Jesus Pentecostalist. Imprisonment of a convicted felon has become immoral. Conviction of a murderer has become politically taboo, and double hex on you if he or she is from a racial minority group. Where do you stop? Charisma is a red bulb winking on the fly of Tom Krane singing at Miami, so all the kids can scream with the outpoured spirit. The poignancy of a child-killing resides in the reporter's clogged nose. The Methodists vote that homosexuality is sacred. The only truth about a black convicted of murder is that he is a victim of white oppression. The priest turns to the people and intones: "Hi-ya! Jesus took the highest trip!" (instead of saying, "Hosanna in the highest").

Either they are so right and the rest of us are so wrong; or the Spirit of the Lord is at his best as a naked boy exorcising the people with his penis, and Jesus Pentecostalist can best be seen as he makes the goldfish on the bar dance the hula-hula. There's no more sense to sense. It is just non-sense within nonsense about nonsense.

Sense for Jesus Pentecostalist has become man's greatest sin. It has bound him in chains of slavish thinking and in the imperatives of words. And what are words? And what is thought? And what is man and woman? Jesus Pentecostalist replies (in jabberwocky): Questions are bad. Because thought is bad. Because words are bad. They swaddled my love and freedom with formulary bands. They strangled my purity with do's and don'ts. They made me kneel to a phrase and pray to a picture and fear a presence. Swallow a little wafer and pretend I'd become you, you me, us us, you all the others.

But let me tell you the secret: tune out of earthly language, open all the portals, hear all noise, smell all smells, become a living tuning fork for my Spirit. I, Jesus Pentecostalist. For if you feel it, man, you dig it, man. That's it, man. There's no more. That's all there is, man. And they have been keepin' you from it all this time. Burst and Jamesey-Joyce your way past barriers of flesh and rules and prickly hedgehogs of formality they've strewn across our path to happiness.

If the sins of the fathers are truly visited on the sons, Jesus Doctor's own true son is Jesus Pentecostalist.

Jesus Jesusite

Are you dying? Are you fed up with the intellectualized values of your parents or your elders or the boss? Disgusted at the waste of our environment? Hate shaving and bathing? Can't stand doing what you're told to do? In short, are you turned off this cesspool full of strangulated yowlers, desiccated with deodorants and mortgages, cosmetized with air conditioners, chrome religion, and scientific phallicism? Then, Sister and/or Brother, you are ready to be delivered. How? Jesus, man. Honk for Jesus. Be baptized in the Pacific at Corona Del Mar, California (loincloth, underpants, bikini, or nothing required), or in Lake Tahoe at midnight. Be renamed. Abner. Abishag. Kelija. Caleb. Shadrach. Deborah. Elisha. Shalheveth-Yah. Barnabus. Simon. Chronicles. Adonikum. Biblically. See? You become a Jesusite. And, man, don't get any phony ideas: this has nothing to do with Jesus of Nazareth. That's all old hat. But this is new! Jesus the Jesusite. The heir of Jesus Pentecostalist.

The idea of being a Jesusite is not new, actually. But today it makes great new noises, has bright new colors, and it offers a solution. It is all simple. Only one truth: Jesus loves you. Only one surefire prognostication: Jesus is about to return and end this human chaos called Earth. Only one way of worshiping: to speak with different languages in the Holy Spirit. Ik Ik Babou Go-Go Panank. Only one holy book or bible: the King James Version (KJV) of the Bible. Get both hands around it, and hold tight.

It is not sufficient to say you have not heard of Jesus or the Jesusites. They are all around: Hollywood and Sunset Boulevards, Dallas, Wichita, Washington, New York, Fort Lauderdale; in Bath, England, and in Essen, Germany; in churches, beat and pop operas, sidewalk theaters, underground cabarets, on posters, records, bumper stickers, sweatshirts, wristwatches, ties, buttons, shorts. Jesusites blitzed the pimps, prostitutes, and porno shops in Times Square. The Reverend Arthur Blessit, with his wife, four children, a wooden cross, a guitar, a tambourine, went Jesus-marching through Britain. There are Jesus love-ins, Jesus freak-outs, Jesus nightclubs, Jesus-lovin', Jesus-kissin', Jesus-rockin', Satan-Jesus-bondings (whatever that means), Nature cementing, hot-gospelers in topless bars and Jesusite sweeties in bottomless clubs. Read the invaluable Jesusite texts: Herman Hesse and *The Cross and the Switchblade;* they will tell you all about it. That God is love. That Jesus is coming imminently. Give me a J, give me an E . . . Praise Gods. Bless Yous.

And they play "Aquarius" from *Hair* in place of the Introit, and something like "Eleanor Rigby" for the Kyrie, at the Roman Mass. They blow gum for Jesus in New Jersey, prayer-huddle in the Cotton Bowl, preach at Texas strip clubs. You *cannot* miss it.

Care to see it all? See Jesus? Be a real Jesusite? Get to a commune, a family house: say, Love Inn, New York, or Coachella, California, or Solid Rock House at Novato, California. Or go over to Bill Bright's campus crusade ($12-million annual budget) and join the other 3000 sisters and brothers throughout 450 campuses. Lots of free bread. Flush those drugs down the john in the name of the Father, the Son, and the Holy Spirit. Read the KJV. Chant, babble, moan, jump, roll on the floor, groan, cry, laugh, whistle, eye-roll, shout. Wear a leather-fringed vest, long hair, flowing beard, sandals. Just like Jesus did.

No need to work, really. Work for the Lord and for your sisters and brothers: The Children of God (COG). And don't worry about the PARCOTOFROSAD, Parents Committee to Free Our Sons and Daughters. The COG have forsworn the world, the devil, and the flesh; they clapped a $1 million suit on the PARCOTOFROSAD, plus a $300,000 suit against Texas officials.

Inside you, of course, man, you new Jesusite, you! Inside, you are going on a Jesus trip. No thinking. No requirements. No rules. No restraints. No accountability. No elders. Nobody who disagrees with you. No limits. Nothing but love. No hate. Except for the systemites—you know, anyone who's not for us and supports the system, any system. You will have push-botton forgiveness, instantaneous innocence, stunning end to your guilt, immediate cessation of all your self-disgust. But for the love of Jesus, read no Bible but the KJV. Forbidden are Krishna, Subud, Yoga, Zen, I Ching, the Zohar.

Men have tried to Jesusite their lives before this. But forget that. Just recite the litany. For this is all you have for your inner thoughts. "Thank you, Jesus. Thank you." "Gonna join you,

Lord." "We're knocking at the gate, Jesus." "Oh, praise Jesus, brothers and sisters; oh, praise the Lord." "We're no longer under the thumb of the world." "Gonna rise right up out of slavery, Jesus." "Gonna sit on God's throne."

On the other hand, Jesus, as far as we know, was not sickeningly bigoted, self-satisfied, intolerant, hysterical, spinning around in fantasies. Nor a panhandler. Nor a streetwalker. And it is all very fine to say: "Hey, man, I've turned on to Jesus. Gimme a dime." But if you surrender your mind voluntarily to other powers; if you proclaim as your mind a state of mindlessness according to which there are no rational solutions to human problems; if you see reason as the root of all our evil; then why not go the whole way to Utopia? Like Hitler. Like Castro. Like Stalin. Shoot the "others," the wahoos and the yahoos in Congress, in the Senate, in the colleges, in the churches, in the unions, in big corporations. Whoever they are: Kennedy, King, Jackson, Wallace, another Kennedy, everybody and anybody. Carve out that great big new world. Or shut your eyes and wish it all out of existence. Do this long enough, and when the Public Health Authorities, the Welfare People, PARCOTOFROSAD, or the whole lot of them finally get to you, Jesusite, you will be a polypus, a human vegetation whose only reaction is suggestibility. Nobody who understands you really blames you for revolting against what has been served up as reason, as religious ideals, and as personal discipline. For one was given you as the product solely of a pseudo-intellectualism, another as a series of man-made figures, the third as a pseudo-science of psychiatry and psychology. And none of them revealed to you warmly that you could think because you are loved, or that you could love because you can hope, or that you could hope because all human thinking, hoping, and loving went beyond the materiality of mechanisms and the hysteria of an attempt to escape from mere physical facts.

Jesus Yogi

Jesus Yogi, long since disappeared into the All-Nothing, has silently reappeared in our day, but invisibly. "Buddhism expresses the theology of the Father, Hinduism the theology of the Holy Spirit, and Christianity tells about the Word," said Brother David

Steindl-Rast to Fellow Ecumenists. And Sister Maria, Discalced Carmelite, has a *mantra*. All her own. Swami Satchidananda gave it to her. Her personal prayer chant. "You see a cup shape; I see an empty space within roundness," Swami says, smiling pityingly. An annual Yoga Ecumenical Retreat is held in Connecticut. Try it; you'll like it. We are finding ourselves in the All and the Nothing once again. Maharishi Mahesh Yogi, who disappeared into the dustbin of contemporary show biz in 1968, has reappeared, and this time the All and the Nothing have ceased to compete in his life. Heading his SIMS (Students International Meditation Society), traveling around in a sleek Mercedes and a helicopter, the Maharishi can claim 100,000 international members, dozens of offices in the United States and Europe, a vast plan for 350 centers, very substantial corporate funds reportedly lodged in Swiss banks, and a definite vogue for his aim of "freeing the nervous system of stress and achieving bliss-consciousness." It was all or nothing for the Maharishi.

Now, let us go back, and, in the language of devotees and adherents, see how it all started. In the beginning (and before that), there was the Nothing of the All. And the All was all of the Nothing; the Nothing was the nothing of the All. And it was over all. And under all. And through all. Throughout nothing was all. Stupendous tranquillity! Soundless. Seamless. Except for the "day of Brahma" (4,320,000,000 years in length) and the "night of Brahma" (4,320,000,000 years in length). That is: the Cycle, the *kalpa*. *Kalpa* after *kalpa*. Imagine an immeasurable number of sausages laid end to end immeasurably. Vishnu sleeping on the cobra Shesha, who in turn sleeps on the cosmic ocean. The Lotus sprouting from Vishnu's navel. Brahma from the Lotus. The universe from Brahma. Man continually plunged by *samsara*, reincarnation, in those miserable *kalpas*. His only hope, to get to allness in nothingness: *Mukti*, release. But, still, the Nothing and the All were supreme.

All should have been fine. Nothing should have happened, except more of the same. For then the All would be nothing. And nothing is all there should be, so that there be nothing but me and my navel, and you and your navel, and us and our navels, and the Swami and his navel and his bankroll and his straw pants. "I have the mind of an absolute idiot," wrote Lao-tze.

LIBRARY ST. MARY'S COLLEGE

As said, "nothing" should have happened. In India and the Orient, over in the West, the All-Nothing would have had its own day. However, the best-laid plans of mice and men . . . Some things did happen: the Jews happened; Paul of Tarsus happened. To cap it: the Western mind, the Greek-Roman-American mind with the industrial-military program and the Pope and Wall Street happened. That was something. You see: it ruined the Plan.

There had been a Plan. To achieve the maximum nothingful purity of allness all over. First in time, the seeping wisdom of Vedas, Upanishads, Brahmans. *Saindhavas* they called themselves; Hindus to us Westerns. It was the era of "Holy Spirit." None of those Christian, Picasso-like doves with light bulbs in the wing feathers. This was purity and highest achievement. And so what if the Hindus had human sacrifices, or fed their infants their own urine, or never found penicillin, or never performed a caesarean?

Then, still in the first stage, Lord Buddha rises, lives, transits to completeness, completest nothingness in allness. This is the era of "Father." Still marvelous, if it weren't for the Jews. The Semite is a figment-maker, a sniveler in a desert of apothegms and mono-gods and single ten commandments and the lot. Distortion! Yahweh, Jehovah, Adonai, The Name. Riding on a chariot of clouds. Roaring with the thunder. Flashing his eyes in the lightning. Whispering in the wind. I ask you! Can allful nothingness do that? But worse: "he" (male, if you please) wept, scolded, threatened, repented, spoke of love like a wooing, swooning, swinging swain; he ranted and raved like a ravished cow; he protected with his right hand, cut down his enemies with his left hand (and we know what people did in those days with the left hand). Worse still: historicity. A beginning, a middle, an end. Can you imagine 4 billion times 500,000,000,000 *kalpas* laid end to end, and then multiplied to the nth, and still having a beginning, a middle, and an end? Semites could, or said they could.

To rectify this anthropomorphological, clay-figurine-flesh-and-blood-and-thunder, this Heaven-and-Gehenna godlet heresy, there was the second stage of the Plan. There came out of the All an emanation of extreme allness in nothing, of nothingness in all. More than any crouching guru or masochistic boddhisvatta. More than Lord Buddha 'neath his Bo tree. More than anything, because really the allful nothing. Jesus Yogi, the supreme flaking off the All Nugget. It was the era of "Word." Now the "trinity" is complete. But in appearances only; not as a "babe" with a mother and a father. Not as a "man" talking, walking, sleeping, dying. How can you crucify an emanation? Jesus Yogi just entered back into the All-Nothing. There was no crucifixion. And all this was done in order to tell us where our true home was: nowhere in the All of Nothing. Immediate *mukti* for you all!

Then what happened? Well, Saul of Tarsus, Paul, happened. Christianity happened. And that was an entire *megilla*. Clever stunted little Rabbinic Paul, with his game leg, with his sting of the flesh and his finessing overlay of Greek subtlety, with his eternal fussing and yelping at Jew and Gentile about what a marvelously privileged little great vessel of election he was. Jesus loves me in particular, says he to the suspicious Christians; have a care! Gamaliel taught me, he said to the Jews. I'm a Roman citizen of no mean Roman city, said he to the Romans. Your philosophers spoke of my Jesus, said he to the languid Athenians. "There are many hard things in Paul," wrote poor old Peter wryly.

Paul rampaged all over the eastern Mediterranean from Antioch, Syria, to Rome, Italy, pouring out written and spoken words, worrying the philosophical bones of Greeks and Romans with Biblical metaphors, flaking Jewish minds with Biblical scorpions. He was an unrelenting gnat on the rump of the world. Finally they crucified him upside down on the Appian Way, to be rid of him. But not before he had transformed the sylphlike wordless Jesus Yogi into a caricature, a veritable Western monster: an overpowering ecclesiastic corroded by caesaropapism, bristling with theological armor, loaded down with wounds and blood and cross and sword and blinding glory. Jesus Yogi became, in Paul's hands, a successful Prometheus. Paul changed spirit into matter and thought into crass actions. Paul taught that if the fire Jesus had stolen did not purify you, it frizzled you up. It lit the way for a long trail of earthly enslavements and sanctified Torquemada's bloodthirstiness. You know the rest. But what a fire! What a Jesus! He and his Christianity "is the only cause of atheism," states Yogi Jesuit Pannikar. Any further talk about Calvary, or redemption in blood, or the Communion wafer, or Baptism, or sin, or Hell-fire, or Heaven, is useless. Well, use it if it helps. But get to a swami as fast as you can and bring your credit card. And do it before he has a stroke, or dies of heart failure and has to be buried by three days because his body will smell and he is not going to rise from the dead after the three days. He's a man, after all.

It is all illusion, I know. But my nose doesn't like the illusion, and I can't help my nose. When my appendix ruptured, I hummed my *mantra*, like Sister Agnes and Sister Maria. But they gave me sodium pentathol and used a common knife to "save" me.

In the meantime, is there a person somewhere who will love me personally and forever? All Jesus Yogi seems to do for me is smile and make sounds. Koan. Mondo. Satori. OMMMMMMMMMMMMMMMMMMM.

"With every gust of wind, the butterfly changes its place," Swami murmurs with downcast eyes. The original sense is nonsense, obviously. Common sense is a cover-up job. Jeeeesus Yogi!

5. Some Jesus Figures for the Reasonable Man

Jesus Apollo

For a long time after Jesus of Nazareth departed, there was no beauty in the Jesus figure. No esthetically pleasing lines. No attractiveness limned in balance grace of limbs. Neither liquefaction of eyes, nor warmth of hand clasp, nor sheen of hair, nor symmetry of stature, nor satin weave of skin. To adapt a phrase of William Blake's, there was no comingness together of inner form and outer shape. The words of Isaiah about the Suffering Servant fitted all the Jesus figures: "The world stands gazing in horror. Was ever a human form so mishandled, human beauty ever so defaced . . . No stateliness here . . . No majesty. No beauty, as we gaze upon him, to win our hearts . . . A leper wounded for our sins . . . A sheep led to the slaughter . . . A lamb dumb before his shearers . . . Imprisoned. Judged. Carried away. Numbered no more among the living."

Then, about sixteen hundred years later, by some inner mechanism of spirit, forth comes Jesus Apollo. Apollo not as Mouse-God, nor as Ridder-of-Grasshoppers, nor as killer of the lovely youth Hyacinth, as the ancient Greeks fabled about him. But as the sun of humanity and the brightest flower of its physique. The

most beautiful of the sons of men, as they say. Standing, striding,
looking, speaking, in the Renaissance painters' images and the
shapes of the sculptors. The paradigm of beauty for Michelangelo's Adam and Raphael's angels. Only with the arrival of Jesus
Apollo could Popes build St. Peter's and lavish beauty on religious cult. Only in the name of Jesus Apollo could a Christian
humanism be attempted. For Jesus Apollo walked the country-
side of man and with him all men could hear the mystery sung
by birds and cloaked in the quiet shadows of eternal trees that
bent their heads to histories of man's eternity on earth, his summers on the snakeless meadows and his nights on the oarless seas.
And this was all fine, until the kiss ate man's flesh, the luring
summer tempted his eyes, and the glory of shape gave man the
pride of life. (But that was long after.)

But this Jesus Apollo did not arrive like a thunderclap or out
of the blue. Before his arrival, to pass from reasoning about Jesus
to intuition of Jesus, you had two stark choices. Two streams.
One flowing from the East told of Jesus and God in terms that
evacuated humanity and stranded it in a frozen instant of eternity
trapped in time. The mysticism of Palamas and of Dionysius the
Areopagite, the tortured beauty of Augustine, and the metaphors
of Jerome. The other came from the brooding North: Piers
Ploughman and the "brutish bane of boneless life by God"; Ju-
liana of Norwich forever nodding in accepted ignorance; " 'Twas
love that did it"; and "the high and the next way" described in
the Cloud of Unknowing; the mystical ethos of Antwerp's Had-
ewych and her divine troubadour; the "ghostly tabernacle" of
Ruysbroeck; and the "spark of the soul" described by Meister
Eckhart. It was all rather lugubrious, spiritually steamy, and left
many adherents examining their breasts, buttocks, bellies, and
genitalia for intimations of mortality, and panting for beer, beef,
and bed—just to be human again. Jesus at Bethlehem was still a
little man-child already judging you. On Calvary he hung, over
against a sunless sky, like a bloody dishrag scoured of fiber. It was
all too much.

John of the Cross provided a third and human way of intuiting
the entire scope of Christian salvation. By a very simple transition, not of fact, but of plane of vision. As simple as saying: They
have told you to see God in everything? See everything in God.

The humanity of Jesus became an intuition gateway, not a veil of flesh to be pierced by nails of executioners and the love of adherents. He became the summation of all human beauty, a vehicle for the existential encounter between man and God in this world *before* the next world.

This pure teaching of John became, in the hands of others, a theology of Jesus the man-God as Jesus the All-Beautiful Savior for all men, rich and poor, sweaty and clean. Humanly, that Jesus was so pleasing! He still remained in men's minds as the Son of God, but the stage was set for change, when the religion of the All-Beautiful Son of God was converted into a humanism of Jesus Apollo. In quick-fire succession, Jesus the All-Beautiful ceased to be a divine savior, ceased to be really God, and became a plastic figure submissive to any molding. Many cultured people needed a Jesus Apollo: a beautiful, ideal human figure with no disturbing overtones. Thus was made possible, for instance, the idea of the gracefully accomplished "gentleman" of the 19th and early 20th centuries, the liberally educated citizen of John Henry Newman's University—gentle in success, charming in failure. It provided Thoreau and Emerson with their fundamental justification for a first-personalism that rivals the egotism of any lunatic pleased pink with himself. And Jesus Apollo found an echo in its most lyrical celebrant, Gerard Manley Hopkins, singing in his pain of Jesus crucified and "the fire that breaks from thee, then, a billion times told lovelier, more dangerous, O my chevalier," of Jesus triumphant as "the hero whose heaven-handling flung me, foot-trod me," and of Jesus his God as "my hero."

But Jesus Apollo, by now far removed from what John of the Cross taught, and so at home among the men who had created him and cherished him, never walked in the sweatshops of Birmingham, the child factories of London, the ghettos of New York, Paris, Rio, and Berlin. Jesus Apollo, in fact, was an elitist for the elite, for the genteels. He was absolutely beautiful, if you had time to find beauty in a rather specialized paradise created by grinding the faces of the poor and in an age of factitious innocence and irresponsible romping of the few at the expense of the many. It was all the fantasy of a few foisted on the many who bled.

Besides, Roman Catholic humanism itself failed, even in its narrow place, because clerics, even with their power of yea and nay, cannot judge poetry, make good prose, or ensure fine painting. And Protestant humanism slipped into rank atheism and materialism, because politics and imperialism mix badly with religion, and because empires were built on dead native bodies. And Eastern Orthodoxy never had a humanism. And in the end, too many women and children were made victims by powdered admirers of Jesus Apollo; and Jesus Apollo did not advocate a living wage, decent housing, voting rights, or care for the aged.

And in the beginning, Jesus was savior before he was beautiful. Jesus Apollo was another fake.

Jesus Goodfellow

The figure of Jesus Goodfellow was really much more democratic than Jesus Apollo; and, while he was everybody's in general, he was nobody's in particular.

As his name goes, so goes Jesus Goodfellow: he is, well, simply a good fellow. Understanding, I mean. And flexible. A lot of people went around for a long time wielding big sticks and talking big: Jesus says you've got to do this or else! Jesus says you've got to do that or else! They put men and women and children into strait jackets, locked them in little watertight compartments and sent them zooming off to eternity capsuled, silenced, debilitated, and, above all, wounded in their personal liberty.

The first time that Jesus Goodfellow came into effective operation was in the 16th century. Martin Luther, Henry VIII of England, and a lot of other suffering personal human beings had found out that Jesus Goodfellow was not at all above permitting a little looting of monasteries, a lot of marriage for the clergy and nuns ("It will aid us to spread the Word of God," they said; it did not, really; the narrow Roman Catholics, with their crunchback celibate priests and nuns, beat all Protestant sects put together in their missionary work over the space of three hundred years), and a lot of fancy footwork around local wars among princedoms and about rather valuable possessions. With this lesson in front of them, some men discovered Jesus Goodfellow and proclaimed him as such. A lot of age-old hacks had described Jesus as God—with the Father and the Holy Spirit. But the fresh thinkers found out that Jesus was just a good fellow who had lived some sixteen hundred years before and died rather a pious death. Some hotheads put across the idea that, even as such a fellow, he was the divine son of God; but the most rational minds said that Jesus was and is really just a very fine man and a model citizen, a good fellow. No "reasonable" person needs more than that.

The chief and best point about Jesus Goodfellow is, of course, that he puts no strain on the credulity of our eminently reasonable minds and none at all on the credibility of our world. For this is where other Jesus figures went badly awry. Faith was the essential coinage. Not so in the story of Jesus Goodfellow, which most people know.

It is an interesting story, even a comforting story. Why, when George Stevens bent all the talents and skills of the motion-picture industry to portray his life—the Greatest Story Ever Told, he called the film—even then, it was no more than a great story. What greater proof? And like all good human stories it ends in the peace of heroic death and the resonance of an exemplary life. The heroism and the tragedy of Calvary are not blurred with what Jesus Goodfellow can only regard as a feeble epilogue of that happy ending, the "resurrection." The whole affair ends like an old-time Western: Jesus putting away a square meal of fish and walking off into the setting sun with God the Father and God the Holy Spirit.

The other and older version was quite disturbing, and not in keeping with the character of Jesus Goodfellow. After all, he said himself he came to lay down his life. "Greater love than this no man has than that a man lay down his life for his brother." These were his very words. So, if he did not really die, the whole thing was sleight-of-hand, a funny sort of ransom. This angels-in-white-clothes and he-is-not-here business makes Jesus' sacrifice an empty gesture. Have we or have we not been ransomed! Well, then, give us a visible cadaver.

Besides all that, it is unbelievable. Reasonable people have seen a lot of bodies, and reasonable people know that bodies do not rise again after being broken, stabbed, whipped, and bloodied. Besides, we all die. It is *natural*.

Is it not more beautiful to think of ourselves, all of us, and that includes Jesus, as painters in God's lovely world, painting our little pictures, using up all the tubes until they are twisted and emptied? And when our last picture is finished, the colors dried, that we lie down and rest for a little while, as Jesus did and is doing today, while the good master-workman, Nature, Outer Force, Cosmic Thing, Evolution, or whatever-it-is, calls others forth for some more painting? And what better model for human beings of this mold than Jesus Goodfellow?

For anyone can like him; he does not present us with such indubitable certainties and such rocklike sureties that all of life becomes tied to one overhanging meaning shared alike by all. We can be ourselves. He will be there. Fluid with haze of history, tantalizing in his possibilities, smiling indulgently at every twist and turn of men and women, he enriches the imagination, leaves our real experience of life intact, and endorses what we "instinctively know" about ourselves: that life can be pretty grim, and the one thing which helps to make it livable is a really good fellow around the place, as long as we are here. At least, Jesus Goodfellow will do, until the real pressure starts: until we are about to leave the place, or until all good fellows—including Jesus Goodfellow—cannot assuage our pain; when, in other words, the bondage of all fellows—good and bad—grips us by the throat and nobody offers any meaning at all that will help us.

Jesus Prometheus

Once upon a time, men below on earth were cold. Very cold. No fire. No heat, therefore. Upstairs: all the gods and goddesses ran about lightly, laughing beautifully. They had all the heat they wanted. They laughed at men in their cold. A certain Prometheus stole a bit of fire and handed the secret to men. Hence, we have fires, steam heat, electricity, bulbs, matches, atomic energy, electric guitars, and other such means of rivaling those gods and goddesses. But the gods and goddesses were angry; had their revenge. They strapped Prometheus to a rock. An eagle gnawed at his vitals. But Prometheus had won. Dying, he saw his gift living on. We have fire. By defiance and usurpation of the powers that be! And thanks to the Hero. Thus said the Greeks.

They were actually talking about Jesus Prometheus. But, don't misunderstand: they never saw him or heard him. Only today and only we have seen him. To understand, you must listen to the strident voices of today's followers of Jesus Prometheus. They condemn all we are—in his name, stating that we are a sick society. According to them, it is only today that Jesus Prometheus stands clear, and it took this filthy, chewed-out imperialistic, materialistic society to provide a stage for his appearance.

Before this, people talked about Jesus' words, blood, crown of thorns, nails, scourging, and his triumph as of a disembodied spirit. And all the rest of it. But cunning little churchmen and pouting preachers tied it all up with their clever laws and little loyalties. They had part of it right. They said: See! Jesus Prometheus has shown each one how to be a person. But then they added: Go, fast for three days. Go, obey me implicitly. Go, scourge yourself. Go, don't make love. Go, pray. Go, submit. Result. Jesus Prometheus was obscured, almost forgotten.

Until today, that is to say. When people once more have got to know Jesus Prometheus, and realized that what he won for us by dying was simply this: I can be myself. Be a person. Nobody can interfere with me. I am the universe. The world is there for me, so that I be myself as on a stage proper to my ego excellence. And any obstacle in my way is to be destroyed. Trash laws. Trash the Churches. Trash the Synagogue. Thump out that rhythm. Beat your hands. And no weakness, mind you. If you meet a tear-stained face, be careful: pity corrupts; compassion weakens; show your zero facial look.

To tell us about Jesus Prometheus, there first came a testament of patriarchs led by Father Abraham in the new image of Elvis Presley. Then came a stream of prophets preceding the modern Jesus Prometheus: like the guttersnipe-angel Beatles with an awesome purity; Jim Morrison hanging out his penis for the sisters and brothers in Miami (to show promethean exhaustion—what it takes to be yourself); Elton John beating out that rhythm to the winking tip of light-bulb codpiece, as the sisters scream; like Mick Jagger rending your mind with a ravening release so that you were Satan, Jesus, female, male, neutral, God, earth, water, fire, sulfur, all in a row, all in yourself; or the Plaster Caster Girl Guides displaying their erect phalluses; like so many others up and down this ravaged land.

Then, as these prophets foreshadowed, Jesus Prometheus! The second manifestation!

You remember his first manifestation? Jesus of Nazareth. The incandescent, revolutionary man walking in Palestine, whipping others up to do their thing, choreographing their heads and stomachs and thighs with miracles and spastic tics of holy personalism. Now, the second manifestation, just like the first one. Except this time, Unisex Jesus Prometheus—Joplin-Hendrix. The Gasser of all time and eternity! Once you *heard* them-him-her, once you lived them-him-her, free! Free at last! They let my people go.

You call them male and female? Forget it, brother. They have the secret. They leaped over that, to be themselves, to show us how to be. Ourselves. MYself. "Don't believe their New Jerusalems," cried Joplin, "don't you go and think we've Paradise in Pensacola, Nirvana in Nixonia, Communion in Chicago, or angels in Los Angeles." Added Hendrix: "My stomach gives me bestial powers beyond all vision. My head can hymn me god or God. But I'm beyond all that now. Live! Be! Yourself!"

And if you think, muddleheaded bourgeoisie, that the only people caught up as Joplin, Hendrix, and the youth are a minority; if you think that you can flee the strong epiphanies of Jesus Prometheus, look around you now and listen to the new sounds. The poets and painters: "We're tired of wearying forms used in the search for beauty of meaning. We prefer the expression of an oversized but ever so exact replica of a Campbell's Soup tin." Priests: "We're tired of being agents who conjure up tattered ghosts and of the god who commands, exacts, demands, expects, imposes norms. We prefer the godliness of our being as we feel and the feeling that our being is godlike." Intellectuals: "We're tired of being charter members in the petty republics of ideas created by antlike minds in the past. Our liberty is threatened, unless we can think all our thoughts, without referring them to others." Journalists: "We're tired of boring impartiality. The world reaches the apogee of its understanding when filtered through our personal reactions." Politicians: "We're tired of being straw men for an ideal set up by past and dead men and of being guardians of a heritage determined by other minds. We need to care only for what is expedient." In sum, as all such Prometheans state: "It is *our* satisfaction which determines how *we* act and thus create our land. Amerika The Beautiful!"

But a collection of human egos whose norm for creating a beauty of life and a beautiful land lacks the harmony of give-and-take between independent people who decide to be mutually dependent, is a collection rather of would-be godlets whose heaven is as banal as the passing days. Time and experience have shown that the unisex Jesus passed away on a pill to unforgettable memories of youth, youth, youth, death, death, death. Salvation? Don't bother me, man. This is my day to be myself. To be Adam, Alpha and Omega, the Ayn Sof, First and Last. Jesus? He is me, for I have replaced him. And in the Graveyard of the Greats, in alphabetical order, but with broken phalluses as wombstones, you will find . . . H for hendrix, J for joplin . . . and toward the end of the alphabet, V for Manson's victims.

Gesù Mio!

Jesus Anthropopithecus

Now that we've all grown up and know Santa is Mom and Dad, we all know things did not begin in this serious world of ours with an apple and a talking serpent. And it's not the year 5872, no matter what the Rabbis say. As for the seven days of world-making by a football-coach god calling the shots staccato-like, together with the mudpie creation of Adam ("the Lord God formed man from the clay of the ground," says the Bible), the rib birth of Eve (a first in obstetrics), the fig leaf and the wailing, that was all laid to rest over one hundred years ago. Really a simple process. A dilemma with the two usual horns, solved by a stroke of genius. And for solid religious reasons.

People had been grumbling for hundreds of years about theologians and philosophers and believers who imposed their views of a creating god on other men. By the 19th century, the other men had had it up to there. For they were given no choice: accept the idea of a creating god. And once you accepted (or even if you didn't) they came around with a collection box or an army; told you when to have children, how to make love with your wife, and what political system you should or shouldn't have.

A man, a genius, Charles Darwin, took a sea trip in the *Beagle*, examining ancient records in tribes and fossils and so on. He hit upon an idea that was simple but satisfying. He assembled all the evidence he could find of those precious fossils. First, he found they stretched back billions of years (out goes the Jewish five thousand years). Second, he found they arranged themselves into groups, orders, and families. Now, if he could only round to third. But there was one difficulty: he could find no connection between these groups, orders, and families over the billions of years. They all arose, flourished, and disappeared. No connection. No transitional forms. Like a string of beads, but without the string.

Charles Darwin formed a theoretical string, in his imagination. There was none in the fossil record. Let us imagine, he said— No! Let us suppose scientifically—No! Let us assert absolutely (for it must have been so; it is very reasonable to suppose, although we have no evidence) that there *was* a connection from the most ancient elements right down to man.

Well. With that reality settled and out of the way once and for all, and an entire system of belief erected and flourishing on that solid basis of empirical knowledge, we now *know* man is descended from Hydrogen, Amino Acids, Nucleic Acids, Viruses, and Other Chemical Compounds. Out goes the Christian 1973 A.D. It is NOW! Approximately 5,000,000,0073 A.H.A.A.N.A.V.O.C.C. Anyway, it is that or admit there was a creating god. And we cannot do that, because there wasn't any. And there wasn't any, because there could not have been any. You have to be reasonable.

Religion is all myth. A myth is something that has no statistical validity—a condition to be abhorred as bad and evil and as the modern version of having no soul. But we will not deprive you of belief. We can replace your belief in a religious religion. We give you in fact (Darwin's theory) and in text (the fossil record) an irreligiously religious idea. Throw away your Bible; ours has photographs. We offer you, in other words, a viable alternative: Evolution. Have we a choice?

One thing disrupted the smoothness of this marvelous guesswork. The story of Jesus. Many like it. At one moment, there you have the world and its total universe spinning around, self-contained and exploding (outward or inward, depending on your politics). Next moment, the meteorite Jesus. Jesus was now in human history. Much like a Green Man from Mars. Came from outside the universe. (Totally gratuitous, said the theologians patronizingly.) He saves us all. Then he climbed into an invisible spaceship and—whoooosh!—off he went again to "outside" the universe. Jesus is now outside history. Until the Big Grand-Bang Day (or the Big Small-Whimper Day). Back comes the spaceship. Jesus steps out. He waves a welcome to the good (the sheep). And God help those who have been naughty (the goats). Then, all good sheep climb into the spaceship. Whoooosh! All scoot "out of the universe" into "Heaven." For ever and for aye. The trouble is: the fossil record says nothing at all about this.

To complicate matters further, some of us not only like the idea of Jesus, and of Heaven, but also Darwin's choice. Well, one thing we have learned: there's a reasonable answer for every need. And sure as the juicy molecules pulled themselves up by the bootstraps and rounded themselves into little green apples (and we know God didn't make green apples), the solution to this contradictory problem comes at us walking on two legs. Like a man. Jesus Anthropopithecus.

Reasonably speaking, evolution is a fact. And it has not stopped, just because we straightened our spine, expanded our buttocks, increased our cranial capacity, grew female breasts (to replace the buttocks as sex signals), and made weapons and poetry. We have obviously been very creative and very busy; but "nature" is still churning up evolutionally; and there is no resting on our laurels.

What is going to happen? Whatever Jesus Prometheus might say to the contrary, all of us men, women, sticks, stones, fish, little apples, and big trees, we are going to acquire a common consciousness. All our entirety is gradually swelling up at one pressure point and to one apex point. The Omega Point. When that is reached, a new consciousness will arrive, and with it—you guessed it—Jesus Anthropopithecus. The Omega Point.

Jesus, like you and me and everything in the universe, has been there all along. "Where wast thou when I laid the foundations of the earth? Declare if thou hast understanding," God challenges the haplessly pre-scientific Job in the Bible. All poor Job lacked was a degree in chemistry and anthropology. Job *was* there (at least mostly), or so Harlow Shapley asserts, for "practically every atom in Job's body—mostly oxygen, carbon, hydrogen, and nitrogen, were in or on the surface of the earth when the foundations were laid." In fact, friends, *we* were *all* there, as Shapley concludes. Including, of course, Jesus. For the same reasons. The same atoms, after all. Us and Jesus. A reverse immortality and better than anything promised man by his religions. God was not alone.

We can forget all the folderol about Jesus, his cross, and the supernatural. "Outside the universe," indeed. Now, it is all much more intelligible and palpable. That Easter story turns out to be the best human story every told: without the feeble epilogue of a happy ending. It even enriches our imagination. Draws a tear now and then. Jesus Anthropopithecus assures us of a glorious end: "John," he smiles anthropopithecally, "join me in a gentle passage from one form of cellular life to another, with Job, the Pongidae, with Anthropus Pekinensis, Cro-Magnon Man, Zinjanthropus, Australanthropus, and with the amino acids of a few billion years ago."

Above all, Jesus Anthropopithecus leaves us free to expect for the first time a very and clear and intelligible future: a row of gravestones, and the silence of nothingness.

Hallelujah! . . .

Jesus One-of-the-Boys

The ultimate point in the disintegration of the Jesus figure is reached with Jesus One-of-the-Boys. The mere description of this figure, as its inventors view it, is sufficient to show you how far that disintegration has gone. As usual in other figures, there is a developed theory and a smooth verbal explanation. It goes somewhat like the following.

Jesus deserves as much recognition and remembrance as the other great figures of history. He should be ranked with Guatama Buddha, Zoroaster, Moses, and Mohammed; with Patrice Lumumba, Malcolm X, Dr. Martin Luther King, and even Kwame Nkrumah ("The Great Redeemer"). In other words, Jesus of Nazareth was one of the boys. So let no one try to diminish his importance or overthrow his popularity. Just make sure he does not get lost in the shuffle. For Jesus was one more, and, in his own inimitable way, quite outstanding leader and pathway-finder for us men. The need satisfied by Jesus One-of-the-Boys is most understandable and to be given its due. As Carl Jung wrote: "Heaven has become empty space to us, a fair memory of things that once were. But our heart glows, and secret unrest gnaws at the roots of our being."

The point Jesus One-of-the-Boys makes to us all is that we are at the most critical turning point in human history. We simply cannot afford unnecessary divisions. Enough of all particularism, exclaim the Chinese and Russians. Too much of sectarian dogmatism and prejudice, assert the Turks. We all have had enough of sects with special signs. Of parties with preponderant Persons they wished to foist on everybody like them. The pluralism we now seek and need as a condition of enduring as a race excludes any role of Jesus but his role as one more great religious leader. Smooth it all over.

For centuries, Christians have insisted that Jesus is unique, that all other leaders are secondary, and that finally all men will have to acknowledge the prime position of Jesus. Such a Jesus is, of course, utterly unacceptable to modern man. But, as One-of-the-Boys, Jesus fits right into the scheme of things. You have a bit of yours. We have a bit of ours; and, after all, there are many roads to happiness. Provided I do not interfere with or hinder your personal beliefs, what more is needed? If you seek a god in Yahweh, and I seek a god in God or Jesus, and someone else seeks a god through Buddha or Mohammed, and still another in nature worship or devil cults, is not that the same thing really? As Joseph Campbell remarks with true amplitude of spirit: "It doesn't matter to me whether my guiding angel for a time is named Vishnu, Shiva, Jesus, or the Buddha." This is an important point.

Besides, and this is the chief argument, what would Jesus himself do if he were alive today? Go about sowing discord and dissension, elitism and enmity, fission and fighting, hate and hubris, a passion for predominating, and a lust for power over all men's minds? This gentle, peace-loving man would be animated by one thing: pity for men. And his words would resemble those of Joseph Campbell: "If you're not distracted by names or the color of hair, the same message is there, variously turned." And he would add some of his parting words: "Love one another, as I have loved you. In my father's house there are many mansions."

It would be great to visit those mansions where All the Boys live: Nkrumah and Mohammed drinking coffee and swapping headgear, Buddha showing his navel to Moses ("Here's how I did it"), Abraham and Malcolm X comparing notes on spears versus bullets, Patrice Lumumba and Zoroaster rapping about race relations, Josef Stalin having a laugh with Pius XII, J. Edgar Hoover and Martin Luther King exchanging information about wiretaps, and a vast concourse or club of Whale-Worshippers, Bird-Adorers, Thuggees, Aztecs, Head-Hunters, Cargo-Cultists, Greek oracles, Roman augurers, Jewish high priests, African witch doctors, Salem witches, Celtic Druids, a few Bull Gods from Crete and some Nudists from Brighton, England, the paleolithic Venus showing her 31,000th pregnancy to the Virgin Mary, and James Joyce translating for the Holy Spirit. All the Boys. With all their gospels, korans, bibles, books of Moroni and Mary Baker Eddy, Sanskrit writings, Niebelungenlieds, Nordic runes, Egyptian papyri. With all their paraphernalia: matzoth, crosses, chains, yarmulkas, skull caps, shawls, chasubles, stoles, masks, rings, seals, wigs, altars, temples, shrines, churches, cathedrals. With all their promises, promises, promises. . . .

Just the Boys—at it again.

6. Some Jesus Figures for the Social Liberationist

Jesus Bleeding Lord

Since the dawning day of Jesus Goodfellow, Jesus Prometheus, and Jesus Anthropopithecus, if you face the facts about Jesus Bleeding Lord, you will admit one thing: *he* is so human, so pertinent to men of ancient history but not to men of recent times, that any ancient man can claim him, but every truly modern individual must find him uncongenial.

Blood and bleeding had a sacred quality once, before they became merely a manifestation of corpuscles, red and white. Today, blood represents a human mess—once outside the body. Something to be studied by the hematologist. Sopped up by sanitation workers after a gangland shoot-out. Mainly menstrual for the woman. Sign of cancer. Surname for Bangladesh, Biafra, Indochina, Northern Ireland, Palestine, Cyprus, and the Sudan. Symbol of John Kennedy's wife holding her dying husband's head as the car sped to the hospital where he died. Red for the local Red Cross Unit. In the twilight of the figures of Jesus, men see strange sights and follow funny fantasies of blood, pain for pain's sake. If Jesus hung on his cross again, and if men once saw his blood and tried to save him, he could get hepatitis from the blood banks of our city hospitals. What can modern man do with Jesus Bleeding Lord?

A Bleeding Lord? So tribal! So anthropological. Like images of Heaven beyond the skies, the Man in the Moon, and witches cooking babies on Walpurgis Night. Vestiges of man's primitive past and preconditioning in an unknown world. But now, at last, Jesus Bleeding Lord is refashioned, made congenial once more to moderns. He is energetically (and with TV cameras present wherever possible) stripped of compassion, love, salvation, miracles, and made altogether quite fit for reasonable men and women.

Today, a Bleeding Lord, say like Jesus, is only useful as one of three familiar things. As a sort of latter-day Prometheus, atop his rock in chains, grinning gruesomely at the fitful rages of a choosy god, paying his debt for having made gods of men; a ravening beak dipping by divine command into the bloodied folds of entrails and the failing organs of his frame; and squatting men below huddled forever over flames which Prometheus lit. "The Führer expects every German to shed his blood for People and Fatherland. *Sieg Heil!*"

Or: as Hero Horatio fighting on the bridge against Tarquin for freedom in Rome, and saving others by his dying act in broken timbers and the sharp bite of weapons that could not reach his people except by passing through his body bright with blood and bent to die, that others might live. "Greater love than this no man has than that a man lay down his life for his brother." Jesus said it. Jesus the Bleeding Lord.

Or: Ché Guevara bleeding from the bullets; Selective Service records dirty with rabbit's blood; kids with ketchup on their T-shirts to prove that war is bad; and Muhammad Ali with a bloodied nose in whitey's land. "They shed the blood of innocents to oil the wheels of dollars," said Frantz Fanon. Jesus Bleeding Lord.

Those are some of today's Jesus Bleeding Lord figures. There have been others. It is a very adaptable figure and useful in many ages. Historically, it was useful chiefly as a reason: if my Lord did shed his blood for you, then be baptized—my Jew, my Muslim, my Christian non-fellow. This Christian undignity went deep. It was a refined blasphemy of Jesus' salvation. "In his blood

he saved us," said the Fathers. "Then accept the blood," said
Christians, "or we'll shed yours. 'Tis right. Only right. Submit to
such love." Such, for instance, was Father Joseph, Grey Eminence to his Scarlet Eminence Richelieu, preaching to the wilting
Calvarian Sisters of Christ's Crucifixion and padding barefoot
from the Cardinal's suite over the walls of La Rochelle to the
General's tent, and planning lovely bloodied death for Huguenots
in the city and for babies roasted by the troops in Pomerania because supplies were low.

Historically speaking—if, at any point, we were to consult
history—all the above was only the dark side of a shining
newly minted coin that Christians flung on the bargaining tables
of the human marketplace. The bright recto side was the knowledge of a loving Lord and Creator who died for love and lived
afterward. Shout about the love of it all, the Christians said. Do
not forget the blood and the pain. In your pains: when you see
your own blood, or feel the lack of it, or are dying because it no
longer supports your life; remember he bled and died before you.
And they contemplated further. His hands were railed together
with his feet and so gave him Five Sacred Wounds. Five portals
of love. His head was crowned with thorns. His heart was
pierced by a lance. Worship his sacred heart. His shoulders carried the Cross. Worship his shoulders. But this bright recto side
excluded all Blutfests. There were to be no mental thrills at pain,
no transference of sexual impotence or sexual prohibitions to the
plane of Jesus' blood.

Apart from history and keeping up with modernity, we now
are quite beyond all primitive things. Science has delivered us;
and technology sheds all the blood we need to pour. Besides, analysis has shown that blood and bleeding things (men, women,
animals, as well as bleeding lords) are primal projections and subconscious webbings for our daylong fears. So Jesus Bleeding
Lord is relegated to the halls of what we know today of
Man-Myth-Magic. Another mere symbol beside all those others:
Aztecs, and the Pygmies, the Borneo wildmen, not forgetting
Stonehenge and the British Druids, Newgrange and the Irish
Druids, and Viking Killfests in the name of Wodin. You can see
what a hodgepodge into which blood, bleeding lords, and all that
sort of thing fit.

So what can man do now with Jesus Bleeding Lord? How can he see him as divine in any way? Or find transcendence in his actions, or salvation won by his pain and death?

The blood sacrifice of Jesus is not understood as having a divine or eternal reference together with divine and eternal requirements. All in Jesus has been reduced to the dimensions and substance of man's will and of his society. By degrees, man has stripped himself of a divine Jesus and of the latter's transcendence and of the transcendence for us in blood that was no symbol but was divine. Having lost sight of that, today's man now casts Jesus in his own pygmy image and cannibalizes himself from then on. This Jesus figure becomes the infinitely applicable model for any cause; on his banner may be written any personal or group slogan; his sufferings become the justification for any paranoia which demands the death of those we do not like; his blood is smeared like rabbit's blood, a symbol, a call to arms, a gesture of mourning or of anger. And Jesus Bleeding Lord, the logical if impoverished heir of the Jesus figures for the reasonable man, in turn heads his own little dynasty, the Jesus Liberation figures.

Jesus the Mystic Gun

Even in this late day of Jesus-figuring, someone will surely say that Jesus died, sits in Heaven now, and shall come back on the Last Day to judge the living and the dead. Well, there are some men and women today who will tell you otherwise: after agony and death, Jesus surfaced as the Mystic Gun. "Revolution comes out of the muzzle of a gun," commented Chairman Mao in the Little Red Book. In Jesus' case, of course, a mystic gun. And he moved and moves around to join the brotherhood of us, revolutionaries of all the world. Feel his considerateness and compassion in the Brothers and Sisters. If you don't, then you are one of the two types of men today whom Jesus the Mystic Gun condemns: as Dan Berrigan pointedly puts it, the first wants to "order the Ten Commandments tattooed on his bung hole in ten colors"; the second "wants the American flag tattooed in three colors on his prick's round." So speaks Jesus the Mystic Gun through his Guru, Dan Berrigan.

Jesus the Mystic Gun came into his own when John the Guru

appeared. Or, so Dan Berrigan and the neo-mystics of the American Catholic Church like to say. This is rather heady stuff; forget your history books; just listen.

John, *Doctor de la Nada*, that is to say (Berrigan translates) Guru of the Absurd, revolted against a sick society. He fled to the Mystic Gun in disgust at the industrial-military complex of the 16th century. Kidnapped. Imprisoned. Falsely accused and tried by rump courts. He opened a new way, a high-wire act; let all monks get out of their religious orders and reject their country and its discipline and march with Jesus the Mystic Gun in danger, in the underground. For, today, there is a war on. Or didn't you smell death?

Now, that's only half the story. Hear the full message they proclaim in the name of Jesus the Mystic Gun. It's Guru Dan speaking again, telling us it's better to have a bloodbath (like Jesus) straightaway, under the sign of the Mystic Gun. And the bloodier the mess, the deeper the death, then the squarer, the holier, the firmer will be our victory. Only you have to follow implicitly what I, the Guru, am saying. For our past heroes, Freud, John of the Cross, Teresa of Avila, young Luther, Gandhi, Martin Luther King, Jesus, Socrates, Buddha, are dead. They "wandered the city of the dead and called men into being once more." Now (as he implies) you have me, "the classicist, the ecstatic, the good fighter, the faithful man, the hound nervous as lightning in the traces, the merciless surgeon of the soul, the Jesus prayer." I am Jesus the Mystic Gun alive again. John the Guru, now called Dan.

But there is still more. And nobody could have dreamed it off the top of his head. It all seems very fine to be on the run mystically, to throw a little rabbit's blood, to create public diversions. But when you go that far down the road, a really dangerous question arises. As some of the Jesus Revolutionaries, specifically the Jesuit Maoists out of St. Louis, Missouri, put it succinctly: "How are we going to overcome the alien, congealed objectivity of the external world and remold the crust of arbitrary factuality into intelligible human relationships?" The secret of the answer (if you can figure out the question) is, of course, this: the mystery of Jesus' own proletarian background. Remember old Joseph the Carpenter? Don't forget him. A proletarian.

Jesus, we are told, was a proletarian. Like his father. Therefore, he was a Communist. Therefore, he was a revolutionary. Therefore, he was a Maoist, is a Maoist. The mystery of his proletarian background is exemplified only in Chairman Mao (God bless him!) and revealed now to those who know the life-giving words of the Little Red Book. "If the rains fall, the earth is watered," stated Chairman Mao cryptically but prophetically. For the followers who have been instructed, all is clear: "Purge yourself of all your bourgeois (or, in particular, your petit-bourgeois) consciousness. Buy weapons, gas masks, knuckle-dusters, some sand bags, etcetera. All the paraphernalia with which Jesus Revolutionary can achieve his triumph." For, although "the traditional petit-bourgeois strata in the West have been liquidated, new intermediary strata—privileged in many ways and tied to the monopolist forms of development—have taken their place"; so say the St. Louis Maoists. The Followers are to destroy them: disarm them, cripple them, trash them, overcome them.

Jesus the Mystic Gun and Revolutionary wants us, first of all, to have a preparatory period—just like his thirty years of obscurity—to be followed by all the blood and victory of his Calvary. Blood particularly. The idea is simple. Grow a Jesus beard. Have a Jesus hairdo. Study Mao Tse-tung thought (Maothink). Burn official records. Blow up Federal installations. Kidnap a few "peaheads in government." Go on the run. Even if they catch you hiding in a broom closet or under a bush, smile, be calm; it's all part of the game. Remember gentle Ché, beloved Ché; and Rudi Dutschke, Red Danny, Camillo Torres; and so many other glorious ones who preceded us. Neither bullets nor court trials can finish us off. Didn't Jesus the Mystic Gun tell us: "Fear not when the fuzz drag you into their courts and precincts. I am with you in that day"? And if any revisionist asks: Can Chairman Mao bring Ché and Torres back to life again in time for our triumphal takeover of power (for the people's sake, of course), or can he bring himself back to life once they proclaim his death?—answer him: Mao is the sun. Mao is the moon. Mao is the stars. He does admirably for the people in China what Leo the Lion did for M-G-M. The whole thing cost, according to conservative estimates, just about 30 million-plus in human lives. Chinese lives. Jesus the Mystic Gun did say: "I have come to cast a sword upon the earth."

After all this, if I leave the message of the Mystic Gun as announced by its latter-day messengers, and search for that history book again, my eyes at least see a gentler scene, my soul perceives a more hopeful (although admittedly less politicized) prospect. Jesus was a gentle man who was God, as I believe. He did not advocate violence. He did not wield a gun, mystic or other. John the Guru in real history was Juan de Yepes y Alvarez (1542–91), better known as John of the Cross, master of the mystical. He never heard of the industrial-military complex, of Indochina, of Harrisburg prison, never hid in closets or wrote a vulgar sentence, and he would never have poured even rabbit's blood on the ground much less on government documents. He never used four-letter words. He wrote ballads and poems and books on the love of Jesus in an individual soul. And "Absurd" is not the meaning of the Spanish *nada*. Nothing (*nada*) is not absurd. Nothing is nothing or, if you like, not anything. And John never read the Little Red Book, and nothing he ever wrote or dreamed cost the life of a single soul much less the liquidation of over 30 million people.

But history is not the issue here. And the new Guru continues unperturbed. "Around me," says he, "I find only nightmares, necromantic projections, pain flung at me by the corrupt and evil-smelling civilization our grand country has become. The power centers have evoked these stalking ghosts of the past instead of exorcising them, so that they can fill the world scene with painful cauldrons of suffering. Even me, me the Guru of the new Absurd, they are trying to measure by most sinister and stereotyped images. They desire each man to be a well- or mal-functioning robot. Each man's soul they would transform into an obedient cretin. They want merely lobotomized victims. Did I ever tell you of the tacit music I hear within my brain even in the subway? If you let me, I shall bring you to walk the resounding solitude of a holiness without holy water, worship without pietistic smirks at statues. Bombs create that solitude. But the tacit music, that is mine, mine, mine . . ."

Jesus Black

You know where Jesus was really crucified? In the Black Man's soul. "Hey! Who's the poor guy those white creeps hung up there all bleeding?" Jesus Black. That's who. Saint Patrice Lumumba mowed down by white Belgian bullets. Our Father Martin Luther King assassinated by order of the filthy white industrial-military complex. Malcolm X. The Soledad Brothers. Fred Hampton. Papa Simon Kimbangu butchered. Cleaver, Newton, Seale, Angela Davis, all persecuted. And millions of brothers and sisters. Millions. For hundreds and hundreds of years. Jesus, the real Jesus, has been killed, over and over again, by white racist Christian society. Because he was not white. He wasn't! A fact of history. Don't forget it. Brown-skinned like David and Moses and Rabbi Akiba and Simon Maccabaeus and Solomon. Café-au-lait like the Trinidadians and Haitians serving drinks in Fifth Avenue penthouses, or like those perky Oriental diplomats driving all those kinky $20,500 Mercedes-Benz's to and fro at the U.N. Secretariat. Not only Jesus. His father, God, is black. A white god is colorless. But God is all things and beautiful. Black is beautiful.

In a racist society, a God has no place. They tried to kill Jesus Black in the Black Man's soul, and substitute their own colorless Jesus. "Savior of all men," they said. "Open to receive and relate to all men," they said. Universal Jesus? Like hell! A lily-white Jesus. Loves black people who want to be white. "Now don't go doing nothing the white don't like," he said. "What whites does is okay." Yes. Think of those rewards in Heaven, the white Heaven; whites will concentrate on the rewards here on earth. The white Jesus Bag.

But they didn't succeed. The Black Man's soul never died. Nor Jesus Black. In his spirit, the Black Man held on, as did Jesus Black. In his soul, the Black Man's fight commenced. The whole infinite ladder of his being was filled with this yearning for the purity of his blackness. His blackness tugged at him in the ancient recesses of his mind. Separate from it by generations, where to look for it now? They looked in Black Man, in Jesus Black —brothers enslaved, exiles from home; they looked while, all around, racist whiteness surged like a night tide. White racist Christians had spent generations building a materialist society, erecting a very surface system of values, dealing only with the surface, not with the center, the spirit of people.

Jesus Black may or may not save; but the need right now is for a good slogan, something to rally the Brothers and Sisters and

make the blood boil. Get the people to the polls and the meetings. Raise that Black consciousness. Here comes Prophetess Bar-
bara Ann Teer in a fire-orange robe and a gold-plated breastplate,
to have words with the Brothers and Sisters. Blacks are a spirit
people. Whites are racist and materialistic. Blackness is a spiritual
value. We are not your old wine-sopped ne'er-do-wells, your
Uncle Toms, your house niggers. We are far away from home,
Brother Jesus. Have been on a bad trip. Set us free. Set free! Let
my people go, says the King. "I feel in myself a soul as immense
as the world," says Frantz Fanon, "my chest to expand without
limit. I am a master and I am ordered to adopt the humility of a
slave."

Now, Black Man with Jesus Black is on the journey home. A
spirit journey. Open up. Liberate. Regain and reclaim spiritual
freedom. Revitalization. Rebirth. Cleansing. Lifting. Loving. The
power is in us. We're going now. Our black bodies are body-
temples. We all have black godliness in us. Jesus Black is indigenous, relevant. Born not once from a virgin, but again today from
Black life and Black faith, surviving and flourishing in a white racist world. Jesus was a revolutionary attempting to build a black
nation.

They killed Jesus Black.

But blackness gives us a new gospel, the gospel of Jesus Black.
Its sign: The Cross? What Cross? The clenched fist at the Communion Rail and outside Temple Emanu-El on Fifth Avenue. Its
goal: Salvation? You crazy? Reparations!

And first and foremost, cut out that theology nonsense. "The-
ology," said the Reverend Pressley, "is by definition what one
does, not what one thinks." "And we will tell the Pope what
Black Man to make Cardinal Archbishop of Washington," says
Reverend Lucas. "He'll be the head nigger in charge." No two
ways about it. But it must not be black Bishop Harold Perry of
New Orleans. "He's a plaything of the boss," says the Reverend.
Dirty old man, the boss.

Now take a good look at yourself, Jesus Black, Black Man.
Leave aside the reluctance. Just a thin line fringes the edges of
your oppression. Beyond lies a world shimmering with distance
and promise. Take a good look at your mind. Wake up! Make
your own magic. Don't wait for it to happen. *You* are magic.

You are *Black*. Testify! Testify! Renew your Blackness in its strange purity. Smile with Black Man's sublime trust in the permanence of Black sunshine in the colored uplands. Chant with the Bothers and the Sisters:

> I do believe I can feel that fire.
> I do believe I am that fire.
> I do believe I can regain that power.

Behind that chant, you can hear the genuine voice of generations of Black people in whom the fire of enthusiasm was drowned in floods of cruel indifference, and the power to develop themselves was castrated by calculated subjugation.

But can anyone—in the name of that scarred past and in the name of Jesus Black—close up the lacerations on Alex Rackley's body, pick out the hot lead from Sam Rapier's body (it's like a sieve), and comfort Judge Harold Haley's widow (she cannot find his head; the Soledad Brothers have hidden it)? For, consider this: the creation of Jesus Black can be no less racist, no less harsh and comfortless, than the lily-white Jesuses of all the oppressors of Blacks. Some Blacks need "an opening of new avenues of thought, redirection. A whole concept of who we are and how we function." But when we go so far in fictionalizing as to say that Jesus Black, White, or Sky-Blue Pink speaks authoritatively and only through the mouths of Dessalines, Papa Joseph Diangienda, Papa Simon Kimbangu, and Frantz Fanon, and only to Blacks, we openly desire and declare God's love to be racist, his salvation a joke on men, and his son, Jesus, another mortal freedom fighter.

Jesus Femina

One of the still enduring misdirections of Christian life and theology concerns women or, if you will, the woman. Of course, Christians inherited much of their attitudes from Romans, Greeks, and Semites—for none of whom woman had any real worth. But the Christian misdirection is all the more striking because, if Christians should have known how to think profoundly and act excellently in any department of human life, it should have been in this question of the character and the role of woman in human society and for the human self. They did not.

The error was further compounded by the Jesus-figuring which marked the development of Christian society. Jesus figures such as Jesus Caesar, Jesus Doctor, and Jesus Monk only drove deeper the Christian error about women: they were chauvinistic both for theology and for gender. Because woman was misunderstood, man and child and sexuality and marriage and love were all incorrectly focused throughout Christianity. One oppression and one injustice fathered many more. We can assign solid historical and cultural reasons for the failure of Christians in this matter; yet their failure still partakes of the bizarre. Perhaps it is this bizarre quality which explains one bizarre reaction today: the totally gratuitous creation of a new Jesus figure, Jesus Femina. Of course, Jesus Femina provides no final answer; it is an interim retort by some women, and is born of their pain and felt humiliation.

Some time before Christians arrived on the human scene, Aristotle had said that the female character possessed a natural defectiveness. Pythagoras had stated that an Evil Principle created woman. Jewish sages held her made from a crooked rib. The Talmud admonishes: whoever teaches his daughter Torah is like one who teaches her lasciviousness. In the daily synagogue prayers, the men prayed: "Blessed art thou, O Lord, for not making me a woman."

The Christian concept of woman was and, to a large extent, still is that the sum of woman is what she is *useful for*: for children, for cooking, for household chores, for satisfying her husband's desires, for managing the home. Whatever she had in common with man (sexual desires, ambition, personality, talents of intellect), and what she had as particular to her (physiology, beauty, softness, sympathy, intuition, creativity), all was admitted and understood within the focus of usefulness—to men.

She served many purposes for man since long before the emergence of Christianity: she symbolized concretely the negative (Sister Death), the non-human (Mother Earth), the dependent (Sister Moon), the vehicle of man (a ship is "she"). Above all, she shouldered man's guilt and was thus the object of a frightful litany of invective which has besmirched woman's head down the ages as a result: witch, gorgon, siren, harpy, whore, the devil's gateway, he-woman, man's pitfall. St. Paul taught that woman was made for man, should keep her head covered in church and also keep quiet in church. And he condoned marriage with her as an alternative to burning in Hell on account of lascivious desires. Woman, Christians taught, was synonymous with chaos, disorder, adultery, weakness, quarrels, betrayals, entrapment, cattiness, passivity, idolatry, the negative principle in nature, the wiles of foul effeminacy, the city of evil. St. Bernard likened her to an open sewer. St. Ambrose said stoutly that her only use was to bear virgins for the Church. Thomas Aquinas, the most brilliant mind of the Medieval Church, held her to be "a male gone awry" and conceived "as a result of some external factor like the south wind which is damp." Martin Luther said that "if she dies bearing, it doesn't matter. Let her die. She is there to do that." And so it can be prolonged. Christianity was chauvinistic, as were its Jesus figures.

In early modern Europe and the United States, a few brave women tried to reform the ill. But male chauvinism prevailed. "Petticoat reformers," sneered every man ready to sell his wife for a quart of beer or an ounce of twist. Some like George Sand attempted to open rebellion, flouting social mores. Some like Florence Nightingale made a virtue out of necessity and a dominion out of what used to be women's drudgery, nursing the image of woman while she nursed the wounded and the dying. Even in the relatively non-Christian world of psychology and psychiatry, woman were given the male image of what she should be like—if healthy. "Due to raging hormonal influences," said Edgar F. Berman, women can go a little beserk.

The errors which ultimately gave rise to Jesus Femina were, therefore, inevitable: concerning man ("over" the woman, her superior, her definer), marriage (woman's only blossom-land, but she as second fiddle to her lord and master), sexuality (woman was the *object* of it, man *had* it), and love (in her case, always implying subjugation). In general, it is obvious that the lot of woman in Christianity did not differ substantially from that of woman before Christianity.

The exaggeration or misdirection—to be more consistent with the facts—should have gone in the diametrically opposite direction and given men an inferior place in relation to women. For the one essential human condition which Jesus chose to require, in order to effect the salvation of all men and women and thus, as he planned it, to make the Jesus Self a reality, was, precisely, a woman: her mind (for her consent was asked), her womb, her birth pangs, her milk, her love, and her care. Time and place and ethnic origins may have been variables. But a woman was essential, for a mother was essential. Woman was thus entwined intimately by Jesus with himself in his humanity and his divinity. But Christian men did not see or did not choose to see this; and they fashioned a theology of humankind, a philosophy of love, and a code of social behavior based on the assumed primacy of man—merely on the pretext that Jesus chose to be male rather than female, and blinded themselves to the intimate statement about women (among other things) that Jesus had made by choosing to enter the human universe through a mother.

Christian men did what the other men had done in all religions and religious history. For even when the divinity was acknowledged to have a "female principle" (e.g., the goddesses of the ancient pantheons), still it was only men who served as chief priests; and women performed minor roles or none at all. Indeed, on the basis of a sorry record, it is safe to assume that Christian men did what they would have done no matter *what* form God had chosen in being incarnated. Had God chosen to be incarnated as a cow, for example—as theologically speaking he could have easily done—men, with impunity and blind eye to ludicrousness, would have claimed primacy in tending such a cow. Their motive would still have been a self-serving shortsightedness; their strength of reasoning purely cultural; and their justification merely that the cow had obviously meant it to be so.

In focusing on the male gender of Jesus, men not only made a paragon of mere humanness (a tragic failure in man's thinking about the divine which, as we have seen, became an exaggerated mark of latter-day Jesus figures), but they then reduced that humanness by half. It would be a pity if women, in reaction finally to this grave error of millennia's duration, would repeat it. But the long-delayed reaction of women has at last surfaced in the extremely illogical and self-defeating form of Jesus Femina.

Jesus Femina is advocated by the Femlibs, or the Sisters, an appellation reserved here only for those engaged in the female liberation movement who champion Jesus Femina theology and outlook and who also advocate in the same breath the total iden-

tity between male and female sexuality (only a mild physical difference, they say) and/or female superiority over man (man becomes the appendage): the Jesus-Mas-Femina principle. The
Sisters have elaborated an entire theology; and they present a
new view of "Jesus" and of his Second Coming.

God, apparently, had and has a male principle (Father-God)
and a female principle (Mother-God). God was and is also a trinity of persons: Father, Son (Jesus), and Holy Spirit. Each of these
was and is paralleled by a female principle: Mother, Daughter,
Holy Spirita. Therefore, a double trinity: Father-Mother, Son-
Daughter, Holy Spirit-Spirita. The second person (in reality, two
principles, male and female) appeared on earth and was called
Jesus. But in reality, it was Jesus-Mas-Femina. "Jesus was a femi-
nist," said Dr. Elizabeth Farians. "If he was not, then he didn't
come from God."

This Jesus-Mas-Femina, according to the Sisters, was something uncapturable by men when it passed over the human landscape. In form it appeared truncated, as only a man. Jesus-Mas.
But in reality it was complete: Jesus-Mas-Femina. Complete, because its unisex tied all human meanings together. It was a revelation. As in a stream, what we men and women have called male
and female were, in this revealing being, as one. In Jesus-Mas-
Femina, the human being was complete: heir of all good and
golden things; receiver of the pure recompense of observing sun-
light; alive to the sounds of water, the nodding of bluebells, as
well as to the depth of thought; winged in foot, poised for flight
among the stars of intuition; bearer of wisdom in heart, in head,
in blood.

At this crucial moment in the history of humankind and its
communication with God (always with a male and female principle), when the miracle of human happiness and balance should
have taken place, there entered the Plot. The Plot was at least
preternatural, if not supernatural: its originator was, of course,
He-Satan. For, according to the binary character of all things divine and human, there is in devildom a He-Satan and a She-Satan.
And at that crucial moment, He-Satan had the upper hand. Playing on the chauvinism of men, He-Satan perpetrated the crime of
official Christian chauvinism. And thus, from the earliest times,
Christian teachers and theologians concentrated on extolling ex-

clusively Jesus-Mas and in affirming a Holy Trinity composed of two males, "Father" and "Son," and of one neutral, "Holy Spirit." The Plot was one which primarily affected theology, the queen of sciences. But it was also a congenial and wholly satisfying arrangement for the male chauvinists. And it had very practical effects: a he-theology and he-teaching, a he-philosophy and a he-morality, he-popes, he-bishops, he-priests, he-angels, he-devils. Jesus Femina was excluded. There is even a suspicion among some of the younger Sisters who have not yet researched the etymology of the word, about the universally used "Amen": they would prefer to use the new liberating and consciousness-raising term: "Awomen."

For "we are victims of a bad theology," says Roman Catholic theologian Dr. Farians, "so we've got to have a new theology"; because "if theology is going to represent God, it's got to be just. You don't need to be a theologian to realize that."

As to the Second Coming of Jesus, the new theology is explicit and quite exciting for the Sisters: "I envision a Second Coming in which a female principle will be offered," said Dr. Farians. "The masculine and the feminine in each of us will be harmonized. The final humanization of the species!" There must a rebalancing of affairs; so Femina must dominate for quite a time. The new coming of Jesus-Mas-Femina will not be through a Virgin Mother, of course, but through a Virgin Father. The terms "Blessed Father" and "Our Gentleman" will parallel the older terms "Blessed Mother" and "Our Lady." She-Satan will have it all over He-Satan. But the greatest effect will be on us, Sisters and Brothers. Again, Dr. Farians: "Each of us will be free to be ourselves, no longer restricted by sexual stereotypes." Women will be seen as persons again. Thus will men and women be able to love each other in unisex, that is in sexual equality, thus echoing the dream of the Femlibs. As Roberta Blackburn put it: "The best definition of sexual equality I've ever heard is that after any sexual intercourse it's uncertain which of the two will conceive the child."

Such is the breakthrough, according to the Sisters, and such is the prospect. Future she-popes, she-bishops, she-confessors, he-nuns, she-eunuchs for the Kingdom of Heaven, she-castrati, she-husbands, he-wives. Away with all the androcentric nonsense: the phallic woman, the "missus," the "lil' playmate." Instead, a glorious intermingly modeled on the Holy Male-Female Trinity.

When all, male chauvinists included, have had a good and justified laugh at that farrago of nonsensical theology, the quiet, insistent questions return, and Christianity has not yet answered them: What is woman? Is Christian salvation as chauvinist as male Christians made it out to be, or as some female Christians would have it? Jesus was a man, not a woman. And at the same time he chose to effect salvation only by means of a woman. Yet, the truth is that Mary did not stand alone but was married to a man—and not merely for form's sake; they were married. And that man, Joseph, the most inscrutable character in the whole history of Christianity, did not stand alone; for all his glory derives from association with that woman and her son. All three, in effect, formed, not a triad of paragons preened in personalism, but a family of dependent love. Let chauvinists of both sexes reflect.

Jesus Gay

The newest and, for the conservative mind, the most puzzling of the Gospels launched in latter years is the Gay Gospel. Its centerpiece is Jesus Gay. The arrival of Jesus Gay on the scene presents us with a dichotomy of feeling. On the one hand, there is a realization that, in a heterosexual society, the homosexual has a grave problem. On the other hand, a disgust is felt at the fact that, in their effort to tackle that problem, some homosexuals have created out of whole cloth a Jesus Gay figure, a new theology, and even a fresh interpretation of the Gospel story.

Up to this point in time, there can be no doubt about it, the attitude of religionists was clear and expressed in a vocabulary specifically fashioned: buggery, sodomy, perversion, bestial carnality, the abomination, the devil's delight, self-abuse, the eighth deadly sin against the Holy Spirit, deviance, the forces of faggotry. The Gay was a queer, a queen, a fag, a capon, a eunuch, a variant, a pansy, a mushy-spongy namby-pamby.

Now, over against all this, homosexuals seek to justify the figure of Jesus Gay from the Bible, Jewish and Christian. They say: The message of Yahweh was clear even in the Jewish Bible, and is quite clear in the Christian Bible. What was the Holy Spirit doing "hovering" over the waters? "Do not give yourself to the love of women," warns Proverbs. How could Yahweh speak to "Israel" (a masculine proper name in Yahweh's Hebrew), saying: "Come with me, my true love. Thou shalt be master of my love." And David and Jonathan? "The soul of Jonathan was knit with the soul of David, and Jonathan loved him as his own soul. Then Jonathan and David made a pact. And Jonathan stripped himself of his robe and gave it to David." How did Elias cure the widow's son? "He laid the boy on his own bed, and he stretched himself upon the child three times, and cried unto the Lord." The symbolism, the beautiful symbolism of it all!

If the thing was not clear then, they continue, it was clear in the New Testament. They still did not see it. Jesus, the Second Adam, the Savior, Jesus Gay! Jesus had a disciple, the only one of twelve others (the youngest and, as far as we know, the only *unmarried* one), John the Divine, "whom Jesus loved," and "who lay on Jesus' breast" at the Last Supper. The same John who wrote in his Apocalypse about the 144,000 virgins "who were not polluted by women"; John succinctly notes that these follow the Lamb, Jesus Gay, wherever he goes. But even today, Jesus Gay would be welcome among the Siwans of North Africa, the Arunta of Australia, the Keraki of New Guinea. Anal intercourse is universal among them all. But not, Brothers and Sisters of the Dream and all Prisoners of the Closet, not in Western churches, synagogues, and establishments. They buried Gays and Jesus Gay in a nimbus of guilt and locked them into a Tunnel of Bondage. The theology of Jesus Gay is built on one interpretation of history: the history of that Tunnel.

The era of the Tunnel lasted too long. The bondage of shame, guilt, black secrecy, agonies of fear of being discovered; of trysts in public lavatories, beneath park bushes, in the back of a car for a "quickie," at obscure rooming houses. The bondage of disgust: feigned copulations with "straight" husbands and wives, the horrors of a heterosexual touch, the labels of "ill," "sick," "queer." No Gay union possible. No acknowledged ceremony in public before God Gay. No Gay home life. No Gay dancing. No public embrace. Job discrimination. Crushing phobic laws. Church segregation. Reverend Gene Legget, avowed homosexual, suspended from the Methodist ministry in San Antonio "amid hate and animosity and derisive laughter." The Stonewall Inn Bust of

June 1971. Men and women kept in a twilight world. A beauty quenched. Gay history was full of lonely cemeteries. Like infinitesimal ghosts, persecuted beings, Gays fled to penthouse dwellings, formed their own mafias for survival in the United Nations, the State Department, in the Vatican, in TV companies, in country clubs. But the greatest of them all, Jesus Gay, was crucified in the hearts of many, killed by the loneliness, by the slur. Jesus, Savior of all men, universal in his appeal. Not to Gays, said "they."

The longer Western civilization lasted, the worse the bondage. Even poor mother-loving Sigmund with his self-created penis envy for Dad and his snaky dreams about Mom, sang the same song. And a cascade of pseudo-scientific terms poured on innocent Gay heads: bisexuals, homophiles, transsexuals, intersexuals, polysexuals, paraphiliacs, the H persuasion, and so on. Even when F. A. Beach coolly proved that 49 out of 76 primitive tribes accepted Gays and Gaydom, the myth and the bondage persisted. The high winds of official Christendom howled around the perfumed isle of Lesbos and drowned out Sappho's lonely chanting.

Still, even within that Tunnel and throughout all its bondage, the dream held on. Gays never lost the dream of a birth. It was a dream dreamt by Alcibiades the Greek, by Tiberias on Capri, exemplified in "Jesus Gay" and his "beloved disciple," but later buried by officialdom. It was borne forward, in spite of that, on the melody of a high music, a homophony, invented by the untouched Jesus Gay, a chordal accompaniment that pained on Calvary as it swooned in Gethsemane, raged at the moneylenders in the Temple, shone on Tabor, and sang through the Sermon on the Mount. A new affirmation came in 1948, with the rediscovered Gospel of St. Thomas: "When you make the male and the female into one, so that the male will not be male and the female will not be female, then you shall enter the Kingdom of God." Ye Gods! From all the way back in the 3rd century A.D.

Suddenly the light appeared at the end of the Tunnel. Sappho had not sung in vain, and the lonely figure at midnight waiting at Hyde Park Gate could start on home. The liberation! No man can explain it, they tell us. Except, perhaps, as part of the Second Coming of Jesus, or as part of the general liberation: of youth from mordant old age, of blacks from racist white civilization, of

Indians from colonialists, of Chicanos from the gringos, of women from chauvinist men. Jesus Gay decided to manifest himself again, to walk again among the Brothers and Sisters. "All things to all men," you said. Preachers of the Word down through the ages? Very well. All men and all women. Vaginophiliacs, rectumphiliacs, polyphiliacs. It was, in short, a gentle-hued tranquil sunrise before a glorious high noon. Brothers and Sisters, studs and fems, suddenly found voice. If "they" can have their churches, marriages, couples in holy union, religious orders, and chaplains, why can't gays? "The homosexual," declared the Reverend Wood of Newark, "is no longer content to sit at the door of the Church singing Psalm 88."

In short, Jesus Gay had a public Happening. As silent as his own birth centuries ago on a quiet, somber Christmas night two thousand years ago! The Gay Church of the Beloved Disciple was founded by Pastor Clement in 1970. He felt the call of Jesus Gay: Stop being merely a "good queer." Be yourself! "Homosexuals have nothing to fear from God" was his motto. Why should they? "An outpouring of love like I've never seen," said the Reverend about the happenings in his Church. It celebrated its first anniversary in 1971 by founding a new Gay religious order: the Oblate Companions of St. John (members wear purple and gray vestments). The Church stresses "the apostolic and the sacramental," says Pastor Clement. "An exciting development," says Reverend Weeks of Holy Apostles' Church. All this joy and love had been lost for fourteen centuries in the Tunnel. The Gays had to go back to the 6th century, Brothers and Sisters. Right back to St. Germain of Paris, if you please. To find his Mass and make a Gothic–Gallican–New York Gay rite.

Thus is Jesus Gay emerging. Everywhere! In the Performing Garage, a theater, in order to mark the occasion, Pastor Clement and John Noble renewed their twelve-year-old vows in a ceremony of holy union, promising "to have and to hold (each other) from this day forward, for better or for worse, for richer, for poorer, in sickness and in health; to love and to cherish in the sight of God." There's more, Brothers and Sisters! Father Marion, clad in his black and lavender, visits Quadrants 4B and 4C of the Tombs (reserved for homosexuals), as emissary of Jesus Gay and His Gay Father. Some people, said Reverend Weeks, "think

Christianity is a club limited to people like themselves." It isn't
any longer.

But you do nothing for the race, say the cavilers and clods, the
fearful straights. No children, say they. We have a bonanza,
Brothers and Sisters: the cloning process! This gives you as many
personal *Doppelgängers* as you want. We all want *Doppelgängers*. Gay ones.

But more still! The first conference ever on religion and the
homosexual was held in March 1971, at Riverside Drive Interchurch Center, New York. Then, Gay Pride Week in June 1971
together with the Gay-in Gathering at Central Park. Sip-ins at
bars. Gays flailing and fighting not only with the police but with
New York City Councilmen. Disputes between curees and invet-
erates before 32 million TV viewers. Banners screaming: "Better
Blatant than Latent!" People realized suddenly that Gays have
the same X and Y chromosomes as straights. (But, as one man
said, "some critics can't tell sodomy from a hole in the ground.")
And, finally, Pope Paul authorized "burial of sodomites" (he has
no better word in Church Latin) in consecrated ground.

Thus the new history goes, the dream is realized. Dreamt by
hundreds of thousands down the centuries: men and women, girls
and boys, eunuched by a one-track Church and a castrated Christianity, who lived and died with their pains and their lost hopes,
their persecutions and their miseries.

"An army of lovers can't lose," said one Gay. Now the Beloved Disciple will be understood (and perhaps his Apocalypse).
"We have found an identity and found something of what Christianity is about," said Pastor Clement. Thus the universal love of
Jesus Gay is at last receiving honor. Thus the preaching of Paul
(only marry women if otherwise you would burn, he advised) is
coming into focus for the first time since he wrote those Gay
words to the Galatians: "There is neither Jew nor Gentile, neither slave nor freeman, neither male nor female. All of you are
one in Christ Jesus." Joy is here now. Gayness is here. Because
Jesus Gay is here. "Homosexuality as a way of life has come of
age. Either the Church will recognize it or die," said the downright Reverend Maurer of the National Drug and Sex Forum. In
that spirit, he should have added: And Lesbians can reach the
Kingdom of God and of his son, Jesus Gay, without the lonely

use of the dildo. And we should add: Many a dead man gave the same challenge to the Christian Church—conform or perish; and they all perished.

Contemplating all this, one could give some quick, pointed, and, at heart, feckless answer, such as: Okay. Now will someone organize a Fund for a Statue to the Poet Horace Who Wrote the Best Odes to Little Boys. For, surely, Jesus Gay has taken *him* home. But the fact remains: homosexuality cannot be swept under the psychiatric rug, for beneath it the soul is also smothered; nor can it be relegated in chains to the ethico-religious hell of utterly depraved human abnormalities, for the love and salvation of Jesus are excluded from that. But neither can it be paraded around beneath the pseudo-aura of a Jesus figure with a narrow gage and the garb of what is called a theology but what is, in reality, theological humbug. For thus Jesus with his love and compassion is excluded; and, without him, in a square world the door of the Closet swings wide open ready to receive once more the refugees.

Jesuschristsuperstar

Since 1970, there has been a new no-nonsense idea of Jesus going the rounds. Let it speak for itself. For years and centuries and eons, it goes, they put the fear of God in every mother-loving son and daughter of a Christian, with Jesus figures frightening the living pizazz out of us all. Cadaverous-faced saviors, stern-eyed judge-gods, bleeding Jesuses, and all the establishment talk: Jesus was poor, not dirty; lived with whores, but never had the weekend off; ate with the rich, yet hadn't a dime. He only appeared in clouds and flashing rays and golden halos. And everyone around him was supposed to be happy. But they never had a laugh. Nobody laughed. No jokes. No fun. For Jesus, happiness was quite a serious matter. Damn serious. Give a belly laugh, and you could end up very far from Jesus. So they said.

But from 1970 A.D., that all changed. There was Jesus, the superstar. Not on Mount Tabor frightening the bejasus out of everyone as he rapped with Moses and Elias hanging in mid-air. Not on Calvary bleeding on a cross and looking mournful. Not in the Vatican wearing little satin slippers. Nor in St. Patrick's, of a Sunday, when the Cardinal (God bless him!) came out to smile on us all and watch the collections. But right where the action is: Broadway. And right on top of a huge phallus made of wood and paper and glue and paint, in center stage. Not as big as Mickey Mouse in Disneyland. But certainly as homey as Peanuts and as regular as Archie Bunker. You felt you had known the guy all your life. So, please, have a laugh. On Jesuschristsuperstar. That's why he came. Y'know?

Not that it really matters where you see Jesuschristsuperstar, in *Jesus Christ Superstar*, in *Godspell*, at the local Jesus Freak clubhouse, or wherever. The point is: the stuffing has been knocked out of reverence. Remember we were always told to be pure and wholesome and clean? That innocence was best? That you have to be quiet and reverential and sit straight up and talk clearly and go about your business seriously and maturely? Well, forget it. It is time to be liberated.

Forget it, because here is Jesuschristsuperstar moping along as we all do, with some squares hissing from a gondola hung above his head, a Judas lad black as pitch, screaming and rolling around, and a groovy Mary Magdalene trying to tell Jesus what's good for him. And all this to the ear-filling, mind-blowing, eye-batting, bustling music that lifts you right to the pitch of yourself.

When you add the pranks, pratfalls, prancings, and marvelous laughter of *Godspell* to the naturalness of *Jesus Christ Super Star*, you *know*, we haven't got to be afraid any more. Ever hear the joke about the Rich Young Man? Or that crack about losing your life to save it? Well, Jesuschristsuperstar tells it like it is. You see, this is *real* religion. Why, here you have boys and girls simply simmering with excitement at the sight of Jesus. And when he's "crucified" on that chicken wire at the end. Wow! It's a real, live, lovely boy standing there.

Out across the land there is a wave of response: Christ songs. Chris Holliday loves it, says he does at least three or four "Christian songs" a night at Harold's Silver Dollar Lounge in Reno. Decca Records loves it—$35 million gross on a double LP record of the *Jesus Christ Superstar* songs. And the clergy love it ("clearly a religious manifestation," says one steamily). And Billy Graham loves it. God is moving among those kids, he says. And the kids love it.

And mustn't God like it, then?

The only question left to be answered, as always, is: What has all this to do with Jesus of Nazareth? If you grow up slow and mature and clean, as they used to say; and if you read books and listen to educators and undergo discipline; obviously you are not going to find Jesuschristsuperstar. But if you are gunned up the puberty corridor like a rocket from a launcher, all heat and noise and trailing hair, and if you take off from language, from work, from what approximately 7 million other "kids" (the squares) are doing and what approximately 206 million other Americans are doing, you are going to be lonely out there.

So will Jesus.

Because he came to stay in the house of man and to dwell in the streets of man's city. Not to take off on a trip or to shake the dust of the city off his feet and disappear in order to do his own thing. He did that thing once. It had nothing to do with Broadway or the Met; only with the morality and loneliness that bring you to either place in a search gone badly awry.

Jesus Take-My-Marbles-and-Etc.

After all men's folderoling and addlebraining about what to do with Jesus and how to figure him, all the way from Jesus Caesar down to Jesus One-of-the-Boys, with the extravaganzas of the Jesus Liberation figures thrown in for good measure, would you not expect some sensitive souls to sniff the air and cry: stop the world! Jesus is getting off! That is exactly what has happened. To Jesus, mind you. Or, to be more accurate, that is what some sensitive souls are telling us that sensitive souls have done. They've said to Jesus: Jesus, you know you've had it. And it is not hard in their view to imagine what Jesus' answer is.

After all, great men like De Gaulle (*"Quels ingrats"* was his re-action to the 1968 riots that toppled his regime), Adolf Hitler ("They are unworthy of my cause"—i.e., the Germans who gave in), and Churchill ("The whole thing bores me"—i.e., British politics) finally got fed up. You can stand it just a certain distance. But the moment of truth arrives, and you pick up your marbles and go home in a huff. Thus, one of the last few Jesus figures to be born is: Jesus Take-My-Marbles-and-Etc.

Probably the two most prominent and, if not articulate, in any case loud champions of this new Jesus figure are Edward Bond in England and Leonard Bernstein in the United States. Bond wrote his drama *Passion* for the open-air festival held by England's Campaign Committee for Nuclear Disarmament, at a London race track, on Easter Sunday 1972. The press coverage was very impressive. Bond's real interest is to get all of us in the West to dismantle our nuclear bombs; then (he hopes) the Russians and Chinese and French will follow suit, and the Japanese, Israelis, and Indians will stop developing theirs. The logic of all that may not be clear, but that is his hope.

The setting, then, for this statement of hope by Bond is *Passion:* the Queen and her Prime Minister meet to drop a nuclear bomb and to unveil a monument. The monument is a full-size cross: on it is nailed a full-size crucified pig, its open carcass gazing bloodily at the audience, its two front feet stretched out and nailed to the side beams. (Bond delicately specifies that the pig is to be obtained from a slaughterhouse and not killed merely for the performance. That, we can assume, is ecological purity, or a tough stand by the local union.) The point of the crucified pig? Well, men have not waited for Jesus to save them; they have gone ahead and relied on their own—piglike—efforts. Pretty soon, along comes Jesus in a robe; here is the Savior robbed of his big day by a pig, his one chance usurped by an animal; he leans wearily on the arm of Buddha, who is clad appropriately for Nirvana in a loincloth. Jesus sees the crucified pig and says: "I am too late. I can't be crucified for men, because they've already crucified themselves." And Buddha, the realist, says: "You see! They are mad. They can't pity each other. So how could they ever listen to us?" Exit Jesus, as he entered, leaning on Buddha's arm.

Of course, the Queen, the Prime Minister, and the others go on ever more madly making more mad bombs. An old woman props up the dead body of her son in a sitting position. Gas escapes from his decaying belly and whistles through his teeth, forming the words: "I have learned that a pig is a form of lamb and power is impotence. Madmen, you are the fallen!" And that must go down in history as the most profound commentary on the 20th century.

It is all a chilling non-theology: salvation only by invitation of the saved, and only if the saved have pity on each other. (Which they have not, adds Ned Bond.) And the Crucifixion of Jesus is as significant as that of a pig. While Jesus flees with Buddha to a safe place, marbles and all, Bond grins a grisly and cynical "wisdom." Then we know: When Pippa passes the next time, let's be frank and tell her that all is *not* right with the world. There is no salvation by Jesus. Poor Jesus.

You may think that Ned Bond is crazy or blasphemous or trivial or naïve or coarse or a scrivener. Whatever the judgment may be of him as a playwright, it is clear that the point he misses is that Jesus is savior, now as then, in spite of men; and that he is not about to exit. And, incidentally, that leaves Bond as the likely candidate to pick up his marbles and shuffle off leaning on the arm of those in his audience he can lull into looking on, in unprotesting calm, at blasphemy-cum-social-relevance. Blasphemy is always relevant.

To give Bond his due, not all the action is on the stage. One is reminded of those theologians who are willing to do away with Jesus' claims, in favor of a little modern recognition; publicity, we call it. They speak of a Christian polytheism: Jesus taking his rightful place with all the other also-ran greats. And all those Christian gentlemen and ladies: bishops, priests, nuns, running around seeking relevance, fuming with feverish fabrications in order to make their Church "live" again, with democratic assemblies, pulsating resolutions, votes, roll calls, statistical proofs, pullulating acronymical organizations, contributions of arms and ammunition to the Third World to kill off Portuguese and white Rhodesians and other unsalvageable human beings. There is, indeed, a lot of hot air around our ears today just as noisome as that in the belly of a dead man. Bond with his Jesus figure is not so far off that particular mark.

There is another version of this retiring Jesus figure in Leonard Bernstein's *Mass*. Indeed, as the title implies, the idea of how Jesus picks up his marbles and toddles off is now presented in the context of a full-blooded Mass—at least as far as the words go. (Oh, yes, there's a little bit of blasphemy, and some curse words thrown in here and there; but that's poetic license for you.) The intent, the whole point of the Bernstein effort hangs on the dramatic representation of a Mass, a Roman Catholic Mass. It has the vestments, the gestures, the Latin words, and all the accouterments.

But *Mass* is, of course, no more a Mass than a *Duffy O'Doyle*

Synagogue Service on the same stage would be valid, in which the performing rabbi and his acolytes tear the Scroll of the Torah to bits and blow their noses with those bits, shatter the seven-branched candlestick, the Menorah, and use the pieces for soup-stirrers, and use the Ark of the Scroll as a receptacle for dirty stockings and jock straps—all to the words of Isaiah, Jeremiah, the Psalms, and traditional Temple music. This would not be any kind of synagogue service. *Mass* may be, as Donal Henehan indulgently remarked, an attempt to embrace in one tear-stained bear hug, us, our children, God, and our common dilemma. But one wishes Bernstein had been urged by his benefactors, if not by his own sensibilities, to keep that particular hug and such staining tears away from what millions the world over still hold sacred. (The mythical *Duffy O'Doyle Synagogue Service* would very rightly have had B'nai Brith, the American Jewish Committee, and the Jewish Defense League hot on its heels. In this context, it is not amiss to take note of the disquietingly acquiescent American audiences and patrons on whose arms Bernstein shuffles off to ponder with Bond on "realism.")

Nevertheless, the work in question is called *Mass*, and so its statement is intended to center on Jesus, salvation, mystery, and man. Jesus does not appear on stage. Except when quoting the words of the Roman Mass, Bernstein does not mention the name of Jesus. Jesus hangs invisibly around the wings like the Yahweh of Moses in the Bible. In fact, the first clue to Bernstein's misunderstanding and distortion of the Roman Mass lies in this direction.

Everyone knows how Moses, having been up on the mountain with Yahweh, comes down bearing the stone tablets on which the New Law has been engraved—Yahweh's gift to the people. But Moses finds that the people had become bored and made a golden calf, which they were now adoring. In his rage, Moses shatters the tablets. It is a genuine take-the-marbles-and-go-home gesture. Bernstein arbitrarily, and with little sophistication from anyone's point of view, transfers the Moses role to the Celebrant of his "Mass" and the Yahweh role to Jesus. A triumph of ecumenism!

The Celebrant goes through the major portion of the Mass ritual, including the solemn moment of Consecration, the whole interspersed with such theological plums as a giving of thanks "to God who makes me happy to be young" (where are all the Senior Citizens?); humble appeals such as "Come on, Lord, if you're so great, show me how"; admiring affirmations such as "and it was goddamn good" (the creation of the world); poetic flourishes of teen-age social Darwinism such as God "created the gnats to nourish the sprats to nurture the rats and all for us big cats" (imagine what a better rondo Bernstein would have had if he had remembered the bats, the mats, the pats, the scats, the brats, the spats, and the polyunsaturated fats, to mention only a few); and a "non-credo" which includes the telling line: "You, God, chose to become a man. To pay the earth a small social call. I tell you, sir, you never were man at all." (It seems, then, that Bernstein's Jesus never put his marbles where his mouth was, in the first place.)

At a certain moment, the Celebrant destroys the symbols of Jesus (Wine and Bread). Then there is one of those terribly *special* silences. "You know it was exciting to see what I've done," says the Celebrant to the other players. "Take a look, there is nothing but me under this," says he, pointing to his robes. Then he makes off, comes back ("dressed simply," says the stage direction), and joins the chains of embracing actors giving each other (and the audience, if they accept it) the "touch of peace."

So, with the central act of Christian worship and its instruments in pieces and Jesus, therefore, excluded, all men join in peace. The Jesus of *Mass* is one who needs no longer to save us. If he does not save, Jesus is nothing. Without Jesus, how even discuss mystery and salvation? We are left only with man. Not much of a trick. Hardly worth the price of admission. And that is what *Mass* does for Jesus, for salvation, for mystery, and for man.

What *Mass* did for Bernstein is perhaps cut from the same cloth. The competent critics of his musicology are not at all agreed that it did for Bernstein what Bernstein intended. As one critic remarked: "If you want to beat *Hair* at its own game, why tamper with Jesus?" *Mass* was meant to rouse up a community feeling. But, again, as one critic remarked, the whole thing had the earnestness of an interfaith conference at a fresh-water university and the repetitious purposefulness of a group-therapy session.

Of considerably more importance is what *Mass* does for its audience. Decked with many lines of subliterate rubbish, strung out on some reminiscent melodies and some mind-blanking silences, Bernstein's achievement in this regard is, in sum, to afford his audience the chance to tamper emotionally and ideologically with the sacrosanct character of Jesus and the central act of Christian worship. All this is presented to us as a cultural activity and an esthetic engagement complete with tears and bear hug and perspiration. "You see," he says, in effect, "the entire mystery of Jesus is no mystery. Let's be human about it, as we can be about sex, apple pie, the war, the flag, our country, personal honor, anything. For nothing is so untouchable that we cannot use it, in order to be human."

But to be fair, Bernstein, like Bond, has picked up a visible cue from the real world and made a beeline to the box office with it. And, again, like Bond's drama, his *Mass* has served to characterize the visible antics of many Christians who have set out to "humanize" Jesus and everything connected with Jesus. Some of the more recent behavior of clergy and people at Mass services is as painful and grotesque as *Mass*. The words used at Mass in such services could just as well fit a midnight celebration at a nudist colony. Sample from a West Coast Mass service: "Take the Body of Jesus, as you will shortly take the body of your girl." That is realism. Jesus, in other words, is fashioned into whatever suits the behavior, including the caprices, of any man and of any woman. The figure of Jesus is used by Bernstein to represent the opposite of what Jesus achieved: salvation for all men. Even in man's modern disorderly theater of longing and even for a Jesus figure, this is an impossible role.

Exit Jesus. Exeunt all.

7. *Satan: Anti-Jesus Figure*

No sooner has Jesus Take-My-Marbles-and-Etc. appeared on the stage, done his act, and taken the final bow, than from the wings we all hear something like a cross between a loud satisfied chuckle and a Bronx cheer. When the whole circus is at its height, we are suddenly reminded of Satan, the Anti-Jesus, the gloomy advocate of the profoundly cruel, the purveyor of gratuitous evil, the sinister possibility of human choice, the reckless anti-figure of the Light in which Satan must stand in order to be able to cast his somber shadow; Satan, that hardy perennial, the one and only, the original, the total anti-figure of Jesus, of God, of whatever is good.

In and through every other Jesus figure, men have sought to control and persuade others, alleging a power greater than their own, and a belief at least in the guise of good. Every other Jesus figure is a fabricated role thrust upon Jesus, or an attribute stolen from him and refashioned in his name. But this classic Anti-Jesus figure is ever set squarely to do open battle with him.

Despite his press and some of his bemused dramatizers and biographers, Satan Anti-Jesus is not really looking for *personal* headlines and does not find undisguised public appearances con-

genial to his methods. Still, if the demand is great enough, he
may acquiesce from time to time. It might be just when all the
kids are out having a weekend: the police discover a series of
dead human bodies bled, like pigs in a sausage factory, in some
fashionable suburban villa. Or, maybe an airliner sets out from
Chicago for Memphis and ends up hijacked in Algeria, and the
police at home find a mound of earth in the hijackers' Detroit
frame house together with a skewered doll and other voodoo paraphernalia. Or, scientists run amok "in the spirit of the times," as
the papers put it, and in the cause of science, and we find in their
wake the satanic cruelty of Nazi experimental laboratories where
men and women were guinea pigs of unspeakable agonies. Or, it
may be when the child-faced "sisters" tell us in court how by the
cleft grace of She-devil Lilith and in the name of Prophet Manson the "family" danced macabrely around the pregnant Polanski
skewered like a cow. Two lives with one stab, two stabs, nineteen
stabs. And so "wipe out the pigs"! But these are rare occasions.
Usually Satan Anti-Jesus prefers anonymity.

Our daily newspapers and magazines keep us informed about
the existence of a rather vast cult of Satan. Obviously, its touch
reaches far beyond even such chilling and dramatic litanies of
evil. In fact, it is sometimes so homespun in its language that it is
like listening to the protests of any oppressed minority. "Something," the Satan cultists tell us, "has been put over on the whole
human race for thousands of years. It cut every man's potential
just in half. I mean, right down the middle." This is the message
you can cull any Wednesday on Lexington Avenue and Fifty-
ninth Street, New York City, from a darksome old man in a
black robe handing out some clean dirty books:

Jesus God, they told us in school, walked among men doing
good! They dinned it into us. From now on: Be good! (they
taught us). Fight against evil! Love your neighbor, especially if
he hates you. Do not return ill for ill. Turn the other cheek.
You're a bag of lusts and lasciviousness. Watch it! Satan is after
you. Don't lie! Don't kill! Don't dishonor! A litany of don'ts.
There's a demon in you. We will exorcise it. So they told us all.
Propaganda! All this was nothing less than an organized masochism, a great injustice to Satan. The cruelty and the blindness of
it all. And a poor life-sized fallen-angel (talk about oppression!)

figure is put forward as the prowling cause of all our ills and the fetish of our deep guilts. But all this has gone on too long. Too much of the reign of Jesus God, the sugar godlet of baroque and Gothic and incense.

Now, suddenly, Satan! Alive and well. Undaunted. Happily evil. Where Jesus God murmured: "Live!" Satan (spelling backward) asserts: "Evil!" There *is* a demon in you? Well, thank your stars! Don't exorcise the demon. Exercise the demon! Channel that demonic power. Ritualize your hate. Invoke your lust. Consecrate your lies. Baptize your murders. Be glad you can be naughty. Satan walks again. Go visit him. Honor him. Be a temple of glorious indulgence. Satan blesses the superb shamelessness of your carnality (beautiful word!), the marvelous miasma of your micturition on the Host and the Cross. Stand up. Strip off. You are offered death, real death in life, a stench in the perfumes, maggots circling the eye sockets of the corpse, the sweat on the body of lovers, the blistering of a child's face as it burns to death in its crib (Mom is on a "trip" with Dad and friends). Glorious!

Not merely a subterfuge, mind you, to shore up the mind against its ruin by mortality. No despairing gesture. No flight to upper regions, nether regions, any regions. This is real death in life. Hate notes for your future. Recovery of lost occasions in the past for most ugly sin. Exaltation of your present evil.

The old man who preaches this withering message happens to like Fifty-ninth Street. But Satan is no mere denizen of a single corner or a single town or country. Nor does he peer through the eyes merely of a solitary old man of enthusiastic evil. Indeed, ever since the mealymouthed Jesus God, myriads have tried to worship Satan, to celebrate their complete and completed being in him: purity-cum-lust, clean-cum-dirty, gentle-cum-murderous, true-cum-false. The range of activity, imagination, and inspiration are easily conjured up in the mind by a glance merely at a few of the more recent names involved: Nostradamus (16th century), Jeanne-Marie Bouvier (Madame Guyon) and Catherine Deshayes (La Voisin) of the 17th century; Sir Francis Dashwood's Order of the Medmanham Franciscans (18th century); Marquis de Sade (19th century); McGregor Mather's Hermetic Order of the Golden Dawn; Aleister Crowley's Order of the Sil-

ver Star; the Black Order of Germany (20th century). No doubt
about it. Jesus Satan is alive and well as a housebroken lion in
Black Pope Anton Szander LaVey's San Francisco's Church of
Satan. *Regie Satanas!*

The diabolist and diabolical view is very articulate and all too
clear throughout the language of the cultists: Men and women
should not have to stand for the stark loneliness of Christianity,
the solemn silence, the stifling of desires. Merely a covenant to
satisfy the flesh. Merely a cross to give joy. And mountains of
don'ts. Nothing but don'ts. No certainty. Nothing palpable, ca-
ressable. No secret cruelties (except in the name of love, if you
please!) No tasteful pronunciation of obscene words. No delicate
mouthing of four-lettered names. No covenstead. No inverted
cross. An occasional nun erotically licking the wounds of a plaster Jesus. But men and women had no access to the full truth:
that sensuality is a jeering, sneering mock-up of our death agony;
that killing is a rape of filthy goodness. Who cares for hymen or
hysteria? Infidelity, so perfect in deceit, that is something to get
high on. "Do you want to love? Please hate! Do you want to be
excellent? Please be bad!" This is the lesson of the Diabolist
taught in dark and noisy places. But, alas, Walpurgis Night always a black secret. Burnings, rackings, lynchings, drownings, os-
tracisms. Many martyrs for Satan: the German Johannes Junius in
1682; New Salem Catherine Selwyn in 1692; the English Jane
Wenham in 1712; the Mexican Queretaro brothers in 1950. "Call
that love, do they, your wishy-washy lovers of Jesus God?"

Now, then, just don't break your sides laughing at the antics of
the Bucklands, the Rogerses, the Adens, the blue-ribbon nudy
nests in Connecticut and Maine, Lady Bett, Lady Judith, Lady
Blaise, and all the cozy, cozening children decapitating helpless
chickens beneath the moon. Esbats. Chants. Potions. Enochian
keys dating far back to the dawn of history (actually 1962 A.D.).
(And there are such appealing back-ups. In the United States
alone, 10,000 professional and 175,000 part-time astrologers, serving an estimated 20,000,000 people who spent—in 1969 alone
—about $150,000,000 on the works.) Take off your clothes,
man. You are quite indecent as you stand. Snaky-waky at the
girl's buttocks. But plead the Fifth Amendment to the precinct
sergeant. Dad will call a lawyer. Or the A.C.L.U. will defend

your American right to be as kooky and as cocky as you like. "Bless me, Father, I have sinned. Last night, I thought I was God. Her father says I've got to marry her." Do not laugh at all.

To tell you the truth, it is far less a laughing matter than you would think. Because Satan is most effective when he avoids the personal appearances and fades increasingly into the general landscape of events where we breathe him in like the air. Increasingly, men and women have understood. Brutality is a vision of agony minus any creative goal, minus any palliative, minus any spiritual recompense. And it lengthens like a chain, advances like a tide, deadens, brutalizes.

A single example, one chain, as it were, will suffice. It has been years since anyone was surprised to know that there was a Mafia, a Cosa Nostra. And it has been generally understood for years that "families" have "wars" and "rub each other out." An innocent enough situation for most of us, given the general world situation during our lifetime. "They" have "their world" and "we" have "ours." While the surprise was never long-lived, there was a shock and a moral outrage at one time when gang wars broke out and raged publicly.

But gangs were not wiped out; they were forced to retreat to "home-base activity," in their secluded and safe areas, so to speak. With time, there was established an effective, lucrative, organized crime net across this and other countries. Good organization, too. Territories, cooperation, coordination, regional and local directors, bankbooks and balances of trade, reports, bookkeeping, group insurance, medical and other fringe benefits, corporate old-age and retirement plans. Sound business practice prevailed; rough competitors kept them on their toes; and they had their own "international business."

And, really, when you come right down to it, they were not much trouble to the law. They kept to their business, and the law kept to its beat. There were bribes, of course; but both "sides" understood the rules; and, after all, a little compromise never really hurt. Anyway, generally, no one stepped casually into the other's territory, unless the heat was on from up above. Then, maybe, a few raids by the police, or a few "hits" by the mob, and back to normal. Life went on.

The chain of brutality had another link.

Somehow, then, that bribery aspect seemed to take on a life of its own. It blossomed. It became a perfectly legitimate part of normal business, if both "sides" looked at it coldly (and why look at it otherwise?). After all, if you worry about the morality of the thing, you just make a lot of trouble for everyone, and get laughed at for a sucker besides. It is much more realistic to spread the word and help your friends cash in. Police friends. Business friends. Wall Street friends. Trucking friends. Export and import friends. Building and construction friends. Military friends. Academic friends. Lawyer friends. Ecclesiastical friends. City Hall friends. All friends.

Altogether, a golden link.

The word spread . . . and spread . . . and spread, and the graft and the takes and the bribes and the influence piled so high there just wasn't any way to camouflage the mountain any more. And just when it almost seemed that there couldn't have been many people left to camouflage it from, corruption investigations began to blossom like spring flowers. Not only in the United States. But in London, Paris, Marseilles, Düsseldorf, Mexico, Rio de Janeiro, Beirut, Moscow, Milan, Rome, Amsterdam, Geneva, Prague, Hong Kong, Singapore, Sydney.

Perhaps New York's special commissioner Knapp spoke for the results of all of them when he not only excoriated the highly systematized level which corruption had reached in law enforcement, but exposed a system so riddled by corrupt arrangements as to make the police and even the courts and judges appear symbiotic partners in crime, big and small. The line separating the "sides" had become blurred beyond all meaning in practical life.

It was apparent how strong the chain had become, and how constricted men had become by it, when the deep effects of the corruption process were unwittingly bared. Corruption, it became clear, is so rife in the areas of gambling, prostitution, loansharking, building trades, consumer goods, military supplies, that —as Commissioner Knapp concluded, the only solution was to legalize the crimes, and so (this was the idea anyway) to do away with the corruption. In all innocence, the serious proposal to remove corruption by declaring its total acceptance is to ensure the success of corruption. Thus, the ultimate societal and legal success of the bribe system. Corrupt your way to legality. Don't even mention the base immorality of the motive. And don't try any argument that prostitution and gambling are socially good or socially evil, or that *anything* is socially good or evil. But legalize the crimes which led to the corruption; and what was the matter with the payments made to achieve it in the first place? What makes corruption corrupt? What makes corruption corruption? What can "corrupt" mean?

At this stage, one cannot stop to reckon the enormous incentive (ultimate success) to anyone with enough money or a big enough machine to go on to the next set in the chain of corruption and the next and the next. Commissioner Knapp's proposed solution is the key to the ultimate annihilation of all laws, providing that enough corrupt pressure is brought to bear.

As if that were not jolting enough, the answers and reactions to the Knapp proposals were equally wide of any moral mark— or even of any moral reference. No fewer than five district attorneys responded to Commissioner Knapp (all negatively); not one mentioned public, governmental, legal, or any kind of moral responsibility on any side of any issue. No one man of high public responsibility talked about good and evil, about any general consensus underlying the law and the daily life of citizens, and supposedly guiding the protectors and leaders of citizens as well.

They probably thought no one would listen if they did. It was as if they had heard the public voice saying: What we've got here is a mammoth problem. So don't preach at me. At least, not about the police or the public or the investigations or the threats.

While the commissions investigated, and the ties of crime to law and business were drawn for all to see, the mobs were having a long, bloody, and very public war. Headlines: "Fifteen known dead in about a year." Blood. Bodies riddled, burnt, stabbed, poisoned, skewered on butcher's meat hooks. And while both the investigations and the gang war were going on, *The Godfather* became one of the greatest romantic best-sellers in recent history, and the movie made millions. Not only success; glamor!

And not only success and glamor: legal protection. When the Mayor of New York City ordered the police to clear the Mafia out of town in August 1972, this brought a widely publicized and sententious warning from at least one ranking legal expert to the effect that such a thing could not be done, if the city could not produce an airtight case against each of the figures involved.

Now, while the rest of us scratch our heads and wonder who is crazy and how it all began, Satan giggles every morning over the breakfast headlines. Any city is safer for the mob, or for any hoodlum or thug (well, to be fair about it, he really should *look* respectable and must have enough money to dole out), than for any of the millions who loved *The Godfather* and laughed and cried for the people in it, but who did not seem to notice that the tables had been badly turned on them. For anything becomes possible as the compromise progresses. And nothing should surprise us: Biafra, Bangladesh, Sudanese massacres, Nigerian expulsions, Belfast bombings, multiple murder-rape, kidnapping, burying alive, and so on. As corruption replaces any moral base in determining law, might is right, and life is cheap, and mind your own business. Look the other way. What the hell. Let's stop worrying about everything.

Not many months ago, *New York* magazine had as its cover story a piece of reportage by Peter Hillman of fifty-eight killings in one week in the city. A story of moral outrage? The beginning of a crusade to restore sanity and respect for life? Not exactly. Rather, it was a cool, very cool, "case by case" recounting of every murder, "focusing on the day when the greatest number of victims were killed." It was statistically very sound. "This Summer's Seven Bloodiest Days" was the bold-lettered cover line. Somehow it was a headline that seemed to invite the reader to conjure up other summers, other perhaps slightly less bloody days.

Then the tone was set for the piece itself: "Reporter Hillman" (said the blurb for the article) "creates a picture of the incredible banality of murder . . ." Finally, at the end of six pages of factual reporting of bloody, wasting, violent death, all recounted in a new-journalism monotone curiously unsuited to its subject, the great question was asked: "Fifty-eight homicides in a single week in New York—how can anyone begin to deal with the toll?" Now, *there* is the moral question to ponder. The answer? Only two suggest themselves feebly to Hillman.

First, you can "count the victims in various ways." He suggests counting them as men and women, as blacks, hispanics, and whites. Then try counting how many were killed by the gun, how many by knife—and don't forget the defenestrated baby. How old was the oldest? How young was the youngest? In what precinct were most of them when they died, and how many victims knew their slayers?

Second, after you finish counting and reckoning, you get the weather report. "You can blame the weather," he says. The rain, the heat, the heavy air.

Hillman is sure on one point, though. And cool or not, it is a signpost pretty far along the trails with Satan: "What you know for sure about these fifty-eight homicides in the one week in July is that the public forgets them—if they ever noticed."

Not very long ago, Paris and New York "traded" (via their daily newspapers) bizarre maps of their respective cities. These maps blocked out for citizen and tourist alike those increasingly restricted areas safe by day and the even further diminished areas reasonably safe by night. For the City of Light and the Great White Way are claimed with impunity by Satan; everyone else needs guides and maps (which our newspapers obligingly supply—their public duty being thus fulfilled); we are alienated and frightened strangers at the short end of a long compromise with Satan.

PART II
FALSE SEARCHES:
THE "HISTORICAL"
SEARCH FOR JESUS

Once you leave aside the figures of Jesus and all the second names conferred on him, the logical step is to turn to what in modern terms we call history, the historical record. Four or five questions arise dealing with the four successive periods of time since the life of Jesus.

What do we know of Jesus factually? This question covers the approximately thirty or forty years of his life, say up to the year 36 A.D. The Factual Jesus.

What do the first written records make him out to be? The records fit in somewhere between 36 A.D. and 110 A.D. The Messianic Jesus.

What did Christians decide about Jesus in their main concepts and formulas of belief? The Dogmatic Jesus. The relevant period is the longest: from 150 A.D. to the beginning of the 17th century.

Finally, what have scientists, those working with the factual evidence at hand and relying on their logical processes, decided and said about Jesus in the period between the 17th century and the late 20th? The Scientists' Jesus.

Any account of Jesus in history would not be complete without a bird's-eye view of the Fantastik Jesus. In the 19th century alone, over 60,000 books and pamphlets were written about him. It would, indeed, be fantastic and unbelievable if nothing fantastik had been written about Jesus then, before, or after, in an endeavor to explain him.

8. The Factual Jesus

In this context, a fact about Jesus of Nazareth means either a date, the name of a place, the name of a person, an event, or an accompanying circumstance, which concerns Jesus and establishes his historical reality and which can be established from sources other than the New Testament. Such facts, as in the life of any man who lived almost two thousand years ago, fall into three categories: those that are historically certain; those enjoying a certain historical probability, greater or lesser; and those that are merely historically possible.

It would be extremely difficult and unscientific nowadays to deny that a man called Jesus ever lived, whatever we believe about him and whatever we think about his identity, his importance, and the movement that arose in his name. Outside the books of the New Testament, the earliest testimonies to his existence and the bare outline of his life come from Jewish and Roman writers. The earliest testimonies to the bare facts of Jesus' life are to be found in Jewish sources; and this is natural and logical. Jesus and his followers posed a real threat to the Jewish establishment. It is chiefly in the rabbinical tradition of polemics against Jesus and his subsequent followers that we find a solid testimony about Jesus. Some parts of this tradition date back to the lifetime of Jesus and to the fifteen or twenty years immediately after his death. Although inveighing against him and his followers, they bring out several points: that Jesus was the son of Mary, that he was supposed to have worked miracles, that he called himself the Son of Man, that he used the very sacred Jewish phrase "I am He" (this was an assertion for Jewish ears that he was God), and that after his execution and death his tomb was empty.

We then come across a series of professionally historical testimonies from the eighties of the 1st century into the first third of the 2nd century. The earliest is to be found in Josephus, a historian who wrote between 81 and 96 A.D. In his *Antiquities of the Jews* there is more than one mention of Jesus. Although most scholars admit that someone, probably a Christian, tampered with the texts in question, it is undeniable that he mentions Jesus and records the fact of his existence.

A second testimony comes from Pliny the Younger, who was sent by the Emperor Trajan in 110 A.D. to investigate corruption in Bithynia (modern northwestern Turkey). He wrote to the Emperor in 112 A.D. telling him about the Christian sect and asking for instructions. Again, it is a direct testimony to the former existence of Jesus. Around 95 A.D., Rabbi Eliezer Hyrcanus of Lydda speaks of Jesus' magical arts and there is no doubt in his mind that Jesus had existed. The Roman historian Tacitus, writing his 132-volume history between 116 and 120 A.D., discussed the events of 64 A.D. in Rome under the Emperor Nero. Speaking of the latter's persecution of the Christians, Tacitus spoke of their founder: "Christus, from whom the name had its origin, suffered the extreme penalty during the reign of Tiberius at the hands of one of our procurators, Pontius Pilate." Tiberius was emperor of Rome from 14 to 37 A.D. Pilate was procurator (governor) of Judea between 26 and 36 A.D. Tacitus had at his disposal the official archives of state in Rome. From these testimonies, then, we know that Jesus existed and that he was tried and executed by crucifixion sometime before 36 A.D.

We have very little other evidence to narrow down the actual date of Jesus' death. But some evidence indicates as a probability that he was put to death around the first Passover after the execution of a man called Sejanus, a favorite of the Emperor Tiberius. There is also a statement in the Talmud (Sanhedrin 43a; 107b) that Jesus "practiced magic and led Israel astray." All indications are that this comes from the records of the Great Sanhedrin of the year 32 A.D.

About the date of Jesus' birth, we have no exact details. Gospel accounts imply that the King of Judea at this time was Herod, who died at the end of March of 4 B.C. With no reason to doubt this statement of the Gospel, one is still left with a large margin of possibility. How far prior to 4 B.C. Jesus was born can be determined with only a certain degree of possibility based on three facts which may be reflected in the Gospel accounts. One is a Roman census begun in 12 B.C. by the Roman Legate in Syria, Publius Supplicius Quirinus. He began the census in Syria and did not start it in Palestine until the year 7 B.C. Such a census is mentioned in the third Gospel, Luke's, and Quirinus' name is given. Luke mentions the census as marking the year of Jesus' birth.

The second fact is the way in which King Herod of Judea suppressed a family plot against him. He discovered that his two sons, Alexander and Aristoboulos, were plotting with some of the notables of his kingdom to remove him from the throne. Herod had three hundred of these notables killed in public. His own two sons he had strangled in the town of Sebaste (modern Sabastiya) in 7 B.C. In one of the Gospels, mention is made of the "Slaughter of the Innocents": Herod is supposed to have had all male children of two years and under killed because one of them was destined to be king in his place. This Gospel account may reflect one of the side effects of Herod's suppression of the family plot.

The third fact is, surprisingly enough, the much discussed and much derided "star" seen by the three Wise Men from the East. We know for sure, from the observations of Kepler on December 17, 1603, and from the observations of P. Schnoebel, that there was a conjunction of Saturn and Jupiter in the constellation of Pisces in 7 B.C. and that the conjunction took place and was observable between the end of February and the first nights of December of that year. We also know that astronomical observation had been developed to an art in Persia and the general area. It is possible, then, that some astronomer did observe the conjunction, regarded it as noteworthy, followed an ancient tradition about its significance, and turned up in Palestine in 7 B.C.

We thus arrive at the conclusion that Jesus was probably born prior to 4 B.C., possibly in 7 B.C., possibly one or two years before 7 B.C., and that he was executed probably in the year 32 A.D. Jesus would have lived, then, for approximately forty years.

No surprise must be had at the fact that Jesus was born at a B.C. date. The error was introduced by a Scythian monk, Dionysius the Exiguus, who lived in Rome between 500 and 560 A.D. He dated the birth of Jesus from the foundation of the city of Rome. Dionysius took this date as December 25, 753 B.C. Actually, the Christian era as now dated is at least four to seven years too long.

About Jesus' birthplace, his appearance, where he spent his youth, when his preaching began, what places he visited, and what he said and did, our only direct sources are the New Testament books. He must have been light-brown-skinned. His eyes were probably brown, possibly blue. His hair was probably black and shoulder length; equally probably, he had a mustache and a beard. He certainly spoke Galilean Aramaic, probably could chat in Greek, possibly knew some colloquial Latin. Some of the places mentioned in the Gospels can be identified from outside sources and some cannot. Nazareth, for instance, where Jesus lived, is not mentioned before, during, or after Jesus, except in Christian documents. To deny that it existed in the time of Jesus would, however, be too arbitrary. His mother's name, Mary, is found only in rabbinical sources; and that of his reputed foster father, Joseph, occurs only in the Gospels. The Jewish historian Josephus mentions blood relatives of Jesus, as do the Gospel narratives, sometimes referring to them as the "brothers of Jesus." But the word "brother" is ambiguous in Hellenistic Greek, the language in which those references are written.

Outside confirmation is abundant for many details mentioned in the New Testament. In matters of dress, food, life styles, public officials, political situations, idiomatic language, religious usages, and mental attitudes, modern research has served to authenticate the picture of Jesus, the Palestine of his time, and the historical period to which he belonged as we find it portrayed in the New Testament. Factually, therefore, we have the bare essentials about the life of Jesus: that he was born of a woman called Mary, somewhere between 4 and 10 B.C., probably 7 B.C.; that he preached and was said to work miracles; that he was hated by the Jewish establishment; that he claimed identity with God; that he was executed by crucifixion sometime between 26 and 36 A.D., and probably in 32 A.D.; and that his tomb was empty shortly after his death.

Side by side with these few facts concerning Jesus, one must set one major non-fact. It has as much force, negatively speaking, as any fact about him. Any historian who looks at the history of the Mediterranean basin in the first three centuries of the Christian era and who does not remember or who omits in his reckoning that with the life and death of Jesus of Nazareth a new human dimension was introduced into the world of man, will be hard put to explain what happened. At best, he will explain away what happened between 32 and 400 A.D.

It has been the fashion, nevertheless, since the middle of the 18th century, to explain it all in function of the New Testament writings and of historical laws. But these give us nothing but, at best, a second-hand, sometimes a third-hand, report of what people of the time thought had happened. And they leave us with this: an obscure man, and a collection of his sayings, some accounts (embroidered or not) of his life and death, and some echoes of both in contemporary records.

There is nothing in the New Testament writings or those records to account, on a scientific basis, for the emergence of a victorious and dynamic community of men and women whom both Jews and Romans tried to suppress, the Greeks laughed at, and Constantine had to acknowledge. History, as the science of what happened and how it happened, cannot explain this. Nor should it attempt to do so. What took place cannot be explained in terms of the Roman Empire, or of the aspirations of merely another Jewish messiah figure stalking the foothills of an obscure Roman province called Galilee, and finally ending up a bloodied corpse on a criminal execution dock. By 400 A.D., there was a new creation among men, a new inheritance in the spirit to live and work and build; a purpose and a thrust started in whole populations which was to make Europe possible and, with that, the basic institutions of our society and civilization. It was a new human dimension, a new selfhood for the individual.

But if, in the quest for Jesus, anyone is seeking historical proofs in the present condition and criteria of our knowledge, he will have to limit himself to the sparse data listed in previous pages. On the basis of those data, there will be no explaining of what happened and no understanding of Jesus.

9. The Messianic Jesus

The Messianic Jesus is the picture of Jesus which emerges from the earliest documents written about him which we still possess today. These are mainly the books of the New Testament, twenty-seven in number. Relevant to the life of Jesus, it is the four Gospels and the letters of St. Paul together with the Acts of the Apostles which count. Up to this day, the earliest copy or fragment of any New Testament document is a fragment of the fourth Gospel (John) found in Egypt and dated reliably to 135 A.D. Recently, it is reported that a fragment of the second Gospel (Mark) dating from around the year 50 A.D.—that is, approximately fifteen years after the death of Jesus—has been found among the documents discovered near the Dead Sea and connected with the Qumran site. But this is not yet confirmed. Doubtless, as time goes on, further documentary evidence will be found coming from the period between 1 A.D. and 70 A.D.

It is generally agreed that the four Gospels appeared in their present form sometime between 70 and 110 A.D.—Mark about 70 A.D., Matthew about 80 A.D., Luke about 90 A.D., and John from the period 50–61 A.D. Both in Paul's letters and in the Gospels as well as in the Acts of the Apostles, Jesus is described

and announced as the Jewish Messiah. We find this picture of
Jesus all-pervasive from then on even in such remote places as
China. There were two Chinese lives of Jesus published around
640 A.D. at the behest of the Emperor Tai-tsung, the second
T'ang emperor known also as Li Shih-min, who died in 649 A.D.
We also have an inscription on stone which tells of Christian mis-
sionaries who came to China in 635 A.D. The inscription itself
dates from 781 A.D. and it pictures the Messianic Jesus, as do the
two published lives.

The basic lines of the Messianic Jesus are simple: God had
foretold to the Jews by means of Moses and the Prophets that he
would send a Messiah, an anointed one, who would lead them to
victory over their enemies and to national happiness. But in the
Jewish Bible, this Messianic victory and happiness is described in
this-worldly and national terms. Jesus, however, is presented as
Messianic in an other-worldly and non-nationalist sense. He came
to save men from their sins, it is told, and to found an eternal
kingdom. Certainly in the beginning, between his death in 32 A.D.
and the fall of Jerusalem in 70 A.D. to the Roman armies, this
kingdom was interpreted primarily as a Jewish kingdom.

The majority of Jews living in Palestine would have none of
the new religion. The Jewish authorities did their best to stamp
out the nascent sect. Besides all this, inherently the message of
Jesus from the beginning transcended the Jewish Law (which it
declared to be abrogated) and the territorial bounds of Israel (all
lands and nations were invited to become Christians equally).
Within a relatively short time, most Christians lived outside Israel
and most were non-Jewish in origin. The sect transcended Jewish
nationalism. In fact, the Messiahship of Jesus was understood
"spiritually." The early Christian Church took the symbols, the
images, the personages, the language, the stories, and the promises
of the Jewish Bible. They applied these exclusively to their own
beliefs, and they looked upon themselves as the new "Israel" and
the spiritual inheritors of Israel's inheritance.

One of the chief architects of this transference was Paul of
Tarsus, who made the adapted Jewishness of Christianity palata-
ble to Greek and Western minds. Many have used Paul's activity
to explain the comparatively rapid spread of Christianity in the

Mediterranean basin, as if he effected this transference by "hellenizing" an originally Semite message. But this is inadequate historically and textually unprovable. What was true was that the new faith made possible a hope that Judaism never had. It had a genuine welcome for all new nations which Judaism could never display and always eschewed.

But the Messianic Jesus thus outlined had Judaic traits which were to cling to it right up to the 20th century. For a long time, for instance, it depended on the ancient Biblical chronology of the world: creation in seven days, an age of four thousand years (Bishop Ussher actually decided that the world was created on October 23, 4004 B.C.!), the centricity of the earth in the universe, and the names Adam and Eve as those of the first man and woman alive ever. Even when science started to disprove all of this, Christianity still clung to the Jewish chronology. Giordano Bruno was burnt in 1600 for teaching with Copernicus that the earth moved around the sun, and Galileo was forced to recant publicly what he had discovered scientifically in private. Christianity also adopted the ideas of Heaven, Hell, angels, and demons from Judaism. More importantly, it likened itself, the Church, to a mystical version of the Jewish people, speaking of the Church's history in terms of the events described in the Jewish Bible as happening to the Jews. The worship and prayers, the theology and the thought of Christian thinkers and their people were impregnated with this. Augustine of Hippo in the 4th century summed it all up epigrammatically: "The New Testament lies hidden in the Old Testament; the Old Testament becomes clear in the New Testament." All, in other words, was prophecy, foretaste, fulfillment, and realization.

The root of Christian-Jewish opposition lies here. Christians thought of themselves as the inheritors of all that Jews ever were given as believers in God. Jews resented this and regarded Christians as apostates. Christians regarded Jews as infidels who had refused their own Messiah when he came to them. Since the Second Vatican Council (1962–65), a détente has been introduced between Christians and Jews. But, clearly, the Christian Churches as a whole and the Roman Catholic Church in particular are not willing to renounce their claims to the entire tradition of the

Jewish Bible. For in the period between 150 and 350 A.D. Christianity solidified its claim to the Jewish Messianic clothing for Jesus.

The new religion spread throughout the Empire. Demographers estimate that by the year 200 A.D. Christians numbered one million. By 300 A.D. they ran to ten million, almost one quarter of the Empire's total population. By 300, official Roman persecutions had ceased. Throughout the Empire, there was now flourishing a religion which looked to Palestine as the place of its origins, which had already phrased its main doctrines within the framework of the Jewish Bible. Their very name, originally a nickname, told of their essence: Christians, followers of the Christ, the Anointed One, the Messiah. They held international councils under the aegis of Roman officialdom, rode down doctrinal revolts within their ranks, and saw the Emperor, himself a pagan, remove the Roman eagle from his battle standards and replace it with a monogram of that Christ, XR.

The Emperor's mother, Helena, visited Palestine, established to her own satisfaction the holy places at Bethlehem, where Jesus was born, and Jerusalem, where he had had been crucified. Churches were built in both places. Christianity had now established its claim on the Palestinian origins of the Messiah. Henceforth, Christianity for over a thousand years would look to Jerusalem as the place where Jesus the Messiah had lived and suffered and to Rome where the Vicar of the Messiah reigned and ruled. Christianity and Judaism were locked together in a historical destiny from which neither could easily break. Christians now turned and during the next centuries developed their dogmatic beliefs about Jesus.

10. *The Dogmatic Jesus*

To understand how Christians came to think and speak of Jesus over a period of almost seventeen hundred years, you have to assimilate first a short series of concepts. The Messianic Jesus of the early period underwent a detailed, scholarly, and thorough treatment. What happened was simple. Men in the West between 150 A.D. and 1600 A.D. applied to Jesus whatever methods of thought they possessed within the framework of knowledge they possessed of the world. When this process was finished, there existed a body of beliefs—dogmas was the name applied to many of them—which in varying degrees commanded the attention and adherence of all believers, and in virtue of which men organized their lives.

Before retailing the principal concepts involved here, one must have a clear idea of how Christians thought of a human being, male or female. The human being had a body and a soul. The soul had faculties (mind and will) and the body had faculties (senses). The bodily senses had power to get sense knowledge. The soul by mind and will had power to have mental knowledge. God could give a special increase of that power to any sense or to mind and will. And that special power could enable the senses or the mind to know either natural things or supernatural things. The word *grace* was used to describe this power. Christians spoke of many different kinds of grace which we need not discuss here: justifying grace, actual grace, sufficient grace, helping grace, efficient grace, and so on. The essence of Christianity, however, was that without the knowledge and enjoyment of God, man could not be happy. God became man in Jesus in order to make this enjoyment possible for all men. Without the power of grace, all was impossible.

The first main concept is that of *substance*. It was a Greek concept which said: Everything (men, animals, plants, objects) that exists is composed of *substance* and *accidents*. Accidents are all you can see, touch, smell, hear, measure. The substance of anything is invisible, untouchable, but is that to which all accidents are attached. Sometimes, the term *nature* is used for *substance*.

The second concept is that of *person*. Only human beings were considered to be persons. A person, again, is not what you see or feel or touch or smell or taste. The person was conceived as the individualized substance of a human being which acted by means of will and intellect and by the accidents of sight, hearing, taste, and touch. The person was the responsible originator of all the actions performed by these means. Nowadays, we think of a person as a synthesis of emotions, thoughts, instincts, reflex habits, and reactions. All these were considered to be accidents attached to the person.

The third concept was of *God*. God was thought of as being one substance, the divine nature, and being three persons. This was the Trinity. The three persons were: the Father, the Son, and the Holy Spirit. With these concepts, Christians came to think of Jesus in the following way:

God, in three persons and in one nature, existed always. He created the world and mankind in it. God wanted all men to be happy forever. Sin was committed and it prevented man from receiving the grace necessary that he live forever. The Son, the second person, took a human form as a fetus in the womb of Mary, was born and called Jesus, lived and preached, died on a cross, was buried, rose after three days, and departed from this visible world having founded an official group to preach about the salvation he had won.

Big questions arose. Was Jesus really a man? Was he really God? What did he know? How did he know? How did he save us? What happened when he died? Was Mary really his mother? If Jesus was God, he could never lose his knowledge and possession of God's nature (Christians called this the "beatific vision"). How, then, could he have suffered bodily? Or how could he have felt deserted on the Cross, as one of his recorded exclamations seems to indicate? The Christian answers to these and similar questions were framed officially in terms of substance, accident, person, grace, and the trinity of divine persons.

Jesus, as a person living and breathing and acting on this earth, was said to have two substances, a human one (he was man) and a divine one (he was God). He was, however, only one person. Of course, he was also a person in the modern sense (a synthesis of emotions, thoughts, reactions, etc.). But the second person of the trinity was really man: his mother was mother of that person in human form; his body was that of the second person. On the other hand, his hair and his nails, for instance, were not God's hair and nails in quite the same way as his human soul and human mind were God's human mind and God's human soul. For hair and nails and suchlike things grew, were cut, or fell out, as in the case of all men.

Because he was God, he had a divine will; and a divine mind. As a human being, he had a human will and a human mind. Two wills and two minds. This fourfold mechanism was centered in the person of Jesus. Its unity derived from his person. As for knowledge, Jesus had four main kinds. Because he was God, he had divine knowledge. Because he was a man who was God, he had that knowledge any man will have once he sees God in the "beatific vision." Also, as a man who was God, he had a preknowledge infused into his natural being. This pre-knowledge covered all future natural and supernatural matters and affairs. Lastly, he had, of course, the type of knowledge all men get by living, growing, and learning in the normal way. How Jesus functioned with this fourfold knowledge was explained in complicated terms and never satisfactorily described.

As regards the conception of Jesus in the womb of Mary, little was said which is relevant to modern genetics, although much was said relevant to other aspects of the question. We must remember that the human ovum was not pinpointed, by Karl Ernst von Baer, until 1827. Genetics is a very modern science. In modern terms, Christians would have to say that, because Jesus had no human father (Mary did not conceive Jesus after having had relations with any human being), no spermatozoon united with an ovum in her womb. We know much today of the genetic code and the role played by the male spermatozoon. Christians must hold that God supplied what that spermatozoon would have done. What was supplied must have had the usual genetic determinations required so that the ensuing fetus be human and humanly viable. If sex determination or baldness, for instance, is fixed by the male spermatozoon, then what was supplied by God must, in the Christian view, have supplied such characteristics.

The main achievement of Jesus was that of saving men from sin and making it possible for them to "enter Heaven," to enjoy the "beatific vision." This he did by willingly dying on the Cross. Thereby he merited the supernatural grace man needed in order to avoid sin and to die in God's friendship and "enter Heaven." Over a long period of time, Christian thinkers developed an entire terminology and conceptuology in order to talk about Jesus and his meritorious sacrifice; to describe the adoration due his humanity, his sufferings in the body, his condition after his resurrection, his return to Heaven, his presence in the Eucharist preserved in Christian churches, his delegation of powers to his representatives, his actions in human history, and his return to the earth at the Last Day of the world's history. All this was done in the heyday of Christian belief in Europe. Political systems, social justice, personal rights, economic distribution, human behavior, all were ultimately determined in view of this "Christology," as it was called. More importantly still, it was all done within the framework of a philosophical system inherited from the ancient Greeks, and before the use of modern scientific inquiry began at the opening of the 18th century.

A long time before that scientific inquiry arose, this Christological network of views had been "frozen" as a system. It admitted no other system as possible. About man, about woman, about God, about human life and the human universe, it was maintained, one could speak only with the words of this system and think only with the thoughts of this system. This was fine as long as the system was moored to the world by two well-tied lines: sociopolitical systems devised in the light of that Christology, and a knowledge of factual reality which was couched in such words and ideas. By the late 20th century, both mooring lines had been definitively cut. The ancient system was floating free on high seas of human events. The dominant sociopolitical systems of the age are not derived from the ancient system. The principal mode of knowledge on which the 20th century world depends increasingly for progress and survival will have nothing to do with the ancient system of thought. Concretely, this means that a thoroughly modern mind has an almost insuperable difficulty in talking or thinking about Jesus. Ways of worship inspired by that system seem empty. Ways of life inspired by new sociopolitical systems and modern knowledge of factual reality provide no easy way of integrating the ancient systematic thought and language about Jesus. The Dogmatic Jesus is practically unknowable to the modern mind.

LIBRARY ST. MARY'S COLLEGE

11. The Scientists' Jesus

There had always been discussions and dissension about Jesus from the earliest times. But until the 17th century, it was never more than a minority who differed with the majority of Christians. Furthermore, no extensive and learned class of men ever set out to demolish the traditional concepts and knowledge of Jesus. When that did happen, it took almost less than two hundred years to dislodge those concepts and dilute that knowledge.

It is important to note that up to the 17th and 18th centuries, the Gospel accounts of the life of Jesus were always read as religious books, as God's sacred "word," as a special revelation. Nobody of significance ever thought of reading them as mere books. All the books of the New Testament dealing with Jesus and his doctrine were officially interpreted only by the Church and its approved teachers, theologians, and thinkers. Some people have put this down to a clerical chauvinism. Partly, it was. But up to that time there was really no such thing as text criticism or a critical appraisal of historical records such as we know it today.

The rather quick process of demolishing traditional concepts and knowledge of Jesus started with the Protestant Reformation, although this was not the intention of the Reformers. The principle of that Reformation was that, in the ultimate analysis, the only criterion of truth for the individual was the individual's own conscience. "It's your decision and your conscience" was the cry. The dogmatic authority and teaching authoritarianism of the official Church was attacked and overthrown (to be supplanted in most cases by the authoritarianism and dogmatism of men like Luther, Calvin, Zwingli, and the other Reformers). Once this happened, in the 1500–1600's, all else followed. People started to think for themselves. About the same time, men in Europe began their modern scientific researches and discoveries, freed from the dogmatism and absolutism of traditional control, with a constant panorama of nature opening out in front of them. There swept through European (and later American) intellectuals a new feeling of mental youth, of intellectual freshness, of great adventure. It was a springlike feeling and an exhilarating experience. They felt the impact of the new knowledge daily increasing and with it a fresh illumination of their minds and lives. It was called the Enlightenment.

At first it seemed to provide every instrument man needed. It gave him new instruments and new measurements of nature and of his world. It supplied him with a reasoned approach to virtue and goodness and peace in the philosophy of Immanuel Kant (1724–1804). A way of looking at human history that seemed both promising and reasonable was outlined by Georg Hegel (1700–1831). It was the classical period of European music. Man's love of beauty and his desire for the infinite found expression in the poetry, the thought, and the life styles of Romanticism. The American Revolution of 1776 and the French Revolution of 1789 both seemed to augur a new era of human dignity based on human reason. For, in its essence, the Enlightenment claimed to have made human reason man's sole guide and rule. All should be subjected to man's reason; and such reason was exercised only by the individual. Pure reason and the sacredness of the individual.

Of course, Jesus and the traditional view of Jesus came under scrutiny. They had to be examined. As early as the 16th century, some men like Michael Servetus (1511–53) and Faustus Socinus (1539–1604) had come to deny publicly that Jesus was God in the traditional sense: Jesus was either the most admirable man

who ever lived or a man specially endowed and rewarded by
God. But even the principal Protestant Reformers of the time
found this a little too hard to swallow.

The real wedge in the door began, however, with Hermann
Reimarus (1694–1768). A perfect child of the Enlightenment,
Reimarus proposed a religion based on reason and he rejected the
idea of Jesus either as God, as savior, or as revelator. One should
read the Bible as one reads any ancient human book—critically
and on the basis of external evidence. Gradually the main thinkers in the Enlightenment renounced all belief in Jesus' Resurrection, his birth from a virgin, his miracles, and his divinity. None
of these were accessible to human reason basing itself on historical evidence.

Now a deluge followed in the 19th and the early 20th century.
A new breed of scholars tackled the question of Jesus. Some were
theologians and philosophers; others were skilled in the developing sciences, history and anthropology and languages and archeology. And really, it was only a matter of time until the
prevalent intellectualism of Europe and America demolished to its
own satisfaction whatever remained of the traditional concepts
and beliefs in Jesus. In 1835, David Strauss published his *Life of
Jesus:* the Gospel accounts of Jesus were based, he said, on
myths; these had been imposed on quite a simple original reality
—an ordinary man who had some good ideas about moral behavior; there had been no supernatural happenings; many things
in the Gospels were not historically true; one could get at the
truth only by an application of Hegel's philosophy to the New
Testament. In 1863, Ernest Renan published his *Life of Jesus:* the
New Testament, he maintained, was a mythical account of someone whom Renan called "an incomparable man." Renan was primarily a Romanticist and an elitist, and perhaps the clearest expo-
nent of the Enlightenment's dream that human intellectualism
and reason should provide a bulwark against both religious authoritarianism and intellectual tyranny. It should guide all man's
destiny. Intellectuals had a special place in Renan's world order.

By the end of the 19th century, therefore, theologians and
thinkers set out to find what was historically true about Jesus, to
detach his historical reality from the web of myth surrounding it.
Religion should be approached, it was said, with a historical and
humanistic outlook. The study of the origin of religions was im-

portantly regarded as a human science having equal value with
the "hard" and "soft" sciences. Charles Darwin's *Origin of Species* (1859) provided all with a new perspective on man's origin.
The only problem now remaining was to explain how it all came
about. The famed historian Adolf Harnack (1851–1930)
showed that the ancient formulations of Christianity about Jesus
depended on non-Christian sources for their concepts and terminology. Jesus could not escape this net. He, too, was a product of
evolution—genetic, as well as cultural.

There was thus initiated the last and definitive phase in the de-
molition of Jesus as a person credible for the modern mind. This
came about in a simple and, when all was said and done, a logical
way. The keystone of the search now was to find the "essence"
of Jesus, the real historical Jesus. But what Jesus, what "essence"
of Jesus, or what historical reality of Jesus could be found was
predetermined by the mental mold of those who initiated the
search.

That mental mold had several definite traits accepted without
demur as prelogical and subject to no discussion. One trait concerned the nature of the proof or evidence needed; and it could
be formulated as follows: "We have to explain historically how
by 400 A.D. the mass of Christians believed Jesus to be God." The
quest had one main presupposition. These thinkers knew that
there had been a time, before Jesus and during his lifetime, when
men did not believe in Jesus as God. The problem, as they saw it,
was to explain the appearance of belief in Jesus. And their presumption was that the explanation was to be found in sociological
and other quantifiable measurements such as sociological actions,
political moments, cultural cross-currents, and anthropological
needs. But inherent in such an explanation and presumption is the
idea that belief does not come about by any form of knowledge
derived from non-quantifiable sources, nor from the experience of
immediate, personal love, nor from the recognition of a truth not
derived directly from "factual" experience.

If one accepted this presupposition, one accepted another statement: "We must abstain from all evidence except the New Testament and contemporaneous documentation." The idea is that
what came after the Gospel period (say, after 135 A.D., as a cliché
date) and in succeeding centuries misrepresented the Jesus of past
history. There was yet a further presupposition: "We must be

reasonable in all steps and look for the nearest thing to a scientific proof or evidence, even if we cannot have properly scientific proof." It was thus assumed that the methods of Science when applied to the New Testament or to the fact of Jesus could elucidate both successfully. Finally, the very object of all this searching was clearly delimited: "The result of the study must be clear and intelligible in terms of human reason and human science." Presumably, then, the meaning of the New Testament and the meaning of Jesus for history and the meaning of historical reality in the case of Jesus were as factually determinable as, say, the presence of oil deposits in the Sahara and the prevalence of schizophrenia in a patient.

The results were predictable and inevitable. Researchers found, for example, that at various times Jesus seemed to have spoken as if he had a firm expectation that the "Last Day," the end of the world, his own Second Coming, and the "Final Judgment" on all men and women by Jesus were events just around the corner. This was tied in culturally and historically with similar currents in Palestine and elsewhere before, during, and after the time of Jesus. This expectation is called eschatology (Greek: *eschata*, "last things"). Of course, things did not end; the world is still with us and we are still with it. Therefore, it was concluded, Jesus had only a limited view and gave instructions for only a limited time and place. Those instructions are no longer useful. Jesus did not provide us with a timeless or universal ethic. He was not a universal teacher. There never was any question of his being God.

Other researchers examined every word and sentence in the Gospels. They found, of course, that they could classify both words and narratives according to certain forms: the parables, the miracles, the scourging-and-mocking stories, the crucifixion stories, the Last Day stories, and so on. Not to have found such things would have meant that the Gospels were not of the period of time assigned to Jesus. For such forms are to be found in literature previous to and contemporaneous with Jesus. It would be as if we did not find any mention of Russia, of the Communist threat, of the Cold War, of the national debt, or of Civil Rights, in the speeches of American Presidents between 1915 and 1970. But, having found this seemingly positive evidence, the researchers felt obliged to go one step further. They concluded that, because all these forms were to be found in the Gospels and also found outside the Gospels, they were just that: forms imposed on Jesus in order to give him a certain stature which, of course, was not historically real.

It was neatly done; they consequently denuded Jesus' life of many significant words and, still more fatally, of many significant happenings. The emergent Jesus turned out to be less even than Renan's "incomparable man." A biography of Jesus became impossible in our sense of the word. An anciently living man about whom we can really know nothing except the distortions of those who came after him is, finally, a zero for any mind. For the modern mind, in particular, such a man without any factual identification is simply not interesting. He has no meaning; for the modern mind, meaning lies only in facts.

In this light, the condition of official Christianity is most understandable. Protestant Christianity has been focused on three aspects, for the last four decades: ecumenism—the drawing together juridically of the various Churches; the reinterpretation of classical thought about Jesus—as in the work of Karl Barth, Reinhold Niebuhr, and Paul Tillich, while abstracting from the validity of the classical Jesus and seeking in Judaism most of the structure and the content of their thought; and, thirdly, the sociopolitical "witness" of Christians. Jesus remains a vague and shadowy substance, more implied than clarified, a stumbling block for the reason but a rallying point for the emotions, never to be brought up as the key but always to be retained as the atmosphere of a fragrance or the resonance of a marching anthem.

Roman Catholicism is crumbling before the eyes of all and as if, all along, some deep rot had been setting in. Eastern Orthodoxy (Greek and Russian) is frozen within national and ethnic boundaries perpetuated by its own momentum, continually harassed by the invading realism of the age.

All, Catholic, Protestant, and Orthodox, can see the horizon lit up now and then by little flares—Jesus cults, momentary revivals, apparent ecumenical progress. But over all of them hangs a consciousness that some vital juice has run out of the systems whereby they function. The outside world cannot know their agony. It can guess at their difficulties about the dogmatic Jesus, understand what happened when the scientists got at Jesus, and be amused somewhat at the Fantastik Jesus.

The world has its own troubles.

12. The Fantastik Jesus

Throughout the 19th and 20th centuries, people claimed to have solved and clarified the whole problem of Jesus in a simple way. Arthur Drews and others declared frankly and without further complications that Jesus never existed. It was much simpler that way. Less trouble. Others added: The whole idea of the birth and life of Jesus was just a Christian version of the story of Romulus, first king of Rome. Paul Louis Couchard objected (after all, the historical evidence was not to be wholly rejected), and said that Jesus "was an obscure person who died in Jerusalem, it is not known how, in an ill-planned attempt at insurrection, and who had the incredible luck to be deified."

Joseph Klausner in the last century found such views inadequate. Jesus did exist and he had some good qualities—mainly those of a simple and slightly hallucinated Galilean peasant. But when all was said and done, he was just that; he loved prairie flowers, wandered alone by the lakeside and in the hills, loved little children, dreamed of Israel's freedom from the Romans (ah, if he only lived today!), and lived and died an uneventful life. Klausner thought, of course, that Paul of Tarsus, the apostate, the Greek-minded rabbi, pulled the real trick: taking the simple dead

Jesus, decking him out in Biblical prophecies and Greek mythology, thus creating the myth of his claim to be Messiah, son of God and saver of Israel. Nowadays, we know more than Klausner knew about Palestine of Jesus' time. We also can read the Gospels with a less prejudiced eye than Klausner. But a number of people still think that Klausner "solved" the whole problem of Jesus.

Anyway, Jesus did exist. His origins, however, are fantastically described. The Talmud, which contains materials that go back to the time of Jesus, relates that his mother, Mary, was a hairdresser of doubtful repute. Married to a decent sort of Greek carpenter called Poppas, she fooled around with a Roman soldier named Pander (or Panther), had a bastard by the latter, and was flung out of the house by the injured and incensed Poppas. To this day, in Bingerbrück, Germany, you can read the tombstone of that soldier, Tiberius Julius Abdes Panther, born in Sidon (modern Lebanon), and whose regiment was stationed in Palestine about 9 A.D.

Some early Christians were extremely bothered by this story and tried to explain it away: St. Epiphanius (5th century) made Panther out as the father of Joseph the Carpenter (Mary's husband according to the Gospels). St. John Damascene (8th century) said Panther was a common ancestor of Joseph and Mary, and that Joseph's grandfather and Mary's great-grandfather were brothers. The Romans of the 2nd century had a popular song sung at pantomimes which ran: "Hey diddle diddle dee/Jesus, did you know that he/ had a father who could make a door/ and his mother was just an honest whore/ hey diddle diddle dee?"

But all this explained nothing. Not Jesus, anyway.

The Alexandrians of the 3rd century said Mary was loose-living and had an affair with her brother. Hence Jesus. Incest at the heart of it all!

The Arabs in the 9th century used a little imagination: Mary, like all Arab women, wore a *mezar*, or kerchief, on her head. The Angel came and breathed on the *mezar* one night and lo! Mary became pregnant. It was just like what Montezuma told the Spaniards about himself: he was the son of Tlaloc, god of rain, conceived in more or less the same way.

Aurelio Turcati, in this century, decided to give the Angel a recognizable form, and he suggested as a definitive solution that Mary's cousin Elizabeth and the latter's husband, Zachary, were just matchmakers: they threw the innocent Mary in the way of a handsome Arab prince passing by in his caravan and he had the most effective one-night stand of all time. Hence Jesus. An affair.

Karl Venturini, another modern, searched the Gospels and finally decided that Joseph of Arimathea, prototype of the "dirty old man," seduced Mary one Eastern evening in a fig grove. But this did not satisfy Heinrich Paulus, who really set out to find the truth. The Mary of *his* discovery was a simple gullible peasant girl. Some smooth-talking city slicker got her pregnant. Then a friend of his came one night, pretended to be the angel Gabriel, told her that her child was a miraculous conception; she persuaded the equally gullible Joseph (her fiancé); he immediately put on a chastity belt and went on making gates, plows, and barn doors.

Perhaps the subtlest fantastik of all was expressed in another opinion, according to which the Holy Spirit in the form of a dove was the "spiritual mother of Jesus." Mary just bore Jesus and raised him. Edmund Bapst, some decades ago, tried to solve it all by concluding that Joseph was Mary's uncle and married his niece. Incest again! But, after all, as the argument actually goes, what could you expect from someone like Mary, whose ancestors included a whore from Jericho called Rahab, an incestuous woman called Tamar, a treacherous woman called Ruth, and an adulterous woman called Bathsheba who played house with King David while her husband was away at the front?

The next thing which puzzled people was Jesus' birthplace. The Gospels tell us that Jesus was born in Bethlehem. But as Colin Cross, Gravieri, and several other moderns acutely if obscurely remark: Who would want his child to be born in Bethlehem? And in winter? Besides, the very name was ungodly, not quite Jesus-like. Bethlehem does not mean the House of Bread, as Christians like to say. It means the House of Lah. Now, Lah was a Canaanite god of dubious character and like many of his kind was associated with human sacrifices and sacred prostitutes and all that sort of thing. A man called Justin Martyr popularized the

House of Bread as the meaning for Bethlehem, sometime in the second century.

More imaginative people said that Jesus was really a Tibetan, a Hindu, a Persian, a Greek, or a Mongolian. Some people today say that he was a Samaritan, not a Jew, born in Samaria. Others still say he was a Bantu Black Man born in darkest Africa. But whatever is proposed, this much is asserted: Jesus was not born in *Bethlehem* or in Nazareth, as the Gospels rather strongly imply.

Colin Cross points out that when Jesus is called Jesus the Carpenter or son of carpentry, we must be careful. Carpenter and carpentry do not mean carpenter and carpentry. With a little ingenuity the word for carpenter in Aramaic can be shown to mean "sorcerer." So, as Cross concludes, "there was more to the carpentry tradition than meets the eye." Of course, this is like saying: Harry the Haberdasher Truman? No sirree! With a little ingenuity Haberdasher (Norman-French *hapertas*, Middle-English *haberdashaere*) can be shown to mean mushroom-cloud maker. In any case, Cross states, we must think of Jesus "without laying too much stress on Nazareth."

Then, again, the date of Jesus' birth was a problem. Originally and up to the 4th century, this used to be celebrated either on March 28, April 28, or May 29. Then somebody had a better idea. It was fundamental that Jesus had lived on earth for thirty years and had been crucified on April 6, in the year 30 A.D. Now go back twenty-nine years and 3 months, add in nine months more for the gestation period in his mother's womb, and you arrive at January 6, in the year 1 A.D. So the Greek Christians, who worked this out, said January 6 is the day when Jesus was born and appeared to the world. The Epiphany (from the Greek word to "appear") was fine for Greeks, but Roman Christians had an added difficulty. The old Romans had a marvelous feast and carnival on December 25, every year, the winter solstice. They called it *Dies Natalis Solis Invicti*, the birthday of the unconquered sun. They really went all the way during this feast (the Saturnalia): slaves ate with their masters, everybody slept with everybody else, all to show how good it was to be alive and love everybody. So the Roman Christians decided: make December 25, the *Dies Natalis Domini*, the birthday of the Lord, and put an end to this nonsense and lechery and running around. Hence our Christmas. But we do not know the actual day on which Jesus was born. And it really does not matter.

Of course, the business of the virgin birth of Jesus (no human father for him) has been solved. We do not find virgin birth (parthenogenesis, the zoologists and biologists prefer to call it) in nature, except perhaps in aphids, phylloxera, and crustaceans. But that is only because it is terribly difficult to distinguish between ovum and spermatozoa in those three. Anyway, parthenogenesis is impossible. Therefore, it did not happen. The Christians, however, needed some sort of myth about Jesus. When they got a foothold in Rome, they found various Eastern myths. One came from Persia: a virgin goddess gave birth to a son. One from Egypt: Horus, the sun god, was the son of Isis, the immaculate virgin and queen of heaven. One from Eastern Magianism: Tammuz was the son of Mylitta or Ishthar, queen of earth. So when Christians put the birthday of Jesus on December 25, *the* feast of the sun, they adopted the virgin-birth myth. Jesus was likened to Horus. Now, Horus is the origin of the name George (through the Greeks, of course). That is why we say "By George!" We really mean "By Jesus!"

In the circumstances of Jesus' birth, the crib, the donkey, and the oxen can all be forgotten. There were no animals present. Some theologians living a couple of hundred years after the birth misread a text of the prophet Habakuk: instead of the word "ages," they read the word "animals." But wherever or however Jesus was born, he lived a rather hidden life with his parents. Some say he traveled to Tibet (that again!), to India, to Stonehenge, to Marseilles in France, even to Tara in Ireland to confound the Druids, and that he worshipped at the Great Pyramids in Egypt. Yogi Ramacharaka quite recently assured us that Jesus took a trip through India, Egypt, Persia, Tibet (where he was a disciple of the Dalai Lama), lived in the Himalayas, and studied Buddhism and Zoroastrianism. Jesus must have. Without doubt.

But it is Colin Cross again who reveals to us how that obscure peasant Jesus came to do and dare all he did. Cross, speaking about a feast at which Jesus was actually present as a young boy, tells us how he saw Jesus lying in bed that night: "Probably Jesus lay awake that night. Since he was of a mystic turn, the events of the day and the solemn ritual of the banquet would have affected him profoundly. A thousand questions must have swirled in his mind, problems. . . . His large thoughtful eyes fixed on the width of the night sky, the moon, and the infinite splendor of the stars, for the first time Jesus felt the mystery of divinity, of that God who . . . now angered by the lukewarm faith of the descendents of those patriarchs seemed to have forgot [sic] his Chosen People and who perhaps was withdrawing his patronage until they should have repented and sued for forgiveness." To appreciate how scrupulously careful and free this is from all the myth-making Cross roundly rejects in his book, please notice the moods and tenses of his verbs (all this apart from the delicate observations about Jesus' "thoughtful eyes" and "his mystic turn"). Cross starts with "Probably," "would have," "might have" (we are still speculating in the conditional mood). Then, see the definitiveness of "Jesus felt." Suddenly this is what is happening. This is truly how to replace unscientific myth and legend with rational facts!

Not surprisingly, given this new scientific rationale, Cross and others know Jesus' character quite well. He was, Cross says, a progressive, sectarian Jew, a vehement man with some sense of humor, enormous skill as a propagandist, and may have possessed apparent psychic powers and skills in healing. Of course, his eating with prostitutes was in very bad taste (many stress this, without giving reasons), much the same as if the Archbishop of Canterbury took a whore or a Lesbian to bed in order to straighten her out.

Dr. C. Binet-Sangle in this century was more precise. Jesus had a pathological fear of food and eating. He was sexually impotent, suffered from dromomania (all that traveling around), had homosexual symptoms, underwent a hallucinatory syndrome and was the victim of theomania (thought he was God). Cross suggests that when Jesus ate nothing for forty days in the desert, he grew weak, hallucinated, and had sort of ecstatic auto-suggestions. J. Soury stated some years ago that Jesus had syphilitic meningeal encephalitis, was genetically tainted by alcoholism in his father, and inherited tuberculosis (all that sweating) from his mother. But Marchesan says no to the last item. He says that Jesus inherited something of the neurophysical trauma which his mother underwent when Joseph found out that she was pregnant.

So Jesus sweated blood too. Marchesan, by the way, a modern graphologist by trade, rounds out our picture of Jesus' character by a notation all his own. Jesus had 85° centigrade (*sic*) of flexibility, cheerfulness with dignity; 75° centigrade of evenness of temper; 25° centigrade of variability. But he had no vulgarity, no larcenous inclinations.

Jesus' appearance was something else. We have one full-length description from an otherwise unknown Roman, Lentulus, supposedly an official senior to Pontius Pilate, the Roman procurator who condemned Jesus: "nut-brown hair that is smooth down to the ears and from the ears downward forms soft curls and flows on his shoulders in luxuriant locks, with a parting in the center of his head after the fashion of the Nazarenes, a smooth clear brow, and a reddish face without spots or wrinkles. Nose and mouth are flawless, he wears a full luxuriant beard which is the same color as his hair and is parted in the middle; he has blue-gray eyes with an unusually varied capacity for expression . . ." Origen in the 3rd century said Jesus was small, ungraceful, and a mere nothing. Byzantine preachers claimed that Jesus was lame in the right leg. Epiphanius in the 5th century was much more precise: Jesus was six feet tall, had a complexion like ripe wheat, a long nose, coal-black eyebrows, a touch of red in his hair (the Jewish in him), and looked strikingly like his mother! Renan in the 19th century added to this, claiming that Jesus had a physical fascination and attraction which no woman could resist. But this must be put down as a Gallic dream. In the Middle Ages, they said that Jesus was five feet five inches tall. But by the 14th century, the Laurentian Code states categorically that he was five feet eight inches. There the matter rests.

Others do not agree with some of the more traditional stories about Jesus and his death. F. Klopstock (19th century) says that Socrates (yes, Socrates) appeared in a dream to Claudia Procla, wife of Pontius Pilate, and told her to plead for Jesus; so Pilate was in a sort of a plot to save Jesus. Then, about eighteen hundred years ago a group of people called Docetists said that Jesus never got near that Cross. The people around Jesus found an unfortunate man called Simon of Cyrene and forced him to substitute for Jesus. Jesus, by his magical powers, changed Simon's appearance to look like his own. The Romans said that it was a donkey which had been crucified; and they mocked the Christians with onolatry (worship of a donkey, ritual copulation of donkeys with young girls, etc. etc.).

Of course, why Jesus did what he did and died as he did has given rise to its own "explanations." The ubiquitous Cross lays it directly on the line. Three possibilities: Jesus' mind was unhinged by religious mania (so he went around claiming to be the Messiah until the authorities got fed up); or, he really made no claim at all to be the Messiah (it was all a mistake); or, he did claim this, was a born gambler, and lost the gamble. If those are valid suppositions, it is peculiar of Cross not to mention a fourth: Jesus was the Messiah, the Savior. Just as a possibility.

Hugh Schonfield in his latest book denies that Jesus claimed anything of the sort. Jesus schemed and plotted very well. He arranged it all so that there would be a crucifixion (what is a Messiah without crucifixion?). There was a lot of bribery around those days, of course, so that everybody collaborated—Roman soldiers and officers, Temple guards, some of the priests, and so on. Jesus was nailed to the Cross. A paid accomplice gave Jesus a sedative when he became thirsty on the Cross. The centurion did not pierce Jesus' heart. Joseph of Arimathea (also in the plot) put Jesus in the tomb, and at nightfall Jesus was taken away, lived a short while, and then died. A marvelous plot! A complete stranger posing as Jesus carried off the part about the Resurrection. There was no real Resurrection, of course. It all rather reminds one of those stories about Hitler being alive and well in Acapulco, Mexico City, or Isola Negra!

Heinrich Paulus, in the last century, did not quite agree with anybody. He had fresh ideas. First of all, Jesus' feet were not nailed. At nightfall, he detached his hands from the nails and simply ran off into the woods and hills. Paulus does not agree with others that the Resurrection was a hallucination (collective or individual) which the followers of Jesus had. Much more prosaic! When Jesus ran off, Joseph of Arimathea dressed his wounds and clothed Jesus in the gardener's clothes. Mary Magdalene, half-crazed with sorrow, saw him, thought he was the gardener; but this miffed Jesus and he called out her name. When she wanted to embrace him, he said: "Do not touch me." For a very good reason. He was aching all over from the scourging he had received.

Then, Paulus concludes, Jesus took off for Galilee, where he died shortly afterward of tetanus infection!

Still others say: No. He did die. His body was stolen. Who stole it? Take your pick: The gardener? Joseph of Arimathea? Mary of Bethany? The Jewish Sanhedrin? The Romans? Person or persons unknown? As I say. Take your pick.

And there, gentle reader, you have the Fantastik Jesus. It is hard to know if you can agree with Schonfield's coda to it all when he speaks of "the deathless presence of Jesus the Messiah" in our modern world. Schonfield even fantasizes for our edification: "Let those who wish to partake of the faith and strength of purpose of this amazing man, seek for him, there in the land he loved, among its hills and beside its living waters." And travel by El Al. After all, there are marvelous hotels all around the Sea of Galilee today.

Perhaps the real coda to any account of the Fantastik Jesus should end with the words penned over twenty-two hundred years ago by a man who loved another man, and who could not get over the injustice of the way in which his friend had been done to death by little men with pygmy minds and pygmy fears of what goodness and truth could do to their comfortable little categories. It was Plato writing in the early 4th century about his friend Socrates, who had been executed in 399 B.C. Plato was not fantasizing. He was reflecting with love and pain on the forced death of his friend. Speaking of his friend's executioners and of their decision, as well as of the death of any man made the victim of plots by fearful men, Plato wrote:

It was essential to destroy his good name; if others believed him just, he would have honor and profit, thereby; then there would always be the question as to whether he had indeed played at goodness for an ulterior motive. . . . Hence, he must be stripped of everything, he must be held to be the wickedest of men . . . whipped, tortured, imprisoned, nailed to a cross, or torn to pieces.

OF HUMAN
BONDAGE

PART III
THE WORLD:
THE GREAT SELVES
OF MAN

13. The Jewish Self

The world had never seen, and the world for a long time never understood, the stark and ineradicable realism of the Jewish Self. In the first place, the circumambient world of the Jews for nearly two thousand years has been Christian. And for almost five hundred years before that it was non-Jewish of various kinds— Persian, Greek, and Roman, successively. All the latter were chauvinist, of course; and the Christian world has been the most committedly chauvinist. For the Christians, Jews were the living proof of Christian faith. St. Paul practically said that , if not in so many words. The result was, as always with chauvinists, that the Jewish Self was likened to, and understood in terms of, the Jesus Self, and thus lost to sight. Even Jews were deceived, and eventually took on non-Jewish traits, including some of the Christian traits ascribed to them by Christian understanding and bias.

Job is an example. The story of Job is essentially a simple myth. It tells of a man's submission to a power in nature and beyond nature, no matter how cruel, unjust, and inhuman that power appears to be. "Man's life is hard enough," Job grumbles, "and he ends, anyway, in nothingness. But why must I have superadded miseries and the betting instincts of a fallen angel?" In Judaism, man is fingered out of the lifeless clay of nothingness by the all-powerful god; breathes, loves, hates, strives awhile; then is pushed protestingly but irresistibly back, whence he came, into nothingness. But Christians took over the story of Job; and it became a message of salvation, resurrection after death, and of immortality with Jesus in Heaven forever. At one point, in spite of his suppurating flesh, Job states the hope that one day, in perfect health, he will worship his god. The Christians translated this statement, making Job say that he believed he would rise from the dead and in a restored body see his god's blessing: "In my flesh, I will see my god."

The Jewish Self was unique because it was oriented to a god who, it was believed, had neither shape nor form nor color nor weight. This god had chosen the Jews and given them a land of their own together with special ethical commandments of their own. The Jew was, by that stroke, alienated from all other people of his time, because all of these adored idols and worshiped the natural elements. Jews had to regard everything in their world as distinct from their god, and therefore as alien to them. They themselves were aliens everywhere, except in the land their god had assigned to them. Between Jews and all the created world of their god there was an initial alienation. And only the presence of their god's signs—Temple, Ark of the Covenant, Priesthood, and the Law—could reconcile that created world.

By the first commandment, the Jew was forbidden to have any images of his god—in his heart or in his Temple. A real mythology such as we find in other religions was therefore impossible. For a genuine mythology, there was substituted a series of communal acts commemorating historical events of special significance to the people as a whole. There was no sacrament possible in Judaism, no communion with Yahweh, no meeting of human and divine, even no desire of that on man's part, and certainly no right on man's side.

The Jewish Self was further afflicted by an alien part inside it. The Jewish Self carried the alien world around because inside each man there was an alien part: "the bad image," "evil." It also had to be reconciled with Yahweh. For Yahweh was felt as a living force responding to the Jewish Self's dire need to mend the inner dualism in each person. Yahweh was the only hope of the Jewish Self to offset the negative trait. For the Jewish Self lived in this world without other defenders, and it lived on because of the Jews who died for Judaism. The Community is all, in the final analysis; that is to say, the Community living on this earth.

Thus, the Passover Meal commemorated and commemorates hunger and danger and safe escape from Egypt and from slavery. But only a memory connects the Jewish Self of today with the Jews who escaped then, a memory and, hopefully, communion in a long, unbroken racial association since that time. Racial connection and purity are of paramount importance. The Jewish Self is locked in a compartmented historicism which makes the Self in each epoch the bearer and the architect of the Jewish destiny. Even when the Jewish Self dies, its vanquished scream of protest shakes the congregated stabilities of men's minds, and whips their lives and opinions and complacencies with the cold wind of anguish, desire for love, and regret at the long night of nothingness closing in. The human bondage for the Jewish Self is, therefore, quite distinct from all others.

First of all, the world began in time. Creation had a beginning in time.

Secondly, death is the end of the human bondage and the end of the Self. As at the death of the Golem in Abraham Rothberg's story, the living-souledness of Jewish holiness is of no avail to the Jewish Self at that moment. "Adonai Elohenu, Adonai Ehad," mutters the Jewish Self, as Yahweh rips the Shem from the gaping mouth and tears the parchment with the holiest name of Adonai from beneath the rattling tongue. Yahweh gently but firmly lets the coagulated dust of mortality fall and mingle silently with the dead debris of matter, and renders the living soul of the Jewish Self back to its primeval darkness and tranquillity. There is no personal immortality and no personal resurrection and no hope of lasting beyond the grave.

In the last two centuries before Jesus, Jews took over some Greek ideas of immortality and some Persian ideas on resurrection and the "world to come." But they Judaized them beyond recognition: immortality was made a corporate affair—the *Peo-*

ple would last. Resurrection meant the non-death of Jews living at the End of all Human Days. The "world to come" was not an immaterial and supernatural Heaven, but merely an ever-continuing life on the planet Earth refurbished, replenished, cleansed, and rid of all the things which used to hurt men.

Thirdly, the Jewish Self was identified only by racial connection with that special Covenant which Yahweh set up with his Chosen People. In fact, there was no other identity possible for the Jewish Self. Yahweh's love was for his Covenant and for the group, for "Israel," for the collective personality of all members as one. As a member of that Covenant with Yahweh, the Jew had certain duties and responsibilities toward his god and his fellow Jews. In virtue of that Covenant with Yahweh, he had certain privileges which non-Jews had not. The Jewish Self was not the carrier of natural rights in our modern sense. Nor was that Self regarded as a person. Nor was the god of the Jewish Self a personal god in the Christian sense. That god was personal inasmuch as the godly commands were expressed in human language and the first-person-singular pronoun was affixed to them. But there is much which is anthropomorphic in Biblical Judaism. And the bulk of later Judaism has rightly depersonified the god of the Jews. The Jewish Self had no identity separate from the People; it was no longer the personal object of a god's love; it no longer owed obedience to a god's wishes. All duties had an ethical force and value which derived only from the Community and not from a personal conscience of the Self responsible to Yahweh.

As the human bondage was distinct for the Jewish Self, so the meaning of human life was quite distinct. The paradigm of existence in which the Jewish Self moved contained no reconciliation with the world as it was to be up to the End of Human Days and no ultimate salvation for the individual Jew.

In Judaism there had arisen the twin ideas of "redemption" and the "world to come." "Redemption" was a term applied to all creation: stones, trees, earth, cattle, crops, mountains, seas, rivers, as well as animals, plants, and men. There was no question of a healing or purifying of men and women by an act of love on the part of an all-powerful and loving god. It was, rather, a question of the god of the Jews being acknowledged by all men at least implicitly in the practice of the basic commandments. How "redemption" applied to inanimate objects was never clear. The "world to come" was originally described in terms of material well-being: numerous flocks, overflowing wine, abundant crops, good weather, taming of wild animals, peace among men. On the "last day," it was said, this "world to come" would become an accomplished fact by an act of Yahweh.

Today, except for the small minority of Orthodox Jews, both "redemption" and the "world to come" have been diluted into expressions of general well-being and happiness within a pacific and secure sociopolitical framework. Gone is any idea of a trans-formation of the alien world by the agency of the god of the Jews. The only "redemption" consists of the improvements socio-logically and culturally which Jews can effect. The only "world to come" is an era of human existence on this earth in which Jews, unhampered by prejudice and unthreatened by any vibrant adversary, mold the prevalent ideas of justice, purity, liberty, personal rights, and personal responsibility to produce a world in which the special Covenant and the privileges of the Chosen People will no longer be threatened, but in which peace with harmonious justice will prevail.

Denuded of any religious reference to a living god or to a spiritual salvation, Yahweh's words to Abraham or Ur still remain the keystone of the Jewish Self: "I will make you a great people. I will bless you and make your name renowned, a name of blessing. Those who curse you, I shall curse. And in you shall all the races of the world find a blessing." The Jewish Self is in bondage to a world in which all hope is confined to this universe and to the continuation of the Jewish race as a vehicle of "redemption" for that universe.

14. The Greek Self

To appreciate the Greek Self, dismiss any idea that the ancient Greeks were a nation of natural democrats and a tranquil population of daylong reasoners seated calmly in colonnaded porticos. Their sun was too hot, their blood too warm, their bodies too active, their passions too alive, their wine too heady, their living too hard, their earth too unresponsive to labors, and their land too intertwined with salt sea and mountains. Greeks were either "of the sea" or "of the mountain," as the lingua franca proverb has it. And those in the cities and towns were of both kinds.

What distinguished the Greek Self was the inexplicable intuition—present in no other culture—that the individual had innate desires to transcend his condition and that these desires were legitimate. For only the Greeks among the ancients formulated the idea of an absolute good, an absolute beauty, and an absolute truth attainable by mortal man as mortal man. They called this wisdom. And their chosen road to that wisdom (their only mistake, really) was reason.

Reason, however, must not be understood as we understand it today. Our meaning for this term derives from the beginnings of inductive science and the European Enlightenment of the 18th

century. And reason, in this tradition, is built on a prime negation and a never-to-be-examined presupposition: that unless the
logic of the human mind is satisfied by a demonstration outside
the mind and by means of quantifiable elements in man's world,
then it is not humanly dignified to hold any view or assert anything as true. Reason, thus accepted, subverted more than one
precious human commodity. Belief, for one, went out the window. Knowledge as an inner forum of feeling and intuition was
also discarded in favor of knowledge as an outer museum of analyzed facts. Only "irrational people" such as artists, poets, lovers,
and religious believers dwelt in that inner forum. The Greeks
never knew this sort of reason. Reason, for them, was a means to
wisdom, not an end in itself.

Where the Greek Self shone was in the luminosity of its intuition that attainable absolutes existed and without their beauty
(not their logic or reasonableness) man's life was not truly human.
The Greek Self was a paradigm of tension. It regarded the human
bondage as ineluctable. The Self was not a slave, but a victim.
The Self was a hero, titanic in effort, straining to outwit a determined fate, conflicting with the powers of nature and the preternatural, pursued by flaws and defects which finally proved the
Self's undoing. But in reaching its destiny, the Self attained its
place in what was for the Greek a hierarchized universe where
the gods sometimes snatched the young and the beautiful and the
noble, and where the old died tired and worn and went to rest,
and where all that was humanly true and beautiful and good
lived and perdured forever in a region of the Absolutes.

Where the Greek Self was genuinely flawed was its lack of any
salvation for the individual. The gods could be appeased for a
while—perhaps. They might even be heard dimly mumbling
secrets of life and death in the Cavern at Delphi. The end could
be delayed by distracting the Three Fates, Clotho, Lachesis, and
Atropos, as they spun the thread of individual life, pulled it out
full length, and then cut it off. And some few fortunate mortals
could win Olympic immortality. But the glory of being a human
being was to go down in revolt against the servitude and in rebellion against the cold solitude of the Field of Asphodels where
dead shades slept and wandered.

Although our word "person" is derived ultimately from the

Greek through Latin, the Greeks had no idea of person as the idea has been current in the West during the Christian era. The Greek Self was personal in one remote sense: as embodied in the Hero. The Hero, by his very being, could claim special treatment and a special fate. He had, in that sense, innate rights and an irremovable dignity.

The human bondage was never transcended. Nor were its blind forces, its destiny and its fates, obviated. At the same time, the Greek Self never accepted it, even when caught in its toils. For the meaning and signification of human existence was actually that of protest. Of protest after protest. Each human grave was a protest that men could think the thoughts of the gods, even if they were powerless to escape a death decreed by those gods in their feckless immortality. There was no transcendence even by perception of the beautiful, the true, and the good. Because, no matter how steadily the Greek Self contemplated them and no matter how they were loved, they returned no love. The Self was no object of love. Beauty, truth, goodness, were static symmetries which evoked love but never returned it; they evoked desire beyond their own reach to fulfill. They never aroused hope. They never satisfied hunger.

But the meaning of human life was not restricted to a material here-and-now. Nor, for that matter, was it laid up for an immaterial there-and-then, a world beyond, a paradise, a heaven after death. For, although there was no salvation for ordinary mortals, the Self was a triumph even in its failure. For it went down to dusty death holding firm against blind fate and as no vassal to the worms which ate the flesh and mercilessly swallowed up human laughter, human beauty, and human thoughts. It was truly the Greek Self which spoke through the inscription put on the tomb of the Three Hundred who fell at Marathon: "Stranger, go tell the Spartans that we lie here in obedience to their commands."

15. The Roman Self

The only true god of ancient Rome and the model of the Roman Self was Hercules, the mythical hero, son of Jupiter and successful performer of the Twelve Labors. Romulus and Remus, the founders of Rome, were liked by the Romans as symbols of their preternatural beginnings. The Romans insisted on the cults of Venus and Diana, Hera and Pluto and others. They worshiped dutifully at the shrine of Jupiter as the Father God and rambunctious Chairman of the Board of gods and goddesses who sat around Mount Olympus cackling, wining, and lechering their way through eons of human misery. But Hercules was indomitable, and his fortitude in the face of incalculable odds was grandeur itself. At the end, so the Romans told, writhing in death agonies, he had himself carried to Mount Oeta in Greece, laid on a pyre, and burnt into immortality. Thus Hercules. Thus the Roman Self. Indomitable grandeur in life. A defiant and chosen leap into the jaws of inevitable death.

The human bondage was accepted as the prime condition for the indomitable grandeur of the Roman Self. The only value of the Self lay in its mastery, its victory over life and life's forces. Might was right. Right gave might. A "virtue" was some form of steadfastness in willed grandeur and indomitability. *Vis*, physical pressure, was also will power. *Fortitudo* (courage), *patientia* (patience), *fidelitas* (faithfulness), all were drawn from the arena of physical struggle, the overcoming of great odds, the maintaining of unity against disruptive forces, and the ever-present privilege of the Self when confronted with an unacceptable choice: to destroy its own life by poison, by the sword, or by drowning. Legions of Roman soldiers committed mass suicide by execution, running on each other's swords with eyes covered, rather than fall into the hands of a superior enemy.

They did not excel as original scientists, mathematicians, architects, or engineers. They borrowed shamelessly and stole unrepentingly. But they adapted skillfully from everyone around them, and they incarnated their dogged imperialism and protuberant grandeur in hugeous viaducts, aqueducts, roads, sewers, and bridges still to be seen and still sometimes used all the way through Spain, Germany, France, Italy, Greece, Turkey, Yugoslavia, North Africa, Egypt, Iraq, and on the borders of Saudi Arabia. They imitated marvelously if with a somewhat elephantine touch. They were outstanding in the factual, the informational: law, civic administration, military operations, economic exploitation, industrial expansion, and commercial trade lines. While engaged in all these hardheaded operations, they filched: art from the Etruscans, carvings from the Spaniards, painting from the Egyptians, mosaics from the Palestinians, and even picked up a sense of beauty and proportion from the Persians.

The ancient Romans could not speculate, although they appropriated for themselves Greeks, Greek books, and Greek thought. They did their best to capture the Greek light and grace in lyrical poetry and choral odes. But, in comparison, the Roman effort was heavy at its best; at its worst, it produced boring reading like watching a hippopotamus trying to pick up a single pea. Besides, Romans were not reasonable. But they were eminently logical men. Beyond the factual, the useful, the predominant and overpowering, there was no other meaning. This, indeed, was the meaning of life for the Roman Self: an absence of meaning but for the victory and the glory of being Roman, of government by might, of perdurability by sticking at the task, in order to put off the ultimate defeat of death and earthly corruption. Their own tribal background provided them with a framework of mythology in which native Italian gods were grouped with foreign and Romanized imports from all quarters of the world. This pantheon, together with a cycle of festivals based on their agrarian origins, provided their time process with mime, theater, and a communality of celebration. A commonality of emotions, attachments, trusts, and loyalties linked the inner life of the Roman Self with an outer paradigm that placed death at the end of all the paining and the grave as the veil of all glory. But it was vibrantly Roman.

The human bondage was accepted on its own terms: a struggle against opposing forces, the imposing of clear and biased laws by force of Roman arms; the subjugation (literally, "putting under the yoke," as of animals) of all non-Roman peoples; and a final bowing to the inevitability of death and of final nothingness. The Roman Self had no "innerliness," no innate or "spiritual" rights. "Personal rights" such as we know them did not exist for the Roman Self. A self was outer-directed and to be understood solely by reference to Rome. The meaning of human life, therefore, was sought within a Roman framework which it could be believed did not share the inevitable mortality of individual selves. Only one element in life promised an eternal grandeur and an indomitable perseverance: Rome itself—the City, its laws, its rule over all peoples, and the fear of its power.

The Roman Self, then, was oriented to Rome as to the one thing in life with the strength and promise of survival. Rome would never die. They amused themselves by watching die gladiators whom they had trained for that specific purpose. In such amusing deaths, they saw Rome continue. And at each death, they saw their own continuance in the only thing of value: living when others weaker than they died. It was not because of mockery, cruelty, sadism, or degradation, but because of this stark realism that they taught their gladiators to stand for an electric instant in the arena and shout together: "Hail! Eternal Rome! We who are about to die, salute Thee!"

16. The Muslim Self

At first glance, Westerners are inclined to say: What difference can there be between the Muslim Self, on the one hand, and the Jewish or the Christian Self, on the other hand? Muslims worship one god, revere the Prophets of the Jewish Bible as well as Jesus of Nazareth, Mary the Virgin, and the Christian Apostles; in the popular persuasion, also, it is held that the sacred book of Muslims, the Koran, is merely an Arabic version or a converted form of the Bible.

Christians and Jews would do well to divest themselves of their age-old prejudices about Muslims and Islam, and to dispel their profound ignorance of what the Muslim Self was and is. The Muslin Self was and is unique, and a precious form of human selfhood in the world of man. But those outside Islam, especially those of Christian, Jewish, or Buddhist persuasion, will perhaps always find it difficult to grasp the essence of that Muslim Self: what the human bondage is for it and what the meaning of human salvation is for it. For those other religionists will each find in some aspect of Islam a resemblance to one or more treasured elements of their own: salvation for the Christians, unique godhead for Jews, immateriality for Buddhists. Their eyes will rest on the montage of the familiar rather than penetrate to see the integral, veritable Muslim Self.

Aside from the problem of overcoming the camouflage of the familiar, as it were, there is the additional problem that Christians and Jews do not possess a suitable conceptualization and language with which to express or capture an expression of that "integral" Muslim Self.

This is so because the Muslim Self resides primarily and pre-ponderantly in a process which we in our Western language and with our concepts can express only badly. We would describe it as the immediacy of feeling knowledge, the intuitive leap over all barriers. And this is accurate insofar as it excludes the process of $A = B, B = C, A = C$. But it is defective because for us a leaping over barriers means going (by leaping) from Point X to Point Y, from "here" to "there," two static terminals in a geometric system. But the intuitive immediacy of the Muslim Self has nothing static and does not move in a geometric system, is not tied to a known symmetry. Not only is no "there" there; neither is a "here" involved. There is a process which is a being, a fluidity of understanding beyond frozen categories; and there is a going which is a becoming. But, again, neither horizontally as from one point to another, nor vertically as from one level to another, nor temporarily as from one instant to another. To use the example of $A = C$, it is as if A and C were both included under the equaliz-ing sign ($=$): the resultant reality is not an amalgam or a unity, but a oneness and an indivisibility of being and becoming.

In the thought and language of the West, whatever about the attempts of Buddhists in their language and thought, the only terms and concepts which lend themselves to some use in talking of the Muslim Self are expressions such as "image," "form," "figure," "spirit." But these have to be refined, because the ongo-ing process of Western thought and culture during the last two hundred fifty years has hardened the meaning of such terms until they have become objects of thought and have ceased to be vehi-cles for vision. A figure for us is an outline of itself, not a trans-parent referent. An image is an object in itself, no longer a see-through mirror of the unimaginable. Spirit for us is either human enthusiasm, or a white dovelike species of fowl, or an abstraction

("In the spirit of this evening, let me state . . ."), or (for Christians) a mysterious person, the third person in a triune god.

For the Muslim Self, the spirit lives and moves among material objects of this universe—men, women, children, animals, inanimate things—and it lights the fire of knowledge beyond the words of wisdom and beyond even the thinkable; it ennobles the soul of man by conferring on him access to God's revelation and the truth of all that exists. And the human bondage for this Self was conceived as the continual danger of interrupting the fluid freedom of that spirit, of blocking the transparency of all images and forms. Every arabesque the Muslim Self created permits the light to shine through subtle curves, almost infinite little passageways, and past subtle corners, angles, and circles. The arabesque moves viscously within that light. But the danger always is that only the workmanship will hold attention, that mortal eyes "mortalize" the immortal, and the light die out. Final deliverance from that bondage meant that one died and attained the happiness of Paradise. But this must not be taken as a luxury resort set in South Pacific surroundings.

At an early stage of Islam, when it broke on the outside world from inside the heartland sands of the Arabian peninsula, the seeking of this vision was all that mattered. Muslims expressed it all in human terms which we in the West take as concrete facts (in the modern sense of the word) but which for Muslims were transparent images of an inexpressible reality. Westerners can read today the Koranic description of that Heaven, but they can fail to read it "transparently": the Believers who die will find "couches set with jewels, on which they recline facing each other, while round them circle boys of perpetual youth, with goblets, and jugs, and a cup of flowing wine, from which they suffer neither headache nor intoxication; and with fruit of their own choice; and bird's flesh, of what they desire; and maidens with dark, wide eyes, like pearls treasured—a recompense for what they have accomplished."

In its early expressions and ambitions, Islam provided its adherents with a vision of the spirit reigning by God's will among the sands and rocks and stones of this world. To attain the heavenly permanence of complete absorption in that spirit, this was the sole object of human life. Islam provided the Muslim with a complete blueprint of life, death, history, and eternity. The world was created by Allah. It will end in the unforeseeable future by Allah's will. There is nothing holy, humanly beautiful, or personally valuable in life unless it is sanctioned and sanctified by Islam. The Muslim Self adores Allah, who is all-powerful and all-merciful and will give the faithful believer access to Paradise as an eternal reward after death—for a life of fidelity to Islam.

What does the Muslim Self do today when he is assaulted, as we all are, by a changing and screaming world of radio, television, scientific discoveries, international organizations, and interconnected nations and human beings? News which once took years, later months, to arrive, and then decades to be assimilated, now arrives in bombardments each second. The Muslim Self finds out that it likes the same things as infidel selves in Israel, perverted selves in Europe, and alien selves in Asia and Africa, and that all the Muslim Selves, by definition like many others, are human beings vibrant with needs, feelings, and aches, filled with a complicated machinery of desires, frustrations, and admissions.

Despite this pressure from all directions, there is in Islam today a vibrancy and a power which cannot be denied. It has nothing essential to do with ruling military juntas or technocratic classes in the lands of Islam today, no more than it depended essentially on the political ambitions and dreams of Mohammed Ali in the 19th century, the Mamelukes of the 13th to 16th centuries, or the Ottomans who lasted until the 20th century. It cannot be quenched by loss of land, by exile, and by the awful nothingness that afflicts, for example, over two million Palestinians. It infuses a whole way of life in entire peoples from Gibraltar over to Indonesia, but it is not that way of life. It appears at this moment to be one religion in which a resident power subsists, whereby the science and technology of the West can perhaps (and for the first time) be ingested, reworked, and transformed. For unless that takes place, the Muslim Self would be lost in the bondage and, consequently, something invaluable for human life would perish in the universe of men and women.

17. The Buddha Self

For all who cannot ask questions of life, or who dare not ask
those questions, or who, having asked them, received neither
yea nor nay, the Buddha Self is the non-answer par excellence.
For those with an appalling sense of loneliness. For him who
stands forlorn because of the indifference of those elbowing and
milling around him. For her who is consumed with sorrow that
womanhood is aimless and motherhood is meaningless and men
are either chauvinists or grown-up little boys. Now, to understand the Buddha Self, the quality of the great non-essence, you
must look at the inventor and the supreme example.

   The man Siddhattha (or Siddhartha or Sarvarthasiddha), meaning "he whose aim is accomplished," and whose Sakya clan name
was Gautama, was born near Padaria in Nepal about 567 B.C. and
died about 487 B.C. Immediately on birth, he stood up, took seven
paces to the north, stopped, and exclaimed: "In all the world, I
am chief, best, and foremost; this is my last birth. I shall never be
born again." And much else besides (as you read in the Acchari-
yabbhutadhamma Sutta). At a youthful age, renouncing pleasures, forsaking ascetic practices, Siddhattha finally sat beneath

the Boddhi Tree six miles south of the city of Gaya—and this uninterruptedly for seven days.

Then he had his enlightenment: deliverance from the human bondage, which is possible only by the Middle Way; and he received his revelation of the meaning of human life and of the human being. He taught both to his followers. Hence he was called Mahasamana ("the great ascetic"), Sakyamuni ("sage of the Sakyas"), Buddha ("the enlightened one"), or Bhagavat ("lord"). He referred to himself as Tathagata ("he who has come thus") and is commonly referred to as Gautama Buddha. When he died, his body was cremated east of the city of Kusinara. His ashes were distributed to eight cairns; another cairn was made for the urn which had held his ashes; and another cairn was erected to hold the embers from his funeral pyre.

The Way is Middle: it avoids worldly pleasures and self-tormenting asceticism. The Way is really an eightfold path: right views, right aspirations, right speech, right conduct, right livelihood, right effort, right mindfulness, right contemplation.

The human bondage is a practically endless cycle of reincarnations. But the ultimate aim is entry into salvation. But salvation has nothing to do with an eternal life with a personal god. It is Nirvana, the consummate peace of not being something or nothing or anything, wherein there is neither birth nor death, growth nor decay, disease nor health, purity nor impurity, joy nor sorrow. It is not neutral or positive or negative. It is Nirvana. If you fail in this incarnation to attain it, the human bondage lands you in another incarnation. And so on. So on, perhaps for billions of thousands of cycles of millions of eons and centuries. Until you become a Bodhisattva and just ready to become an Arhat, a saint, who enters Nirvana. But, hallelujah! You can, at that point, decide to hold off on Nirvana and help mortals to attain the enlightenment. Or you can go straight into Nirvana.

During human existence (if that is your incarnation; or it might be flea existence, or cockroach existence, or plant existence), in the cycles of pain, in the face of our institutionalized madnesses, infinite questioning, unsatisfactory answers, increasing ignorance, and multiplying problems, there is no need to engage or commit yourself. For thus you lose the meaning of it all. The meaning of it all is attained by detachment. Believing that any human value in human affairs is unbelievable and unacceptable. Having a substantial hope that all human things are hopeless. Striving to love a human situation in which lovelessness and un-lovingness are the prime motives for sustaining that situation. Thinking, with the intent of abolishing all thought. Feeling one's way to a stage of psychophysical numbness where all feeling is impossible. Willing so purposefully to attain not willing, that the will is suspended by the neck until it dies quietly. Positioning the limbs in preconceived places and the body in pastiche postures, so that places and human things in places became pallid with non-sense. Speaking with a language so evacuated of concrete mean-ing that speech does not communicate. Impoverishing the imagi-nation of images, so that all is unimaginable. Eviscerating the strong urge of passions, so that their nakedness might explode. Immobilizing consciousness at a zero point, so that conscious ac-tivity atrophies.

In clear light of reason, the Buddha Self realizes that what was yesterday, is today, will be repeated tomorrow. The wave rises, falls, rises. The wind blows, fades, and blows. Man dies, is born, dies, is born. The corn grows, is cut, grows again. The rich man gives way to the poor man and the latter to the rich man, and the latter to a poor man. The sun rises, sets, and rises. And the Colo-nel's lady and Judy O'Grady are all the same under their skin, as the old British army doggerel ran. All is the same. The same is all there is. In supreme banality. Go look at a Buddha. The smile of Angkor on the colossal Buddha of Angkor Thom is not enigmati-cal. And its expression is not elusive. It is as consoling as the smile of the Mona Lisa. And as doubtful in quality. It reflects, not in-ward blessedness and not achieved enlightenment, but rather the closed-eyes, hands-off-you-poor-incarnated-mortal look of a sa-turnine metaphysic. It is a composite drawing in stone of an ob-session with an alien unity whose stereotypes were derived from refined nothingness. It had, traditionally, thirty-two major and eighty minor characteristics to be incorporated by any artist: among them were long pierced ear lobes, ringlets, a finial of flame issuing from the scalp, a parrot's beak of a nose, an egg-shaped head, a chin like a mango stone. The whole thus formed gestured in silence at man's protests, offering him merely signs of reposeful nothingness. It was the ultimate answer to human banality.

Salvation from that banality does not mean to be loved and saved. It does not require one even to be human—in any sense or degree; that detail is quite immaterial. It does not mean to go home to warmth and welcome. There is no love. And there is no person to be loved. There is no Other waiting. There is no there there. There is only the passing shadow and show of cyclical reincarnation and the diligence of the Bodhisattvas. As Gautama Buddha said on his deathbed: "Behold, brethren, I exhort you saying: death is inherent in all component things. Work out your salvation with diligence." Work, in other words, for your nothingness.

18. The Hindu Self

Americans can be proud of their Constitution as the oldest living constitution in our modern world. But compare that span, says the Hindu Self, with the more than thirty-five hundred years of development in art, architecture, literature, and social institutions of Hindus and Hinduism. New Yorkers think the north-south, east-west arrangement of the avenues and streets in Manhattan Borough is quite marvelous and original. But at Mohenjo-Daro in Sind, thirty-five hundred years ago, the streets were laid out at right angles to each other in a north-south and east-west arrangement; and all the brick houses had excellent bathrooms, plumbing, and drainage systems, and the kitchens had garbage chutes.

There must, however, be a difference somewhere between America and Hindu India. Indeed: Hindu India is a class-locked society, and the Hindu Self was never a person. In fact, the Hindu Self could not be a person. One *would* rather be a person in Harlem, the Appalachians, San Francisco, or Nogales, Arizona, with some sort of fighting chance, than—let us say—a member of the excrement-carrier caste in Hindu India, a man whose father, grandfather, and all forebears were excrement-carriers, and whose son, grandsons, and all descendants (whatever civil law may or may not come to say about it) will be excrement-carriers.

When you say thirty-five hundred years of the Hindu Self, you are talking, of course, like just one more uncomprehending Westerner. To begin to have a bare glimpse of what reality is for the Hindu Self, take the god Vishnu, as a fair example. His present life span is one hundred years in duration. At present, he is only fifty. But watch it! Each real day is equal to 4,320,000,000 of our years. So please multiply 365 (the days in our year) by 4,320,000,000, then multiply your result by 50 (Vishnu's present age), and you have the present age of this universe, which is almost infinite in space as in time. Actually, the present eon of world history began in 3120 B.C., and it has 400,000 more years to go. When Vishnu reaches his hundredth year, he returns to the Absolute All for an indefinite period of time. Then he starts a new set of those very long hundred years. And so it goes on, and on, and on.

This is the time frame of the human bondage for the Hindu Self: never-ending; composed of *Sat* (what exists) and *Asat* (what does not exist); it especially includes mortal things with souls—men, women, plants, animals, insects, birds, and the like. The most poignant aspects of that bondage is the existence frame; I mean, what a human being is. And this gives us the meaning of the Hindu Self's human bondage. All the bodies and material things which you see around you are really an illusion (*maya*). Inside, in bodies, is the soul (*atman*). This individual *atman* is a spark which has jumped out of the great, one, absolute, real fire, the soul of the universe, the *Brahman*. In fact, the only truth is pithily expressed: *Tat twami asi;* "Thou art Thou." And *Brahman* is Thou. Each one of us is a spark of the great Thou, the Brahman, the soul of the universe, the essence of everything, the superpersonal because non-personal, the neuter because non-male and non-female.

Clearly, the human bondage is a process of that spark imprisoned in illusory matter endeavoring to get back into that fire. It does this by an inexorable process of reincarnations (*samsara*). You can become a grain of corn or rice, a bee, a worm, a tree, a bear, an insect, a dog, a pig, a cloud—anything, in your endeavors to purify yourself. If a human being does succeed, then, as is written in the third part of the Mundaka Upanishad: "Like flowing rivers disappear in the sea, losing their name and form, thus a wise man freed from name and form, goes to the divine Person who is greater than the great."

But do not confound that great Person with the "personal god" of the Christians. Ramanuja (about 1100 A.D.) did describe "it" as one, eternal, almighty, all-wise, life-giving, all-merciful, with love and grace and mercy and life-giving ascribed to the Christian god. But if "it" loves you, you cease to love and become "it." If "it" has mercy on you, "it" absorbs you so completely that you can receive no more mercy. If "it" gives you life, you cease to exist altogether.

The meaning of this bondage, then, is submission to the foreordained scheme of things and, hopefully, final negation in what is. As Sankara (about 800 A.D.) said: "Whatever is, is in reality one. Is Brahman." You submit to your social position as a member in one of the four classes or the innumerable castes and clans. You have temples for sacrifices, and thousands of Brahman priests and ascetics to tell you what asceticisms in fasting and self-torture to undergo, for purification's sake. You must follow festivals and pilgrimages and a lunisolar calendar.

For reading, you have oceans and oceans of books: Rig-Vedas, Yajur-Vedas, Sama-Vedas, the Mahabharata, the Ramayana, the Sutras, Puranas, and Tantras, to begin with. In the sky you have gods like Dyaus, Varuna, Shiva, Vishnu; in the atmosphere, Indra and others; on the earth, Sama, Agni, Prthivi; beneath the earth, Tvastr, Yama and Yami, Prajapati, Aditi, Vitra, Dana, and all the demons. In all, about thirty-three major gods with hundreds of minor ones. But keep your eye on Vishnu (he preserves all things) and on Shiva (he destroys all).

Femlib has no place in the Hindu Self. You have holy men like the Bengali mystic Ramakrishna Paramahamsa and philosophers like Sankara. For your eyes, you have magnificent art and architecture: go and contemplate the Kailasanatha of Eliva or the Kandarya of Mahadeva at Khajuraho. You will not easily develop anything like a humanist culture such as was possible in the West. Nor will you really ever delight in the beauties of nature or have esthetic ecstasy. For all that is illusion. And you are forever reincarnated just once more.

But take heart. The great Vishnu himself has already had at

least ten reincarnations (as a fish, a boar, a tortoise, a man-lion, a dwarf, as Rama-with-an-ax, as Ramachandra, as Krishna, as Gautama Buddha, and as Kalki the Warrior). And he will have at least a couple of million more. The only consolation for the Hindu Self is the possibility that, in the words of the Upanishads: "Like the skin of the snake lies on an anthill, dead and rejected, thus shall lie this body of mine. But that disembodied immortal spirit in me is Brahman only, is light."

19. The China Self

The next time you read the Little Red Book of Chairman Mao, or hear a broadcast from the People's Republic of China, do not allow your Western chauvinism to take over and presume that you perfectly understand what they mean by "state of harmony," "state of equilibrium," and the "Great Society." These phrases were first uttered (with a lot more of the same ilk) by a man who was born in 551 B.C. and died in 479 B.C.

K'ung Fu-tse ("Master K'ung") or, as we know him, Confucius, had a miserable life, high principles, many disciples and followers, has been the most plagiarized author of all time, and died in extreme melancholy after dreaming of his own death. Yet, his basic ideal of a human being became the kernel for the China Self. You can recognize it today in Chou En-lai and Mao Tsetung, as in Sun Yat-sen fifty years ago, or in any traditional China person, male or female, whom you come across. That is why Chairman Mao and Radio Peking can quite legitimately quote Master K'ung. They mean it. Not quite as Master K'ung meant it. But still they mean it.

First of all, Confucianism is a misnomer. It and the China Self have gone far beyond Confucius' pietism and truistic teaching.

Confucius had a very simple outlook, was a religious-minded man, busied himself all his life with odes, rites, records, and music when he was not engaged in civic administration, and taught a system of social behavior that was both ludicrous (women should walk on the opposite side of the street to men) and edifying (no hiking of prices in the marketplace). In addition, he was nine feet six inches tall, was born with a huge bulge in his skull, had an impressive gait, a quiet voice, enduring patience, a boring logic, and, apparently, a gift of persuasion due as much to some trait of personality as to his ability to wear the other man down in argument. He lived in an age when men revered spirits of trees, rivers, crops, and animals; when they worshiped gods of a faraway land, and believed that their ancestors lived on in some shadowy existence after death. It was a simple religion, and he did not disturb it. He believed in a sort of personalized "Heaven," in the traditional gods of the sky and earth, and in spirits and ancestor worship.

The human bondage for him was simple: fulfill your essential duties on this earth (systematic instruction in truth, knowledge, human-heartedness, fortitude) and die peacefully. The elemental, animistic, and ancestral spirits took men over then.

Hence, in his thinking, the state of equilibrium: no emotions of pleasure and anger and sorrow and joy. Hence the state of harmony he advocated: emotions that surge up, but all in tune. "The state of harmony is the Highway of the Great Society," as Mao's placards call out today the principle of Confucius. Hence those oldsters doing daily calisthenics in black pajamas all over Red Square, Peking, today. They are after that harmony.

The China Self developed further. Confucianist Mo-tzu (478–381 B.C.) taught that "Heaven" (again, not exactly *a person;* but, all the same, with an intermittent resemblance to the personal) loves people; therefore, people should love each other, practice frugality, and avoid offensive warfare. Confucianist Mencius (372–289 B.C.) said human nature was good: men should do good in order to express their innate goodness. Confucianist Hsün-tzu (320–235 B.C.) asserted that human nature was bad. Goodness was acquired only by training which external authority set up and enforced.

Over a period of a thousand years and into the Chinese Communist state of the 20th century, government after government, ruler after ruler, used this traditional cast of the China Self for political purposes. "Heaven," god, and spirits withdrew into vague mists. Membership in the "Middle Kingdom"—as China was called—became synonymous with that peculiar flavor of Confucianism watered down and diluted with some Taoism and Buddhism. It was worldly-wise, fatalistic, submissive to authority, knowing no salvation from "Heaven" and, finally, no home on earth except that provided by authority. It was a nationalistic religion. To be Chinese was to be this. Much the same as for the Roman Self, for the China Self ultimate satisfaction is in being of China; and the only eternity possible is identity with an eternal China.

Thus, by the Christian era, the China Self regarded itself as a being cast on its own resources between a completely depersonalized Heaven and an inhospitable Earth. Advancement was by one's own efforts under the direction of authority. Authoritarianism became an in-built element of the China Self. Those spirits and gods of the ancients were finally recognized as plain superstition and as the errors of ignorance.

Further elements were added to the China Self by Buddhism and Taoism. Tao is the Way to happiness. You submit to external authority—whatever it is. In yourself, you empty your spirit; for being empty you can commune with the universe and realize your true place as a grain on the infinite sands of time. Calmness, therefore, and tranquillity in life, no matter what happens. Obedient joy and happiness, even song and laughter at the behest and requirement of authority. It was a mysticism of this great, big world around us, which we find today echoed in the writings of Westerners like Buckminster Fuller, Loren Eisley, and Teilhard de Chardin. Coming from the society they do, however, these latter are hard-hat mystics, as it were. The fatalism is there, but the submission is illusory for them as they seek to build new worlds and to cement pebbles of knowledge with the slippery glue of a mitigated mysticism.

Of course, ignorant people—the peasants and those unlettered in science—invented again and again a huge hoax of Saints, Genii, Perfect Ones in Heaven and Pure Ones above the Clouds, deities in the Skies and Demons in Hell, an Elixir of Immortality, and the Isles of the Immortals. But the China Self has nothing to do with all that. Its human bondage is conceived as a passive intake: external circumstances and authority determine what is good or bad. Justice is a sliding scale. Kindness is by ukase. Cruelty is not cruelty but a duty. Love of one's neighbor depends not on what that neighbor is worth, but on what the norms of authority say about that neighbor.

The meaning of the human bondage is to attain calmness in obedience and joy in obeying if need be. The cream on the cake is, of course, the attainment of that communing with the universe, to let the Light of that universe stream in. Buddhism has contributed this much to the China Self. Sit upright, cross-legged, and comfortably. Look with both eyes on the tip of the nose. When one fixes one's thought on this mid-point between the eyes, the light pours in spontaneously. But there is no love, no incentive of love, no goal of love. For life is an illusion and insignificant. And for the China Self, as Master Chuang-tzu taught, "By and by comes the Great Awakening, and then we shall find out that life itself is a great dream."

20. The Japan Self

The Japan Self, like the China Self, is exclusively national and nationalistic. Even more extremely than in China, there were concentrated efforts by more than one government to identify the religion of the citizen of Japan with the well-being of the country as one nation. Being a good and loyal Japanese citizen was identified completely with being a good and loyal member of the established religion. Like the China Self, too, the Japan Self has taken over two thousand years to develop. And only in today's world have its characteristics been somewhat frozen into permanent lines and into a stereotype which one can classify.

It is a composite and complex Self made up of very ancient and indigenous Shinto (the "Way of the Gods"; the term was invented in the one-year reign of King Yomei Tenno, from 586 to 587 A.D.); of Butsudo (the "Way of the Buddha," which was introduced into Japan in the 6th century A.D.); of Chinese Confucianism and Taoism; of civil and nationalist elements; of borrowings from a transient Christianity, particularly of the Pentecostalist kind; and, finally, of a steady input of Western ideas, ideals, principles, and life styles. Thus, in some ways, the Japan Self is most modern; in others, it is most ancient. But it has one general concept of the human bondage, although the meaning given to that bondage varies somewhat according to the degree of Westernization undergone by individual Japanese. There are signs that the idea of the human bondage is changing as a result of the enormous industrial, economic, and urban transformations effected in Japan since 1945.

Shinto, in its original condition and before the modern period, had a populous pantheon of gods, goddesses, spirits, demons, and ancestral beings known by such intriguing names as Master-of-the-August-Producing-Wondrous-Deity; Pleasant-Reed-Shoot-Prince-Elder-Deity; Mud-Earth-Lord; Oh-Awful-Lady; Male-Who-Invites; Female-Who-Invites; Heavenly-Eternally-Standing-Deity; His-Brave-Swift-Impetuous-Male-Augustness; Heavenly-Alarming-Female; and Prince-Rice-Ear-Ruddy-Plenty. Some of the names defy any Western analogue: Ama-tsu-hi-daka-hiko-ho-ho-de-mi-no-mikoto (which means Heaven's-Sun-Height-Prince-Great-Rice-Ears-Lord-Ears). Deities were worshiped at shrines, and within a yearly cycle of festivals and folk celebrations. Most rites were originally fertility cults and for purification purposes. Functionaries were shamans, heads of families and clans and hereditary families of priests. Some gods dwelt in a distant heaven, a sort of Valhalla, to which a few privileged human heroes were transported on death. Earth was the home of mortal men and women forever at the mercy of the whim of those gods. Death was the end. Depending on the Buddhism, the Taoism, the simple Shinto, or the sophistication of the person dying, after death there was either the All-Nothingness of Nirvana (or reincarnation), the All-Universalness of the Way, refuge with the shadowy existing ancestors, or the nothing of non-being.

There was never any trace of philosophical speculation or theological refinement, until foreign influences—mainly from China—entered Japan. Buddhism, Taoism, Confucianism, lived side by side with Shinto, at times fusing and at times separating. But Shinto as the life style of the Japan Self always preserved the distinctive note which emerged in the classical period of its history. This was a combination: a very hardheaded and practical here-and-now attitude toward all aspects of human life; a social and familial context of customs, ceremonies, folkways, festivals, and celebrations based on the ancient mythology but not on a be-

LIBRARY ST. MARY'S COLLEGE

lief in that mythology as reflecting any historical reality; and a striking, almost complete, absence of what was paramount in Western civilization: the individual moral conscience. Instead, the most vibrant motivation for the Japan Self was attained in the thirties and forties of this century when Emperor Worship became the inspiration for national work, national wars, and eventually for the unsuccessful attempt to found the Co-Prosperity Sphere in the Pacific Ocean.

In place of the individual moral conscience, the Japan Self adheres to a detailed code of exterior behavior oriented to family, neighbors, friends, work, and the state. In modern times, successive governments endeavored to regulate and inculcate this code through schools and civil law. The Japan Self has duties; but no "inner" law imposes the observance of those duties. Guilt feelings, as experienced and admitted in the West, are impossible for the Japan Self. The most poignant self-denunciation is loss of face in one's own eyes as in the eyes of those one respects or fears. On these bases, a code of ethical behavior, exterior decorum, lawfulness, fidelity to one's promises, and respect for others has been formulated and taught in public schools by government order. The motivation for imposing such a taught code was, of course, nationalistic. The motivation for observing it, for being morally good, is never sought in a law of inner conscience private and personal to each individual. "Sin," in the Christian sense, has no place in the Japanese tradition, is an unthinkable concept, as is modesty, purity of heart, personal rights, interior submission, humility, and discretion in the face of the "will of God."

The Self has no endowed rights because the Self is not thought of as a person in the Japanese ethos. The Self is never considered to be a person, because essential to the person is the "innerliness" traditional in the West. And the Japan Self has no innerliness. An individual could never find himself in the noblest state possible to him by any form of self-transcendence. He transcends himself only by suicide; but that is the end of the self—except for the resonance of his act and the fond memory of his example within the familial, societal, and national context of his day. When Japanese decry the atomic bombing of Hiroshima and Nagasaki as "immoral," they are not thinking of immoral behavior in the Western and Christian sense—that is, that the bombing violated an absolute law independent of the like or dislike of any man, American or Japanese. They just did not like being bombed. It goes no deeper. "Immoral" in this case means a violation of what the Japan Self expects *others* to do or not to do.

Even before it is fully crystallized, so to speak, the transformation of the Japan Self is already under way. As the most Westernized population in Asia, the Japanese are evolving in a quicksilver fashion toward a practical concept of human life which, predictably, resembles that of the modern British: preserved symbols complete with an acceptable mythology; a social and national tradition; a total absence of any adherence to formal religious practice and the cultivation of what once was called "virtue"; and an evolving concept of communal and individual goodness and even nobility—without a noble caste or class. Japan is full of revivalist movements, "back to Shinto," neo-Christian, neo-Pentecostalist, and still more esoteric forms of latter-day Messianism and science-fictionalisms.

A Japanese form of Buddhism, Zen Buddhism, was also developed, which in the practicalities of the life of the Japan Self turns out to be an indigenous Japanese analogue to the idea of the English gentleman developed at the height of British Imperial power in the 19th century. But it reflected the human bondage traditional to the Japan Self. For that Self was considered by Zen to be a kind of illusion, a dangerous illusion issuing from man's egotism, destroying man's identity with the totality of life as englobed in man, plant life, animals, stones, and all things. The human bondage in this case, the egotism of man, is mitigated by gratitude for being alive, for simply being. This should give rise to harmony, work, serene outlook, even humor and common sense, and a final calm in the face of death with its gripping darkness and its perpetual silence.

In other words, the Japan Self adapted to a human bondage which includes only the eternal cycles of man's universe, the never-ending wave of generations succeeding generations, the endless development of scientific discoveries and technology, and the toil, the joy, the pain, and the death of men. The meaning of it all is in that cyclical eternity and the passing flash of the individual's life.

In the quaint language of an ancient Japanese collection of

myths, the Nihongi, but with a direct relevance for the Japan Self of today, the goddess Amaterasu told her Prince Grandchild: "This Reed-plain-1500-autumns-fair-rice-ear-Lord is the region of which my descendants shall be rulers. . . . Govern it. . . . And may it, like Heaven and Earth, endure forever." As for the China Self and the Roman Self in their day, so the only permanent value for the Japan Self was and is finally laid up in the permanence and ultimate glory of Japan's earth and sky. But the Japan Self is thus wedged in between an unattainable Heaven and a hard-to-win Earth. Just as Taoism had to do, and Buddhism succeeded partially in doing, the Japan Self seems to be slowly adapting to the changing times. Modernization and Americanization of the way of life in Japan can possibly mitigate the harshness but will not break the bondage to which the Japan Self is constricted.

21. The Christian Self

Christians, enjoying the facility and the promise of the Jesus Self, have been, at one and the same time, its historical bearers and its worst enemies. They never freed the Jesus Self from entrapping Jewish filaments: Messiah, Israel, Prophets, Chosen People, Gehenna, Paradise, Satan, and so on through a whole *megilla* of myths. Furthermore, within a few hundred years of the death of Jesus, Christians had enshrined Jesus, his message and his salvation, in an Occidental imperialism. And this was bad enough; but at least its trappings were merely exterior—the swift onrushing of spears, the gold and satin of elitist groups.

Within a thousand years after Jesus' death, the Christian Self had emerged. All talk and thought about Jesus was tied in to one system of human thought about human beings. The chief elements which made the salvation of Jesus possible were identified with the names, tags, and theories invented by an excellent but quite ancient Greek philosopher, Aristotle, who had lived approximately fourteen hundred years before. The Jesus Self of any human being was identified with Aristotle's "substance" or "soul," and the saving god with Aristotle's First Cause. Jesus, his Father, and his Spirit were described as a trinity of Aristotle's "relations." And one pet theory of Aristotle ("act and potency") was used to explain everything from creation to procreation, from sin to sanctity, from birth to death to eternity and the course of the unfathomable stars. There thus arose the Christian Self.

Worse still, because this system of thought and talk was consecrated as supreme and granted almost the same permanence as was attributed to God himself, it imposed on Christians and on the Jesus Self the thought molds and the language of one passing cultural epoch in human history. When that epoch died, the system was preserved. Inevitably, the Christian Self shared in the obsolescence and inapplicability of that past epoch.

The Christian Self was modeled on an image of a Jesus wholly imaginary and adapted to suit the changing cultural moods of one epoch which had stretched from roughly 200 D.D. to 1600 A.D. It was then reinterpreted almost at will to serve the ethnic bias of several races. It was Romanized, Gallicized, Germanicized, Anglified, Hispanicized, Africanized, Sinicized, Japanized, Celticized, Americanized, Russianized, Hebraicized, Arabicized, Copticized, Hellenized. Most recently, it is becoming ecumenicized. As we now go, the Christian Self will be universalized in the wide-eyed but unseeing attempt at social egalitarianism in which all men, to qualify as Brothers, must level, merge, and finally renounce even those differences of individual identity, much deeper than the social differences, that constitute the very bases of one's "sense" of self. What happens when anyone is universalized? He ceases to be human, even in concept. It is small consolation to tell us that there is no end in sight and that hair will grow even in the grave. Thank you. But we wish to live as individuals forever.

All of these adaptations have been attempts, however shortsighted, at working models of Christianity suited to a particular place or age. But the chief model of the Christian Self through the ages is what presents the greatest difficulty for that Self today. The Christian Self was spread-eagled on an intricate cyclical arrangement of hours, days, weeks, months, and years (sometimes millennia). His worship was organized officially and as revealed truth, from Advent (in the autumn) through Christmas; the Epiphany in January; then Lent, the season of invisible growth before spring; then Easter, on the first Sunday after the first full moon after the twenty-first of every March, the first burst of spring and of visible life; then Pentecost; then the pentecostal period swinging through late spring, summer, right up to Advent in the autumn; and then down the yearly turnpike all over again.

But modern man is not seasonal at all. Spring, winter, autumn, and all that are dates on a calendar, not milestones in his life-producing processes. For we are not tied to the earth directly and immediately as something that determines our way of life, our food, our work hours, our riches, and our death. We are not cyclical, as the earth is; and the year has no cyclical quality for us, nor has the month, the week, the day, and the passing of the hours. The whole cyclical character of Jesus is meaningless. The association of his "mysteries" (conception and gestation in Advent, birth at Christmas, etc.) is out of date. Neither is there any further human value in the cyclical week or the cyclical month. Sunday can have less work than Monday; then again, it can have more. December is just as significant for praying to the Virgin as May. And June as the month devoted to Christ's love means nothing to us. Every and any month, Christians can devote their prayers to this end.

The essential units of the cyclical Christian Self—the minute and the hour and the day—these have lost their oppositive value. Our day is a twenty-four-hour day. Some of us never see the stars, sleeping in the daytime and working at night beneath arc lamps that darken the twinkling faintness of stars in the sky. Our internal time clocks are no longer spoken of as of day and night but of sleep and awakedness. To worship at the rising sun or pray at sun's setting has no sense. We rise long after sunrise and rush along to work separated from all sight and thought of earth by millions of miles of cement and asphalt; and when we retire, away from machine noises and TV glare, hours after sunset, our closest reminder of the importance of the cyclical year may have been a news report of a drought in western Oklahoma; and a reference to the dust-bowl days worries no one. All the finely intermeshing time cycles developed over thousands of years in harmony with our own body locomotion are disrupted. Distance is the time it takes to travel technologically; and time is the ticking of a speedometer; and direction is a gyroscope steering by the stars, beneath the waters or between the planets and the stars themselves.

Not only was the Christian Self cyclical, he was localized: certain spots or places were sacred to him. The local parish church. The family cemetery. The national shrine. Lourdes. Rome. Jerusalem. Fatima. Guadeloupe. La Salette. Lough Derg. The tombs of saints. The sites of martyrs. Today, man is quickly losing any identification with place as such. We no longer have a sense of place as being part of us. As people we do not carry the flavor of light and the color of landscape emanating from one location. The inner tension which characterizes the self each of us individually is, does not depend on the circumstances of a physical place for its quiddity and substance. We have ceased in this sense to be one with nature around us. For we have poured over nature a sameness, a monotony, and a repetitive banality that forbids individual appropriation: asphalt roads, concrete avenues and streets, rearing skyscrapers and buildings, billboards, cinemas, shopping centers, schools. It is a new earthly form in which we wander as nomads, able to call no place our own, belonging to no place as to home. Place is one more coordinate of the self which is invalid. But the Christian Self is tied to place as to a rock. These fundamental changes in human time and human space around the frozen form of the Christian Self constitute a bondage from which it is not able to escape.

In that Self, Christians have anchored one cultural adaptation of Jesus and of his meaning for human beings. The constricting character of that bondage is to be seen and appreciated in the helplessness of the Christian Self, either to change its ambient or to adapt to it. According as the men in that ambient draw further and further away from the thought process and the life styles required by the classical form of the Christian Self, that ambient becomes more and more alien to the Christian Self. Because it is not in tune with that ambient, the meaning given to the ambient becomes more and more dislocated from correspondence with reality. The Christian Self is now simply out of vogue because another and a strange identity for the human self has already been ushered in on the world scene.

Pliny said that the color amethyst approached but halted this side of wine. This is what the Christian Self did and was. It was as beautiful in its day as a faceted gemstone, but it was not faithful to Jesus or to the Jesus Self.

PART IV
THE WEST:
DEHUMANIZATION
AS FREEDOM

22. Brute Time

In the life of any individual, time is the most important element. As time goes for an individual, so goes his life. If time ceases for him, his life ceases. If he successfully dominates time so that it becomes the framework of his self-expression, his life exceeds time and becomes timeless. If time becomes a wild and giddy seesaw between a deadening point-to-point shuffle and a wild madcap dance, then his sanity is near extinction. If time measures what he does, all he is, and how he becomes what he becomes, the human time of that individual is out of kilter. Time, in that case, is not the iron-wrought grillework enshrining our view of him, like the approaches to a privileged garden or the railing giving onto desired countrysides and hoped-for ocean waters. It is the zigzag interlacery of mindless happenings, planless views, outworn feelings, aimless efforts, spent energies, inevitable births, and deaths. And we are very close to the unblinking, steady stare of a schizophrenic melancholy and the transfixed rabbit's motionless acceptance of the snake's death bite.

According as Jesus figures fade in importance for the modern individual, time gets out of kilter more and more; it goes awry. And as this awryness of time grows to excess, those things by which human beings live weave out of kilter: the basis of man's sanity as man; culture, woman (for man lives by woman), Jesus of Nazareth, together with the institutions spawned by them and the human identity initiated with their beginnings.

Time thus reduced to its barest outline is not fit for humans. Taken to be merely a sordid point-to-point process, be it slow or quick, a shuffle or a leap, time has become as unhuman as the process of a train from sleeper to sleeper, the mechanical swing of a minute pendulum, or the drip-drip of icy water from the dark roof of an underground hole forming a stalactite century on century. The only meaning seems to be in sequences—a mirror, in time, of the impoverished world of sequences of facts that point to nothing beyond themselves, except the next sequence of facts.

Just so, the only function of time today is that every "before" be preceded and followed by an "after," every "after" preceded and followed by a "before." Each "before" has the aery unsubstantiality of a point—position but no magnitude, identity but no color. Each fleeting point has a sweetness. Each point-to-point passage is as bitter herbs to the tongue. In between the points there is only motion. And that motion itself has no purpose or character save to get to a point which must be immediately left for the next point, and so—conceivably—*ad infinitum* and *ad nauseam*.

In no age before this was man satisfied or forced to think thus of, and accordingly to live, human time. Men and women have hitherto tried to give this point-to-point process of time a timeless dimension.

Certainly, the point-to-point process is a basic grid as inescapable as the inhalation and exhalation of breath. A condition of being alive, being human. Stop doing it, and you stop living. Together with stones, plants, animals, and all beings who travel time's one-way direction, human beings must exist in time. "He lived between 1921 and 1986." Time is one of the two principal coordinates of human existence.

But human time, or humanized time, is distinct from the time of all other beings. At least, to make it so has been the effort of human beings. They alone of the beings we know have sought to do two things with the time process: to arrange their passing of time's moments according to their own choice, thus not to submit mechanically to the point-to-point process in their own movements, in the dawn and dusk of their inner thoughts, emotions, and reasonings, and in the deterioration and extinction of their being; secondly, to transcend the wear and tear of time by outwitting time's final conquest of their being—freely chosen self-perpetuation in race, in monuments, in achievements, in memories, and in immortality; these are characteristic only of human beings.

It is as if an unspoken condition of being human was this effort to humanize time. In this effort, the time process was liquefied with lambent tongues of substantial hopes and moistened with the glowing eyes of all our yesterdays, not as dead and past points reached and—as soon as reached—deserted, but as aging honeycombs storing the sweet nectar of all the moments and the bitter wax of all the fleeting days.

Nowadays, we are finding this increasingly impossible. More and more, the time process is escaping any humanization. For, more and more, we are failing to escape the imposed arrangement of point-to-point. In fact, a condition of our human advance in science and technology is the increasing mechanization of our human dimension. Our planned and desired humanness is thereby diminished; in a human world going increasingly awry humanly, the first major coordinate increasingly out of kilter for that humanness is time.

"Out of kilter?" queries the modern, with one eye on the steadily moving hands of his electromagnetic, shockproof and waterproof, automatic timepiece. "Nonsense. It's now exactly 1432 hours and 17 seconds, Greenwich Mean Time, the twenty-first of June, a day that had 86,401 seconds exactly. And my second is defined exactly as $1/31,556,925,974.7$th of the tropical year. What's out of kilter?" The point-to-point, second-to-second, day-to-day, year-to-year process is in perfect working order. "And isn't that time?" is the final dismissal.

But the awry condition of time is noticeable, in part because our principal human achievements in technology and science promise us nothing more than infinite series of refinements in the single points of the process. "I will increase the number of points you can travel in your lifetime," claims modern medicine. "I will decrease your need to work at every point," asserts modern industrialization, "and often your need to think." "I will let you travel greater spaces, see more things, experience a greater and greater number of events, facilitate your killing a greater number of other human beings in a shorter time," state the physicist, the electronics engineer, the technologist, "by my communications media, by my spaceship, by my inertial guidance system, by my computers." All on one condition: that you submit your life, your self, to systems that are tied inexorably to a point-to-point process, to brute time.

As a consequence of this, we today become more and more poignantly aware of the narrowing down of our humanness to times and destinations and sectionalizations, to a staccato of actions. Our awareness of ourselves is thus reduced. We are not any longer, as we sometimes were, in a broad and still lake, or, as we alternately were, in a deep and swiftly flowing river.

That lake was at one and the same time a tranquil merger of all the points of flowing consciousness into a liquid radiance and a single state of knowledge possessed, of will satisfied, of memories completed. That river was vision and hope and onward thrust defying the cutting sectionalization proposed by the point-to-point process. For time, in its points and moments, could not stop us. The radiance would preserve us in movement; and the vision would unify that moment beyond time itself.

Now, in our modern world, time is an iron-clad frame clamped over flat surfaces, angled with one-way asphalt pathways, winnowed by commanding signs: onward, forever onward, onward to left, onward to right, onward at increasing speed with decreasing thought. Live this day! Spend this week! Exit from this month to the next month! Walk the next year as you walked last year, no matter how the scenery changes, until those years come wherein you say: "I have no pleasure in them. Now they drag. I'm bored. Time has ceased to be that gleaming frame placed upon the warm fires of life. It is mechanization seeping into and transforming one of the most basic and defining qualities of my life as lived."

Pause and note at any given moment: Where are you? You

have just emerged from the last hour, from a yesterday, from last month, from the previous year. Upon you and already enveloping you is this present hour of sixty minutes, this today of twenty-four hours, this month of thirty days, this year of twelve months. When they have finished flowing, and you with them, you will immediately enter another hour, another day, another month, another year. You cannot use brute time, but merely exist within it. You are not even a pillar of waiting, nor an actor watching a drama from the standing wings, nor a star hung over a changing landscape. You are a bundle of dailiness, monthliness, yearliness, a helpless incompleteness always moving to another incompleteness in a perpetually incomplete motion. You are an inexhaustible separateness perpetually denied oneness. Neither your motion, nor your imaginings of rest, nor your proposed tenderness, nor the songs of joy you shout, nor the worship you offer, none of these will loosen you from the steadily changing grip of time or your gradual approach to the deep sleepless moments of physical death. Your love will not melt that embrace, nor push off the arrival of your term, nor make your death a sleep; for all sleep prepares for reawakening. And you will not reawake. The points of time are inexorably one-way and you have traveled all the ones permitted you.

Sometimes you will see a man or woman who apparently has decided to outwit the awryness of the time frame and to take us along with them, if they can, on the wings of that neat trick. They succeed for a while or in spasms, a Sean O'Casey in theater, a Ruth Anderson in soap opera, a Sylvia Plath in poetry, an Adlai Stevenson in politics. They are all movement and moods, episodic laughter and sudden spurts, foxy reserve and quicksilver intellect. Not cool, not hot, not tepid; unpredictable. But this atypical mixture of thought, choice, and behavior traces merely the configuration of lanes, alleyways, highways, and byways wherewith they seek to baffle and outwit brute time. Their gentleness is that of a disguised cherub with an on-guard gleam in both eyes. Their wisdom has an unreleased anger and an unspent love. The comfort they give is that of the mythical leprechaun —the Gaelic version of the cosmic clown, that half-comic, half-tragic, less-than-human, more-than-human character which emerges as equally pathetic and triumphant from the Celtic twilight of Synge and Yeats, as from the Shadow Plays of Mollas and Seraphin, the antiks of Till Eulenspiegel and Karagöz, and the misfortunes of Charlie Chaplin. They have no epigones; for while many guess their pathways, none but God can trace their steps. And, in the end, each one comes—as we all do—to the cul-de-sac, the blank unscalable wall, and the turn-around for the moment-long resignation sufficient and necessary that they, like all human beings, say: "This is it."

Of course, fundamentally speaking, man refuses to say "This is it" to brute time. He will not accept its mechanical domination. Our search for mastery over time, especially brute time, continues at an increased rate. A state of increasing tension develops. It is as if we are passing through an interim period brought on by our universal search for mastery over all things, and brute time is a passing passion, a temporary by-product, and a necessary consequence of our subjection to the nearly total dominance of our scientific and technological thrust at that desired mastery. But what men seek is a human situation, not a brute condition.

It was inevitable that human time would go out of kilter, once the Jesus figures went out of kilter. For time, since Jesus, had been modified in view of those figures. Men had conceived of time as a process of becoming something free of time's process (this was the dream offer implied in the Jesus figures). Jesus was thought of in two roles: as posted at a point prior to the time process in the yawning maw of an eternity which had no beginning; and as a stationary end term at the finish of the time process.

We broke from this lock-step concept during the last one hundred and fifty years through the advances of science and technology. Jesus as a nodal point, as end knot in the ropes which bound us into the ancient and encrusted view of human life, has been dissipated. For both ideas, Jesus as Atlas at the door of prior eternity and as stationary end term, cannot be assimilated to, or reconciled with, time as we live it today. And, seemingly, nothing on our human horizon and nothing in all our human potential can reinstate that Jesus figure as end term or detach us from the grip of the processional points of time as such. There will be no further domination by Jesus figures. But in order to reach where we as a human society are going, we have to pass through the narrow and painful defile of brute time. The partial and temporary domination of our lives by less than human time is in its very brutality a guarantee that it cannot last, will not be accepted as human.

23. The New Image of Man: Humanness and Insanity

An individual human life gridded uniquely on the inevitable point-to-point process of bare, brute time has to be organized uniquely around the knowledge of facts. Knowledge of facts, on our modern lips, means knowledge acquired only according to the techniques of objective inquiry established and approved by science and technology and their applications. A fact is a fact uniquely if it is quantifiable and measurable by those techniques. Patently, the point-to-point process of knowing is, in itself, like the similar process of time, out of kilter with the full human dimension. By meachanizing, it reduces an individual's humanness to what can be scientifically established, but everyday experience shows that same individual that there is much more going on inside him or her than the facts established by the methods of scientific and technological inquiry.

What is not so patently clear is that the conferring by society at large of unique privilege on a knowledge of such facts—that is, the establishment by society of this body of knowledge as the *only* valent knowledge, and of this manner of investigation as the only means of search for knowledge—this jars society itself into a position out of kilter with the human dimension. It is not so patently clear, and it is almost impossible to discuss or make clear. For all the relevant terms by which to discuss it—"knowledge," "knowing," "learning," "rational," "thought," "reason," "reasoning," "objective," "objectivity"—have been wrenched from all previously valid use and appropriated, with new meaning, as terminology exclusive to this knowledge of such facts.

It is thus that a modern educator will tell a parent: No learning must precede understanding. If the child does not understand something, he should not be taught it. But to "understand" on the educator's lips means the grasp of proofs, of factual verifications. The child will only memorize, insists the educator. And it is this memory-learning burden which oppresses his mind later and hampers his development now. Consequences for child-teaching are one-track and fatally biased, though defined now from the lexicon of unique privilege as "objective" and "unbiased." The child cannot "understand" God or sin or honesty or patriotism or poetry or love or religion or cleanliness or discipline or order or politeness or kindness or self-sacrifice. The education and learning processes of the child and young person "must" be left to develop "freely." They must "choose" their own way. Slowly but surely, growing human beings will learn how to "understand" and "decide" on that basis how they want to live. The growing human being is pontificated to be the new image of man: an empty receptacle made to receive facts. Period.

With "knowledge" and "learning" and "rational" and all such terms segregated for use only concerning scientifically or quasi-scientifically established and technologically applied facts, there is no way left open even to discuss human knowing and learning and rationality in any other spectrum. Such a discussion becomes lost in a new tautology in which immediately a whole area of human experience, inner to each and mutually shared by each, is swallowed and lost, branded as a-rational, irrational, unobjective, non-factual, mythic. Psychiatrists or behavioral psychologists will aid us to dissect these inner experiences, objectify them all, reduce them more or less to quantifiable terms, understand their "true" meaning and significance—if any. We are thus "restored" to "rationality," to "objectivity" of assessment, and to "reality" of human life and human society, all of which are subtly redefined in the process. We are quantifiable and controllable and constitute no problem that somebody can't deal with. The tautology fulfills itself. But the circle is drawn in too small a dimension. Within it as human beings we are seemingly bound as by hoops of steel to the new time process and to the endless succession of facts we are able to establish.

The result is the least human of all the images man has formed of himself in all his history. We are judged capable of knowing the fact provided we stick to the rules of objective inquiry. Abstract knowing—that is to say, knowing which is abstracted from tangible reality—can sometimes be entertained, but you have to be very careful! There are, admittedly, two different kinds of abstract knowing; the abstractions of an Einstein are very different from the abstractions of philosophers, theologians, religious thinkers, and humanists (artists, poets, painters, etc.). The first is fine: it ends up in tangible reality. We value this kind of abstract knowledge as much as factual knowledge. The second is defined as pathetically useless myth and trivia of no consequence to man except as possible entrapment of which he must rid himself.

It is at this point of self-realization in our modern consciousness that the virginity of words and the luminosity of language itself are lost to today's version of a self-fulfilling prophecy: we amputate the same dimension from language as from ourselves, by denying any knowledge but factual knowledge. We appropriate all the words and deny credence to their earlier meanings, and sooner or later we make communication of all but facts nearly impossible. As Charlie Manson said: "He who thinks is lost. . . . Words kill. . . . The original sin was to write it down."

The predictable next step is upon us when we find that the facts themselves do not need us or our language: there can be communication by a non-verbal language; machines we make can use this non-verbal language better than we can; and already the management of our lives, especially for all-important phases such as national security, exploration, medical monitoring, banking, weather control, can be entrusted to an ever more perfectible and sophisticated "family" of computers which—we say—"talk" among themselves, exchange information, think by themselves, make decisions in common, can be self-repairing, and eventually can generate their own kind. And all of this "talking" and "communicating" is done in numbers, is literally composed of quantified facts which produce tangible, usable, practical, and visible "responses" that "qualified" people can use to our "material benefit." "What else," those qualified people ask us portentously, "can you ask of talk and communication?" A certain hesitancy in the answer is only to be expected; we of today no longer expect to understand. Even experts are qualified only in their own fields; there is no over-all resident expert.

So *all* of us expect unintelligibility. On every side. We expect life to be more and more unintelligible. Books, therefore, and language and art reflecting the world around them as they always have, are, predictably, unintelligible. We accept the images they evoke. We do not question their meaning or whether they have meaning. We may submit to an explanation by the author or the artist as to what *he* meant; or we assume he knows, as we assume the machine "understood" what the technicians meant; and we assume that if all this does us no good, it does us no harm. Anyway, it has not hurt much—although it smarts in the soul from time to time.

With the devaluation of language, those more ancient modes of self-expression—poetry and theater and music—fall into desert wastes. The ancient search for meaning in philosophic speculation or theological thought is effete. Anyway, why pile thought upon thought, idea on idea, where there is no cognitive value for humans? Those modes of self-representation—painting and sculpture and architecture—once held as man's means of expressing himself, speak less and less to the inner things we think or we thought we knew and shared with others. In any case, we leave it increasingly to machines to do our expressing for us.

Architecture must reflect predominantly the geometric and sharply defined contours of all-determining facts. But, not all quite gone down the road of facts only, some still look around cities rebuilding themselves and ask one another why all the buildings are the same and all so boring. They are really asking: "Where is the rest of me that the architecture of my time should help me to know and express?" The answer is: "They are amputating it with slide rules; they know and are expressing accelerated square-foot rental rates."

In human painting and sculpture, we must rid the human form

of those traits which the irrational fastens on; it must be made to conform to the minimum of human shape and must emphasize the block-and-cube clarity and might of facts. And color. Quantifiable, measurable, unequivocal, primary color. In squares and straight lines, if possible. In an insanity of riot, if not. Art, if it must be fanciful, should express only the transience of fantasy and the permanence of factual forms: Andy Warhol's Campbell's Soup Tin Chalice replaces a Sears, Roebuck Holy Grail Beaker for five-o'clock cocktails.

The language of love—a last bastion of the "irrational" and the "non-factual"—if it is to be at all expressive, must resort to those human motions so primal, so uncontrollable, so self-felt that their impact cannot be denied, is summarily factual: the language of defecation, of urination, of physical orgasm, all encased in pithy four-letter words and epithets. Preferably nothing you cannot get onto the available space on the wall of a subway car before the train pulls out.

For the rest of it, we should acknowledge past human actions; but we should never try to burn by such a light as led past human beings into errors. And as to keeping ourselves human, well, we shall face that problem when . . .

Come to think of it, once this latter stage of self-realization is achieved, there is no objective reason why the hope and the purpose of human existence should not be completely revamped. Perhaps, as William Blake said, we never know how much is enough until we have too much. Of factual knowledge, the current view is, there is never enough. The purpose of perpetuating human existence, this view continues, should be to arrive at a complete objectivization of the human being, a richness of tangibles, a total absence of perspectives.

With such a statement, we create a new set of conditions for human living and success: the elimination of emotion as a norm of conduct; no mercy for the helpless or the offending; no love for the pleasing and no curiosity for the fascinating; no trust in the word of another (we would have the facts). No loyalty freely given; all would be *duly* given. No instinctual care for the maimed, the defective, the dying.

The ultimate dream of "humanity" would become grotesque: eventually all therapy, all repair work, all extra-sustenance, would be unnecessary, because all non-objective behavior, all non-regulated behavior, would be impossible. It would be a hope that the billion circuits of the computer would replace, not repair, our fleshly brain lobes; that never-failing mechanisms would replace our hearts; and that self-regulating and expendable machines would walk over the earth where once we humans wrestled weakly for some billions of years with the impossible greatnesses of our infinite desires and the pygmy dimensions of our biologisms which spewed forth dirt from seven ill-constructed apertures and finally joined that dirt on top of the compost heap of dead matter.

As with brute time, we all recognize that this recourse to the quantified redefinition of our individual humanness is an inevitable (and somewhat angry and fearful) consequence of our struggle to be free of ancient and hindering concepts. But, as with brute time, the image of humanness that emerges is so poverty-stricken, so pitifully limited and limitable, so badly out of kilter with the fullness we know is our heritage, that its very adoption at one moment of our progress virtually assures within us a tension that will catapult us beyond that image. Men will not go backward; they are on their way to achieving humanness as it was never achieved before. The true dream, the human dream, is not of Cyborgs.

24. The Glass-Slipper Culture

Culture within any given society of men and women was usually an invisible web. It embraced the individual and the community, the private home and the public building, personal activities and public administration. It was the invisible but recognized character of where the individual belonged. Its features stretched over the lines of its architecture, its streets and roads and bridges, were visible in the eating, the work habits, the causes espoused, the celebrations, and the very physical characteristics of the participants—the clothes they wore, their gait and manner of speech, their impatience and their patience, their kindness and their indifference. Each one thought of himself as an individual. But this thought did not clash with his belonging. Nor did belonging threaten or clash with his sense of his individual self. Each had an overriding conviction that he was a part of something greater than himself or any other member. Not to belong was to be not at home, to be in an alien culture, to be an exile.

Yet even to be an exile in an alien culture did not mean that the kilter between individual and culture was gone awry. It was unnatural to be not at home. But to be not at home meant one was away from home. The invisible web of the cultural home stretched that far, and it consoled.

The peculiar trait of our modern culture is that man, at one and the same time, is at home in his proper place, that the web of culture still claims him as a due member, but that in this home place culture has been reduced to its outer structuralized components. The inner vibrancy of culture, its sustaining supply of intuition and human feeling, its fine delicacy of perception, and the subtle shades of foretaste and foreknowledge as second-nature handmaidens for softening and refining man's grosser ambitions, all this has ceased to be. Small wonder that today the position of woman—the first correlate of human culture—is as deeply troubled and shaken out of kilter as the human condition itself. Culture has become merely useful.

The most visible and universal contribution and effect of culture today is the unceasing drive to build impersonal systems around us, realms of large-scale performance systems, life-supportive and life-service industries, tier upon tier of supplies, supplements, gargantuan mechanical servants and slaves, quicksilver messengers to us from the outside and from us to the outside. It sets us afloat in a pervasive bath of news, information, views, advertisements, attractions, ambitions, possibilities. It says: Your motto will not be pure Windsor: *Dieu et mon Droit.* But Windsor revisited and modernized, eliciting just your assent: "Right. Right. Right. Right. Right. Right. Right."

Now there is the torture of tearing pressures in man's culture, and it lies in the unfairness of the demand made on him. In the official language of the computers and within the metallic administrations of both the machines and the machinelike services of bureaucracy and officialdom, man is no more significant than a single dancing particle in the Brownian movement and no more effective than a very small cog in a large mechanical system. In Thoreau's formula, he has been turned around once with his eyes shut to the world, and he is irretrievably lost—in his own world.

But simultaneously the efficiency of this entire system depends on the voluntary attachment and belonging the individual exercises, the patience he prolongs, and the insight he brings. All the innerliness increasingly denied him is also called upon to further the system that denies his innerliness. In short, he is denied any effective reality, and therefore any value, within himself. He thus becomes increasingly isolated. Culturally, he is purely an externality. Spirit becomes a word to express his behavior, not an essential element within his make-up that is seen and valued and shared by his culture. Everything that happens to him concentrates and compresses his sense of self into a closer and more dense ball of consciousness within him. His sense of beauty, his delight in unshackled thought, his pathos at human failures, his desire for pleasant commonalities, and his need to celebrate with others, he must harbor these sparks simmering behind his forehead. As he is swamped in dehumanizing systems, he is driven unceasingly by that pressure to the counter-pressure of a more intensive, a unique, nearly mad, individualism which excludes any thought. An individualism that insists: Your motto will not be pure Descartes: *Cogito ergo sum;* but Descartes redreamed: *Sum ergo sum:* I am therefore I am therefore I am therefore I . . .

   This modern version of culture, then, involves no sense of not belonging, and no diminution of, but rather an increment in, the individual's intensity of self. But an uneasy feeling washes over his mind: this home, this culture is no longer an invisible web with its felt beauties, its silent lessons and whispered consolations, and its experienced tendernesses. Nothing, in fact, is invisible any more. Anything that is, is visible, tangible. Including the individual in all his individuality. The culture is rid of any invisible treasures from the past; all is in the present. Nor has it any unseen contours that weave into the future forming his vision of tomorrow, of an aftertime, of a gentle twilight to his life, to his love, to his values. It offers immediate gratifications and here-and-now rewards. No one looks to a distant future. There is, therefore, no "should do this" or "shouldn't do that." For any such peremptory "should" can be given and accepted only in view of remoter moments within a long-range inspiration based on the innerliness of being. The latter is being defined out of existence. If there are imperatives, they become categoric only with the urgency of the day at hand and the need to be served. Culture becomes a visible surface badge worn for recognition like a union button, not an invisible binding of one to others and all to a whole. It is as though culture has been arbitrarily altered from its full and natural form; reduced and prescribed to fit the incompleteness of the new time and the new view of humanness, much in the manner Cinderella's Ugly Sisters deformed their feet to fit the Glass Slipper.

And yet, as by instinct, we know that the minimum demand we make on culture is that it help us to reflect and reinforce what we are innerly. With every tier of integrated systems, and with each platoon of impersonal machines that flesh out his culture beyond invisibility and beyond his comprehension, man is aware suddenly that he is not enriched by the good things which he has desired (the desire diminishes as the things turn out not quite so good) and never fattened on the regnancy of being he has dreamt of in his youth. Rather he sleeps and wakes with a dormant fear that some vital part of him is extinguished in the functioning of the culture that should define his dreams and point the way to more than what he alone can be; that something vital is probably extinguished in all the other members; that no current carried in culture runs between them all, except perhaps a fear: that all are touched as individuals by something they have allowed to be made greater than any of them, but which has no compassion for any single one of them.

Thus is nurtured a quiet panic sucking silently on the rinds of aloneness in the midst of thousands of others. There is a realization that, while many are in charge, nobody is responsible; that the irresponsible may be removed only to be replaced by others equally irresponsible; for that which nurtures responsibility is denied as a value merely, and has no status as a fact. There is no ultimate court of appeal and no place where the buck will or must stop. Our civic culture becomes a maze of nuts and bolts and struts where all must climb and balance and perform but never sing together at a summit or lie down in common slumber and at peace on the ground beneath.

Culture for us is, then, even less than it was for the Romans, in whom there had not yet developed the whole inner propensity for genuine transcendence within themselves. There has developed such a propensity in us. It belongs now to our humanness. Not as an added quantum, but as a due development of what each man innately is as man. And we will not allow it to be merely defined out of existence, Glass Slipper be damned. Culturally, therefore, we are strung out in tension between a false concept of culture and the neglected state of our inner selves which culture was meant to serve.

We know that in that neglected state, we make no progress in our humanness, in our "inner" selves; that our present constant moving and shifting all really happens in the same place, always within bounds rigidly and artificially set by definition: at certain times much like a carousel rigidly fastened to its endless and meaningless rounds that are defined by nothing more profound than the circumference of a jerry-built platform and accompanied by an endlessly repeated lilt of human ennui.

Clearly, we will not be thus confined indefinitely. The present situation has come about almost as reaction and experiment, after we broke from earlier unfair rigidities and confinements. But we will not have made that long fight, in the hope of finding the completeness we still sense will be ours, merely to be reduced to more confining and less meaningful bounds. We will achieve our humanness. Our present state is one of becoming, a brief way station on the road to achieving that humanness within an ambit as wide as the whole of human society. Culturally, nothing greater than the smaller individual culture groups has yet emerged. There is, therefore, nothing to give us as men the needed cultural reflex. But the process of liquefying structures that will be replaced by the new involves our present painful transition in which small-group culture has become a mere badge.

25. Woman

The first correlate of human culture is woman. This is not because she is a physical source of human reproduction—so, indeed, is man. It is because, over and above her role in human
physical generation, and in direct contrast to the role of the male,
her grasp on the order of human reality is anchored in a special
faculty for that innerliness without which all culture is impossible.

It is an accident of civilization that what men have termed
logic has been denied to exist in woman as it was supposed to
exist in man. This is a male chauvinist assumption. Human innerliness does not exclude human logic; but human logic is a tool
made human by innerliness; innerliness presumes logic, but while
innerliness is always human, logic in itself is no more human than
a satisfying equation, or the processes of a computer, or the quan-
tification of scientific data.

In the present condition of our knowledge we have no clear
means of deciding conclusively and cogently what is the source
of this grasp of innerliness in woman. Nor does it matter whether
some theoreticians claim it is something "innate" to woman,
woman's nature as distinct from the nature of man. (They have

nothing but theories to buttress this argument.) Pragmatists such as the proponents of Female Liberation insist that it is due to male chauvinist domination and ill treatment under which woman had to develop an inner strength in order to remain intact in spite of this ambient. (They have nothing but rage and unfounded suppositions to support them.) It is enough that in the practical order we find that woman has this inner quality. It is hers to a degree and in a way it is not man's; and this is the point of value.

A special faculty of innerliness does not imply that woman is "naturally" wrapped up in herself, in her feelings and intuitions and femaleness. This by definition is introversion or, at best, smug and overriding self-interest, a limitation from which both men and women can suffer. Innerliness refers rather to the way in which the human reality is approached, perceived, and preserved as a predominant guiding rule for human activity.

In human activity itself, there is no difference—except that imposed by male chauvinism—between man and woman. As for strength, women have as much if not more will power and stubborn perseverance than men; in health, they are sturdier; it has yet to be established that they are by nature weaker, say, for physical combat and sports. Culture has assigned them a physically weaker role; but this has already been made ludicrous in view, say, of the stamina of the pioneer woman in this country. It is in any case becoming obsolete with the increasing invention, perfection, and use of labor-saving, heavy-duty machinery. As to moral stamina, it is a necessary part of any successful woman's equipment. Without it, woman would fall apart, placed as she is continually in situations which no normal man could cope with. Men are wont, for example, to speak in especially pained anger when humiliation comes their way. "His pride was hurt" is a common explanation for a man's anger. Yet the history of woman is a long jeremiad of humiliation: daily acceptance of a second place, daily and mute subservience to a male judgment, a male preference, a male-dominated situation; it is a detailed litany of silence and retirement, of treatment meted out to women on the presumption that she is not equal, that she must be "helped," that she is there to subserve man.

In logic, in mental agility, in intellectual thrust, and in judgmental capacity, there is no proof or indication that women are lesser than men; there is considerable evidence to the contrary. Of course, tradition and culture have assigned a second place to women in all these respects. But it is precisely this unbalanced treatment that Female Liberationists are tackling and intend to set right.

There is a single appreciable difference between man and woman. It is irreducible; and, if denied, it would do away with something irreplaceable in the human scale of things. All gather from it a basic life substance which has no other source in all our history. But it is not a difference which makes either sex superior or supreme. It originates in woman. But it is of value to neither man nor woman unless used in complement by both. That difference lies precisely in woman's capacity to grasp the innerliness which man lacks in himself but recognizes in her. Cliché words and phrases can easily dim or distort one's perception of this capacity or wrap it up in disdain. Yet, in any view of woman not colored by a prejudice, it must be admitted.

This grasp of innerliness is itself an innerliness of being, not of thought or of operation. It is a certain mold of character, a construct of the spirit, a form and a shape and a contour rather than an identifiable content or quantum contained in a form or within certain contours. Of course, it dictates more or less how a woman will react specifically as a woman, and so it does lead to thoughts, feelings, and actions. But it is, and it functions primarily as, a filter to receive the particularisms of a factual world and as a crystal reflecting those human inner things which alone can humanize all particularisms.

Man, for instance, bent on actions—brute actions—can take each and every action glittering in its efficiency and verve and hold it up to woman's consideration. As in a mirror, woman will reflect for him not merely the action itself, its details, its promise, its challenge. She reflects that action within a human wholeness governed by what is vital for our humanness—hope, inspiration, beauty, harmony, trust, self-sacrifice, home, earth, heaven, peace. The primal quality of woman, her association with all the primal forces of human life—waters, wind, oceans, fire, ships, earth—is not a paltry Freudian identity, a sexual twist. Nor is it merely man's version of woman as mother, wife, soft flesh, and welcoming hearth. Something not of the material order but something encased in the matter of this human universe shines around the woman's view of life's particularisms and sectionalizations. It "interiorizes" a human action, and forces a man to think on himself. It elicits an expression of meaning for concrete objects. It liquefies the stiff contours of the factual world, and brings a smile of harmony and a touch of beauty to what otherwise would be a still and dumb solitude of events.

When human culture goes out of kilter, it is not surprising that the concept of woman tied to that culture goes out of kilter. This is all the more so if, as has been the case, the concept of woman entertained in that culture has been one-sided and underdeveloped. From the very beginnings of human society—even in its so-called matriarchal forms—woman was defined in relation to man. In their scientian daydreams, anthropologists and cultural thinkers have conjured up various reasons for this "inferior position" of woman. But, reliably, we can dismiss these reasons as the products of overheated minds and not of objective science. We simply do not know. In its essence, this relation of woman to man implies no inferiority at all. Quite the contrary; she was so necessary that, without her, man could not live and flourish. However, social mores and male chauvinism took it from there.

From the beginnings of Christianity, the essence of the womanly was encompassed in waiting. Woman waited while Jesus saved. While men preached. While men governed (the Church, the State, the City, the Home, the Company). While men decided to marry her. While bearing children. While children grew up. While she grew old. While men, doing the same job, sometimes with less efficiency, earned twice or three times as much. While men took jobs forbidden her. She waited. She was supposed to wait. In the modern analogue, she went through years of "when" and "soon": WAIT was the sampler women sewed their days to. Wait: until you can wear make-up, strap on a bra, have a date, go steady, get married, bear his children. Wait: until your man makes the money and brings home the bacon, until you can have a meaningful relationship with your husband, until you have time to be a grandmother. The waiting game.

"If I am," she said to her man, "you do, you act." To her children: "As I am, so shall you act." And forth he went to the real

world, secure in the thought that while he did, she was. And
forth they went, molded in their days by her image. Yet for her
this did not quite ring true. For every good in her life had the
look of use. And still she was not anything. Watching a central
fire rage somewhere in her, she had to warm herself at its reflection as in a mirror. A being still and always thought of and defined in terms of others, and with a protean ability to compromise. Educated to educate a family. Taught to love, so she could
love her husband. To dress so as to please a man. The greatest
twofer in the human theater.

Only at one moment, it seems in retrospect, did Christianity
make an attempt to solve the problem. It was in the 13th and
14th centuries. A cult of the Virgin flowered in Europe; from it,
there blossomed the notions of chivalry, chivalric love, and a
consequent respect and devotion to woman as a being in whom
were reflected with a special intensity of meaning all human ideals of beauty, of truth, of peace, of hope, of warmth, and of all
things eternal and permanent and worth fighting for. The Lady,
not specifically as mother—but not exclusive of her motherhood
—became the ideal shimmering on the human male-female horizon. The presumption was: If women embody all this, then all
else—motherhood, home, physical ecstasy—is included.

But it was an abortive thing. It was confined to an elite. The
theologians and philosophers waded in to rarefy it all in the service of a very sociopolitical-minded Church. Dogmatists proceeded to congeal their theorems. Church authorities hinged their
clerical domination on the idea. The Reformers attacked all
honor ascribed to Mary merely as a handle against Rome. Then a
long, hot stream of Latinate thinkers proceeded to drive the cult
of Mary as a coach-and-four through all obstacles. By mid-20th
century, Mary as the Lady and the ideal had been forgotten. Besides, the wide world of man had departed on new conquests.

Institutional Christianity went out of kilter; it had been the
first and primary source and justification for intuition and innerliness; what place now had intuition and innerliness, female or otherwise, in structuring structures? Syllogisms are not built on intuition; they are reasonable. Jesus as God was fighting off the
God-blob; "feeling," "knowledge" which is not "factual" knowledge, or purely secondary in the cultivation of a logical godhead,

located in a non-universe of shining concepts and utterly diverse from plants, animals, and humans. Then the inadequacy of the fraudulent Jesus figures became widely felt. Whatever their separate attributes, those figures were, one and all, male chauvinist conceptions through and through. A final weakness became evident when woman examined how the Jesus person had been applied to her. She was an individual, to be sure. But she was recognized, defined, and described in terms of her relationship to man; beyond it, she was nothing of value in that world.

Of course, the lot of woman in other religions, cultures, and civilizations was no better, often far worse. Actually, the idea of woman in Christianity was largely based on an old Jewish model with a Christian transmutation. But, as far as that goes, it could have been a Japanese, a Chinese, or North American Indian model with some transmutations.

Wherever it comes from, if this idea is the real essence of the story of woman, and of woman and man, then all the male chauvinists are right. The whole matter of woman and female goes no deeper than the *petite différence*. It has no trailing causalities in the blood and bones of our human identity. It is a struggle in a jungle; oppressed female and male oppressor; would-be oppressor female and self-defensive male, the *petite différence* be damned, and God take the hindmost.

Fortunately and unfortunately, this has not been the whole story. Men especially, and primarily in the Christian civilization of the West, took a very peculiar turn in modern times, when they decided that only the knowledge flowing from scientific observation and experiment and verification was real and valuable human knowledge. What had been called intuition became just animal magnetism, sexual undertones, a matter of synaptic joints, or chemical states of the organism. As a consequence, all those areas of human interest and activity—sympathy, loyalty, trust, hope, desire, esthetics, sensuality, companionship—were inferior, had far less bearing on the "reality" of human existence than men and women had imagined; they were nothing more than the chemistry that had produced them. (A paradigm of this 20th century view was reached in Hitlerian doctrine; and it was a very logical paroxysm, granted the premise. The only mistake, in fact, the Nazis made—in this distorted optic—was to wear jackboots while making love, hasten the death of millions, and interfere with the finance, trade, and possessions of too many other countries at the same time and too soon. They were too frank, too interested in quick results. Hitler was hasty, too hasty.)

All this continued into the time of the Theater of Man's Longing and the shrinking dimensions of the individual's identity. Women panicked. And Femlib moved in. "Stop waiting," they said. "Now is your moment," they said. Some said: "You're really as good as a man." Others: "You're really the same as a man." Others still: "You're far better than a man." The matter became ludicrous; and, in becoming ludicrous, the point of woman's enduring kilter amid all the insanity was lost: no matter what the abuses of woman, she was the source of innerliness for Man.

Now, being finally freed from the male chauvinist imperialism which had enslaved her, woman was suddenly represented as a neutral human being, as just like a man—with a little difference (and some arrangements can be made concerning that). Her innerliness, at stake and in high danger in the awryness of human affairs, is the last element about which all the activists bother.

In the dust and turmoil that seemingly must accompany her fight for the redress of very ancient wrongs, and quickly, the real awryness of woman's position today is lost to sight. Woman is out of kilter with the most powerful element she possesses: her non-verbal power of communication, her non-visual and non-sensual intuition of fuller reality and, consequently, the vast domain of human interest, human endeavor, and human value over which she exercises a unique influence. And the dilemma of woman is a symptom of the age and the plight of the human individual. This is why the majority of women will have nothing to do with the extremism that attaches itself to Femlib; and why the vast majority of Female Liberationists merely want such equitable things as equal pay for equal work, equal job opportunity for equal talents; and why only a small minority scream for identity with, or superiority over, men, or total separation from them. The majority of women feel threatened by the denial of innerliness specific to them.

It is not merely that in this innerliness the difference between man and woman is defined. There is much more at stake: that innerliness is imbued with a value and a meaning of wholeness by which both man and woman can transcend their individual particularisms, thus obviating any merely political necessity for the reduction of each to the level of sameness.

Woman enters today the fullness of participation and due prominence for the first time. In an era of structuralist arguments, she too adopts these arguments, and forges them as weapons against chauvinist repression. But the fundamental question about her has not yet been answered. It does not even hang in the balance. It is out of vogue. To liberàte herself, what must she become? Just like a man? A person living in a single dimension of outwardliness clothed in male capacities and rights and privileges? And when those clothes lose their unessential maleness, as they will, then a person plunged in the Theater of Longing as deeply and helplessly as a man?

If she will make no different contribution center stage than men, but only more of a sameness, the waste to us all of her subjugation until now either has not been great, or it has not been redeemed in her liberation. The only change to emerge from such a condition would be painted in a sorry diptych: both man and woman impoverished, she of her real strength, he of what he vitally needs in order that he be man.

In a world where the non-intuitive, the closed-in Me Empire individual walks across the sands of last-refuge beaches in self-addressing glory and solitude and self-appointed finality, the innerliness of woman is threatened. Yet, it cannot be set aside, lest the instinct of woman for the needful otherness of men and for her own unique yet needful strength be stifled.

Woman along with culture is at the end of an era. All her life hitherto was one of escaping the sands of those last-refuge beaches shifting in drift. Until a minute ago, her life was absorbed with sea and spray and taken in by evening tides, until man's shoulders with promise of rock's security gave her firm ground, granite for her feet to stand, his body warm for her hands to find seeking home and strength. Always had she dreamed so, no matter how desert the days or how winds blurred the skies with clouds.

Now she stands on her bend of that whirling sifting beach, her eyes showing with light that sometimes beads in drops of water, surely about to fall and to disappear. Standing there, she must ask, for the fullness of us all, if she will merely engrave her love on stones and join the townsmen and the citymen and the jobpersons with bones as bruised as they and share the darkness of their merely masculine day.

26. IBM Christianity

It stands to reason that Christianity as an institutionalized religion—that is, specifically in its institutions—is out of kilter. Stripped of its concepts of Jesus and its theological formulas as acceptable working terms, Christianity in its institutions is left bare and naked to cope with the awry condition of that part of human society in which it exists.

Religious institutions are by their nature reflective of something. Christian ones have stated that they are reflective of Jesus and of God. They were and are actually reflective, in their behavior, of *concepts* of Jesus and of God. Without those concepts intact (and this is the situation today), and being still reflective institutions, they now begin to reflect the merely human order of things around them.

It is thus that a rather extraordinary set of circumstances has arisen. If a late-20th-century visitor to Earth from a planet in another galaxy were to examine the various official bodies of organized Christianity throughout the world, he would choose one common characteristic as the apparently most progressive and as the one certainly common trait shared by one and all, whatever

be their individual differences. This is their over-all preoccupa-
tion with structure.

Every day sees ever busier structuring, de-structuring, re-struc-
turing, merging, de-merging, discussing the conditions on which
to re-merge and re-structure or to reword the verbal formulas
and the arrangement of concepts which will allow greater mutual
identity on one day or which will more sharply define separate
identities the next. There are meetings, agreements, disagree-
ments, caucuses, interviews, communications, communiqués, new
and intermediately new and old styles, within Churches and between Churches. And all this is undertaken with a febrility of
words and paperwork; a feverish output of critiques, visitings,
tractations; a mustering of mutually organized cadres of social
workers all got up in regalia, of mutually shared sociopolitical
protests, of mutually agreed upon portfolio policies, and mutually
arranged prayers and pleadings that the structurings go faster,
that the functional agreements grow thicker and more solid, and
that all human beings involved (over one billion) accommodate
themselves to the love of Jesus and his message of salvation. . . .

But the various Churches, particularly in their leaders but also
in their members, seem to be the first to be affected by a deep inability to accommodate themselves to that love, not to speak of
proclaiming that salvation in their outward lives. Their attempts
to practice that love mutually appear to the outside world as a
rather ineffectual hankering and slither of Christian ecumenists,
ecclesiacs, and ecclesiastical bodies. Continually, they seem to be
negotiating risk-ridden pathways and perilous gorges among the
unscalable mountains of an inhospitable land. This is far from the
Biblical picture of sons and daughters, brother and sisters, sitting
down in the wondrous harmony of their Father, in their Father's
house, together.

The wide world stood either aghast or amused as it watched
the preliminary Peace Talk negotiations in Paris between the
Americans and the North Vietnamese concerning the *shape* of
the conference table. It was tortuous, painstaking, terrorizing,
time-consuming, and ultimately pointless and ludicrous. Yet the
punctilious expectation and barren insistence on the actual *arrival*
of the Russian observers at the Second Vatican Council in October 1962, and the actual *entry* of Russian members into a meeting

of the World Council of Churches for the first time in the fifties, came within inches of that same pointless human stupidity and ludicrousness.

It is, then, only a question of inches, a matter of degree. Religious institutions ape their surroundings, when they should rather be a source of enlightenment for those surroundings. They propose to supply their world with moral fiber and majestic direction. But, when we consider Christian ecumenism and Church action, now every day of organized Christianity's prolonged existence is the Day of the Helpless Slither and its every year is the Year of the Hankering.

This brings us to the heart of the awry condition in which organized Christianity finds itself. Here we have a multiplicity of human groups, each one claiming to represent Jesus and to be the sole, or a unique, source of the Spirit Jesus promised to his followers. But the only element apparently not moving among them is that Spirit. The officials, leaders, spokesmen, spokeswomen, thinkers, writers, and organizers among them are, indeed, moved. But nothing in their motions and movements seems to indicate the freedom and the successful pervasion of humans by the Spirit. Congealing and melting structures and formulas are purely human in origin and in effect. The organizational and public life of the Christian Churches and bodies seems out of kilter with that inner liquefaction and spiritual unity which the Spirit infuses as a first sign of presence. There is no subtle luminosity in the House of Christendom today. Nor is there any growing coagulation of hearts and minds, gently, subtly, and effectively.

Rather, that which bound them all together as leaders and led, as subjects and overseers, as pastors and sheep, as children and parents—namely, the faith as religious members that they, the organizers, represented Jesus—this faith is gone, because the Spirit is not with them. It is withdrawn; and every day it is more withdrawn. The rank and file are rolling away from Christian institutions like loosened stones from a once-solid wall. The *visible* portion of the living face of the "Church" is falling away. And the organizers and leaders, in the thrall of those who persuade us that structure is all there is, are increasingly reduced to the status of official residents in an ancient castle or the prescriptive occupants of a vast manorial house gathering in knots throughout empty halls and corridors, whistling commands to the watchdogs who no longer watch and formulating imperatives and schedules for the household members who have fled the household for the safety and the light of the wilderness all around them outside.

The absence of the Spirit is a deeply poignant characteristic noticeable in the negations that have become the hallmark of Christianity today. There are held to be no answers; only problems and questions. It is impossible to single out acknowledged leaders. There are only members who refuse to be led.

Above all, Christianity has no special formulas of its own to propose; it seeks them feebly enough in the world of men around it. It has no specific structures of its own to erect, but is continually assimilated to the sociopolitical structures spawned by men's commercial living. It does not multiply, except as it either seeks bureaucratic increase, paper theology, and artificial worship forms; or as it undergoes the corruption and decadence found in all human institutions and brilliantly outlined in Parkinson's Laws.

It is all merely human. And it affects all people, the body of each Church group, as well as those who contemplate them from outside. For both, the awry condition of institutional Christianity is the sign of a fatal illness, or at least of deep disease and trouble and boding. For the institutions of Christianity will die out if they simply reflect a human order of things which is passing away. Reflecting merely their ambient, they will become just another set of social clubs.

They should reflect the intentions of Jesus, whom they need and whom they should await. And for man in the Theater of Longing, they should mirror, not Jesus figures, but Jesus as he will save and vivify the emergent human being in the emergent order of human affairs.

As with human time and culture and humanness, never in its whole history has institutional Christianity been in such a reduced condition. In its present humanized form, and because of that humanization, Christianity is also in transition. The Church as the testamentary presence of Jesus, as the ecclesial Jesus, will endure, but its inadequate structure must change.

The above considerations force us to a spontaneous conclusion—the critical one arising in many hearts and uttered

only silently by many minds to their institutional leaders: They
who juggle and tinker with structuring, ever-structuring, on the
human models of their human ambient, and who do not vibrate
with the Spirit, how can they have the answer? For we, the people, are afflicted with just that: an ever-multiplying structuring of
all our lives and of every part of life as citizens. We do not seek
to know or need to know how Lutherans and Romans *say* that
Jesus is present in the Eucharist; or how the Anglicans and Romans *think* of the priesthood; or how the Presbyterians and Bap-
tists would *govern* their few millions. It is of no real substance
for the answers we seek, to be told how *far* Episcopalians can go
in the cult of the Virgin Mary; or how the Greek, Russian, Ar-
menian, and Coptic Orthodox Churches can reconcile the Roman
Church's centralist authority with their own method of govern-
ance, match their Sobornost with Roman Papacy, Holy Synod
with Holy Office, Pope with Patriarch, Priest with Pop, Ikon
with Crucifix, Christ Pantokrator with Christ Holder of Keys,
the cone-shapeed *kalimmafki* with the seven-tiered tiara—and
so on *ad nauseam.* Your glory in these is weary romanticism, and
your dressing up of old forms and ancient arguments in democratic garbs is still only a conjuring up of tattered ghosts.

Feed us *faith* that shows up where we are today. And give us
light to brighten every gathering cloud of darkness around our
every urban culture. Give us truth to live by, not merely ancient
husks gathered long ago and dried now in desiccated systems.
Give us living truths to live by, not dead and quite inapplicable
formulas and internecine squabbles that are your imitations of
what we already have and hate. Do not palm them off on us as
gifts of faith. You betray all the signs of being human, merely
human, as we consciously are. You and your activities are, therefore, as casual, as transient and transitional, and as undefinitive as
everything within our human scope. You provide us with a pit to
jump into, not a bridge to cross. With you, we do not walk in
salad days beneath the eye of eternity; we wander in the dog
days of weary time. We can do that in the halls of IBM.

PART V
THE WEST:
THE THEATER
OF LONGING

27. *The New Humanism*

To Be Human

An outline of our modern Theater of Longing must trace the parameters of our modern landscape. All modern persons are born into a world whose attitudes and facets press upon each one, clamoring for answers to three perennially returning human questions: What does it mean to be human? What do I mean when I claim that I am a human individual? What is my human destiny? The answers to these questions involve the inner things by which each individual defines his world.

Our modern concept of what it is to be human is provided most conveniently by the commonly shared vision of the quality of humanness which defines us all. By our time in history, the meaning which the word "man" used to have, has been exploded almost into nothingness. It was formerly used about all men, with the implication that all men shared in a common "nature." And by the subtle alchemy of delicious male chauvinism, it somehow or other included woman as appendage, as a sequela, as what you

presume will be there if something else is there. But this strictly
Western idea of man's nature, originating in the philosophy of
the Greeks and refined by Christians to fit their beliefs, is no
longer common coin today.

Each person's own vision of himself is reduced (as, in other
times, it was expanded) by the common vision in which all share.
He reads of his humanity most often now as a bundle of solvable
puzzles and of trigger-response mechanisms manipulatable for the
"good" of an equally impoverished reconceptualization of "society" encapsulated and entrapped in brute time.

Each man, so reduced by the concepts of his era, finds himself
in a modern Theater of Longing where he acts out in stiffness his
newly constricted roles; where he reveals his sense of impoverish-
ment, and casts about for new contours against which he might
form and measure and give life and color and outward expression
to what he knows (albeit in a new and lonely way) to be his self,
his unquantifiable innerliness which no other man duplicates and
which unifies his every part into the whole and unique self he is.
In a certain true sense, we can see the current, rather heady, Jesus
interest among the young and the dramatists as a last miming, as
an overture to a new drama. Jesus as God is becoming unacceptable. And Jesus as man is rapidly becoming so within the Theater
of Longing.

Now, each man wonders increasingly not only if his voice is
heard but if anyone knows he is there or cares. Business and government are huge; they seem to use him, but to give him no
meaning and lend him no destiny. Through the philosophy and
science of his day, the pressure is on him to abandon recourse to
any traditional font of meaning, dignity, or any other such values, suddenly become unsubstantial if not downright shameful
and certainly unprovable.

While we continue falteringly to speak of "man" and "human
nature," such nomenclature is placed on the new comparative
scale: We agree it is not as erroneous as saying "The sun rose at 5
A.M.," nor quite as metaphorical as calling someone "a dirty dog,"
nor as fictitious as Santa Claus. Even in our dislocated modern
minds and language there remains a shadowy but unyielding bor-
der between human and non-human nature (with intermediary
grayish patches of the inhuman and the subhuman being pro-

posed and theorized about by those who look to Dr. Leakey in Olduvai, and being ignored and defined out of existence by those who look to Dr. Skinner among the pigeon pellets).

The prime presumption in our structuralist time about a "human being" is that this is an organism empty at the beginning of any characteristics save: physical organs—head, trunk, limbs, etc.; physical capacities essential for the maintenance and defense of the physical life of the individual—breathing, digesting, walking, making throat sounds, seeing, hearing, smelling, touching, tasting, acting with hands and feet and genitals; and internal capabilities, immediate and long-range, which are serviceable beyond the bare maintenance and defense of life—thinking and recalling, talking, imagining, reasoning, feeling. These last are singled out by the addition of the hyphenated term "psycho-" to the term "physical": psycho-physical. "Psycho-" in this combination merely means "internal," but non-digestive and non-circulatory.

The human being is, in the totality of this concept, a composite container of physical organs and psycho-physical operations. Organs and operations cling, as it were, to each other in a coagulated whole: the first is meaningless without the second, and the second is not at all without the first.

The container and its contents are put together over a nine-month period of animal gestation. Each container takes about eighteen years to grow to its full capacity and ceases to function after a certain number of years. That ceasing of function is called by a nonsense term, "death." This is a nonsense term because we really do not know what it is or understand it. We know only what happens: Primarily, oxygen ceases to reach the brain; there is brain death. Other organs may still function: a heart beat, a kidney function. The heart ceases to beat. All other organ systems cease. Each cell of the organism dies—that is, each component of the cell ceases to function. "He" or "she" or "it" is "dead." For esthetic and hygienic reasons, the container of the dead organism is buried in the ground or burnt (cremated). The container can no longer receive or act. There seems to be nothing to measure. A "human being" has ceased to exist.

Into this container during its lifetime, we are told, we pour a variety of psycho-physical "fuel" called ideas. The known history of man shows that people changed the inflow of ideas according to the changes in their culture (that is, the particular way in which particular things are done in a particular group) and in their civilization (that is, the sum total of all those particular ways as a way of life shared by large populations).

In the beginning and up to very recent times (about 1700 as a cliché date), men did not possess precise knowledge of the organism's parts. So they poured in imaginary ideas: myths, legends, religious beliefs, and so on. They even described details of the organism. For instance, a once prevalent idea was that of the soul: an inner pincushion invisible, untouchable, unmeasurable; the pins sticking out of it were likewise invisible, untouchable, unmeasurable—the will, the intellect (actually, medieval philosophers gave the souls even two intellects), the imagination, the memory, the emotions or feelings (formerly called the passions). Based on all the welter of religions, moralities, humanisms, and ethics, men poured into the organism ideas about "spirit," "inwardness," "substance of soul," "immortality," a few subterranean tendencies called "sin," "the demonic"; a complex of "virtues" and "vices"; outer monitoring agencies like "god," "angel," "devil," "saint," priest, pope, minister; spiritual acts like prayer, sacrifice, heroism, worship; and shadowy places of destiny like "Heaven," "Hell," "Limbo," "Purgatory."

Of course, none of this inner furniture or outer landscape has been found by modern science. What science has found is merely the functioning container and its contents of physical organs and psycho-physical actions.

While the general outline of the new structuralist creed remains the same, modern thinkers (in this respect at least, strikingly like those who came before) are ever refining the details of their particular concept. The refinements, consistent with the creed, are based on increased structural knowledge of the organism and of its environment. In the "hard" sciences, whole new areas are developing within the welter of fields that now claim primacy of right to pour ideas into the organism: genetics, molecular biology, cryology, etc. In the "soft" sciences, men ably represented by Noam Chomsky in linguistics, Lévi-Strauss in the history of culture, Jean Piaget in child development, are groping to demonstrate the existence of some basic trans-cultural structures of knowing intrinsic to organisms everywhere. A psychologist like Erik Erikson catalogues the various psycho-physical states of man and woman from infancy to old age, by which data, one assumes, we are to be portrayed at each stage of life in a quantified totality, an "average," which will be defined and defended as the true human totality, and against which each human shall be gauged, and in which each human being can expect to be increasingly submerged as a self.

Those on the farthest ramparts of the container vision of man bring us abruptly to its logical conclusion: the human container requires enlightened engineering. As David Cooper says in his *The Death of the Family*, the next due revolution in the organism "will only become a total enough reality, when white men can assume all the colors of blackness and then have babies too."

Thus, it becomes apparent, and it is important to note, that what scientists are doing is redefining the organism's structural character, and attempting to establish it as man's only essential attribute.

The new ideas and arguments used to support such a view are chameleonlike. They appear to cohere perfectly with, because they do not on the surface appear to threaten, the sociopolitical ideals of America and of the West. A "human nature" endowed only with structural dispositions recommends itself as almost infinitely plastic and endlessly perfectible. Therefore, it is "by nature": free of all need that cannot be satisfied by law; uncolored in will; basically equal and identical, wherever it is found on the face of the earth; optimistic in outlook, because it has or is nothing to be pessimistic about; made for freedom, because self-moving; has "natural rights," because it is by its container definition expected to be capable of this or that or the other action, given only the proper "inputs," the correct conditioning, and the necessary corrections for the old mythical ideas and ideals.

Blank as it is, however, the human container concept obviously makes the human person, by definition, highly conditionable, mass malleable, formable, controllable. It is only a step from there to oblivion for all the concepts on which the American sociopolitical ideals are based.

It is precisely on the engineering of this container organism that two bodies of experts are visibly working: a group of psy-

chologists called environmentalists or behaviorists, and a rather
vast array of technicians expert in the use of the communications
media. The first are developing techniques by means of which
the organism can be trained to behave in the best possible way
for everybody's "good" and "happiness." The second group of
people broadcast continually, in print, on radio, and through television, the results of ever more quantified and standardized "research" and packaging techniques (packaging of ideas and concepts as much as products and services).

These results so broadcast form the new vision of what the
container person should like or, as a consequence, does like,
should look like, smell like, sound like, walk like, talk like, think
like, wish like, smile like, live like, die like, look like after death.
In the end, the new vision provides a mirror in which the organism, Narcissus-like, recognizes itself and reinforces its own image.

This double cadre of behavior engineers, not altogether witting
partners, provides us with the new technicians of human hopes.
They draft the plans and programs, draw up the schedules, figure
the ratios, express them in parabolas, actuarial tables, polls, and
quantified proposals which are taken *in themselves* to be the total
stuff from which will be achieved the greater "good" for the
greatest number of human containers.

Such is the vision, and such are the consequent pressures having a profound and dislocating effect on every person's knowledge of what he most deeply is in relation to his sense of what he
is expected to be. Each person, so molded or, at the least, under
the increasing outer pressure of such a mold, is an actor in what
can only be a Theater of Longing. In the twinkling of an eye dissected and measured with calipers, he is tied once more to a
human bondage, but this time so brutal as to diminish his individual humanity to an analogue of his peristaltic workings, and his
shared humanity to an animal equation in which no x factor is
admitted.

In defensive reaction, he begins feebly but unceasingly to insist
on his innerliness, on his "individuality." But these by now have
become lonely things. The Longing is upon him, together with
all its attendant circumstances. Fear, for instance: he has a fear of
losing what he considers his greatest and most precious
acquisition—the capacity to inquire factually and to obtain

objective truth. Disbelief: he shuns all belief of the traditional kind as an unholy threat. Loneliness: he does his best to bypass the first promptings of his inner self telling him that he was never more alone. Weakness: he must devise methods—even gimmicks—to cope with an inherent weakness of man individually and collectively.

In his efforts and his longing, he becomes a modern Sisyphus. All the boulders have been lifted to the tops of the mountains by his machine inventions. But he has a new unceasing labor far more taxing than the frustrating pushing of his ancient paragon: he must hold strong within himself to what he instinctively knows he is. He must find a new expression for all that he feels is greater in him and his actions and his destiny, greater than his new man-made mold, but inadmissible by the very standards of that mold.

The Fear

"If you would measure a man's hope, measure his fear," Tocqueville once said. The fear of man in his modern condition tells us rather precisely what dimensions the object of his hope possesses. The basic idea is that the mind and brain of man have passed through a scarred history, a desperate struggle to be free for the great challenge of being human and the great conquest of the human universe. Though scarred, this history is sacred. For it is the arena in which man's effort to be free of myth and legend is clearly seen and preserved. That effort has been almost five billions of years long. And today, almost at the peak, the threat of oblivion or worse—the return of myth and legend—still looms over mind and brain. This is the Fear.

The mind and brain are viewed as a precious duo. Like violin and violinist. They have struggled to play the pure music of objectivity and factual truth for so long. Turn anywhere you will today, you will find that word pictures are daily drawn for us in the poetry of the proselytizing scientian: we are minutely described as we struggled up the steep path of physical and psycho-physical evolution:

Shuffling through the insensate coils of amino acids and chemical compounds within the fertile haze of the "mystical hydrogen" amid primeval swamps. Zigzagging in and out of living waters. Slithering and gasping onto inhospitable landmasses. Shutting gills. Sprouting wings. Enlarging thorax cage and lungs. Developing and adapting organs: spine, cranium, buttocks, superorbitals. Listening to the precious feedback of brain discharges. Managing the little circuits. Forming synapses. Finding the oppositive thumb: to hold thus a tool, a weapon. (Eureka!) Scratching images on paleolithic caves. Striking fire. Weaving a cloth. Bending an oar. Stretching a sail. Smelting lead, tin, bronze; then iron; then steel. Diversifying into cultures and civilizations. Onward. Ever onward. Sumerian. Assyrian. Chinese. Babylonian. Persian. Indo-Ayran. Greek.

Ah! Those Greeks had a word for it: knowledge. *They* almost made it. And with them the world nearly made it. Mind and brain almost came into possession of objective truth. But, after all that effort in the swamps and caves, etc., well, man's nerve failed him.

It happened like this. Man's grandest accomplishment is the brain and mind that made possible his highest achievement. This latter we know to be the rigor and neutrality of objective truth. This is the truth which he attains in science and technology. And, of course, the neutrality and objectivity defined by scientific standards place themselves quite beyond question. The Greeks found out and practiced that objective rigor and neutrality. There is no need to be chauvinist and point out that the Greeks also added a few non-objective flourishes—they talked about a wisdom beyond and more than factual knowledge. One can surely forgive them that, when we look at the roster of names and achievements: Archimedes in mathematics, Euclid in geometry, Eratosthenes in geography, Ptolemy in astronomy. So many more. All this would have remained bottled up in the parochial atmosphere of homeland Greece if Alexander's empire had not exploded north, south, east, and west. Thus the seeds of scientific rigor were sown over as far as the Ganges in India and as far west as Gibraltar. Then the rough and ready Romans came, hewed out a unified empire within which all sorts of outlooks, initiatives, lifestyles, and attitudes of mind and brain were mutually challenged, fought fiercely, and fructified abundantly.

Now the mind and brain of man were ready for the great leap.

Imagine! About 100 B.C. or 50 B.C., they already had the steam engine in Ptolemaic Egypt to pump water to the top of the famous Lighthouse; they could have had dishwashers, television sets, radios, satellites, Caesar's theory of relativity, the atom bomb, genetic coding, air and ear pollution, the Kinsey report, 747's, blood plasma, offshore oil drilling, the Pill, organic food, and so so much more, if two things had not happened.

First, that failure of nerve. Peculiar thing. The bold, confident spirit of Greece and Alexandria suddenly and inexplicably weakened. Men turned away from science and started to look for comforting myths. Don't ask why. The myths came in horrible hordes. Stoicism. Epicureanism. Mithraism. Gnosticism. And so on. But all these would have been ineffectual against mind and brain, if it had not been for the supreme myth-maker: the Christian and Roman Church. It appeared in some strength about 150 A.D. By 390 A.D., it had taken over, imposing its view, outlawing reason and understanding (mind reasons, brain understands). Jesus Caesar and Jesus Doctor were getting around. It rejected the world, including that world on which mind and brain worked, in favor of personal salvation. (It is difficult to explain why this sudden dichotomy was felt as necessary in terms other than a fear which gripped the religionists of that day, as today it grips the men of science.)

The new and supreme myth supplied men with the sterile consolations of private gratifications and a save-me-Lord-I'se-sinking ideology. It said: Be more than human. Otherwise you perish. Forget your brain. Stuff your mind with unreason, with cherubs, angels, the Virgin, the Crucified One, the Pope, the Priest, Fish on Friday, Confession. Burn the heretics. Hate the world as bad. You are a pilgrim, shortly to leave this place of pilgrimage, this vale of tears.

The result was catastrophic. Faith smashed science. Mind was covered in darkness. Brain was befuddled with chanting and incantation. Empires crumbled. Science lost its momentum. Technology stopped dead in its tracks. The best minds turned to devising abstract formulas for personal sustenance, some self-contained source of dignity and serenity. By 500 A.D., it was all over. An absolutist Roman pontiff sat in Rome. Ancient libraries were burnt to rubble. Europe, and the mind and brain of man, entered the Dark Ages. All the way from 500 A.D. to 1600 A.D.; and in between singing monks, hairsplitting egghead philosophers, abstract theologians, cruel ecclesiastics, corrupt clergy, groaning serfs, oppressed peoples, useless wars, ignorant aristocrats. When someone dared to indulge in science (like the Baghdad Sufis who invented the electric battery), or to argue that the warring division between science and faith was false, unnecessary, and fatal (as Roger Bacon attempted to do), such as these were crucified.

You cannot, however, suppress mind and brain forever. In the 1600's, the scientific writings of the Greeks were rediscovered because the Arabs had preserved them. Once again, men turned to face the ancient challenge: conquer man's world using objective truth obtained by means of scientific rigor. Faith had smashed science; turnabout became fair play! The reflowering of this discipline of mind and brain in man took almost four hundred years. As in ancient times when Alexander's empire and the Roman empire helped, so too modern imperialism helped; and our technology-based world-wide communications have brought the four corners of the world into a painful but fruitful confrontation.

But there is again, as in ancient times, an attempt to stifle mind and brain. Some people are declaring that science and technology are irrelevant. Some others are trying to persuade us that mind and brain are not the whole of man's instrumentality for knowing. Some others still are claiming that there is also a knowledge possible to man other than the knowledge given by science. There is a concerted attempt by religions, especially residual Christianity, to limit the effect of science.

Now, after all we have been through, it is perfectly understandable that the effect of these attempts on the mind and brain of man is the Fear. Fear that man's nerve will again fail. Fear that once more irrationality will triumph, that unreason will prevail. Fear that the false consolation and private gratification of little salvations fabricated by rules and wispy myths will again swamp the mind, paralyze the brain. Fear that we will be forced back into such a Church, back to cower in such a Sanctuary, to kneel in the Confessional for Absolution, back to Holy Water, Agnus Dei's, the Virgin cult, fingering the Rosary, reciting Catechism lessons like mindless children. In short, fear of mental bondage locking out thought and reasoning. Fear of brain cloggage with fairy stories and inane superstitions.

No! Not all that again. When Kafka said to G. Janouch: "Most men are not wicked . . . they are sleepwalkers, not evil-doers," he was talking of those caught in this thralldom out of which science is awakening man. But we moderns must mind: those who attack or criticize science's supremacy are to be seen as wicked; they are evil-doers. And it must be clear—after all we have been through—our saying that about them is *not* the same as their saying it about us.

Belief

Because there is fear, and particularly because of the nature and the pervasiveness of this fear, belief is impossible. If you fear being stultified, strangled, and deceived by any religious faith, then such a faith or belief becomes abhorrent. For any act of faith seems like a concession which will entail total thralldom; any "I shall consider" heralds an enslaving "I believe," to be followed by an irresistible "I obey," "I contribute," and so on.

Ironically, to believe is characterized as a failure of nerve: believing is seen merely as a way to subserve a power structure built on some innate human weakness; and to partake in an organized religion means to be utilized for purposes that are hidden and for the subtle plans for an elitist caste in whose minds very pragmatic ends justify all and every means.

As a result of this attitude, a modern man can perform an outward act of piety only as indulgence toward those he pities or loves, or to demonstrate his tolerance. He has, deep down, a shrinking suspicion that he will be made impotent by superstitions concocted by celibates in conference; or be programmed powerless by paternalistic prescriptions patented in a presbytery; perhaps be made servile by incantations plastered on his lips by pirouetting priests, on his ears by pontificating preachers, on his waking thoughts by contentious confessors and the cajoling charladies of his conscience—a wife, a sister, a mother, a nun, a friend.

For the modern person, there are ingrained hells in the accouterments and accompaniments of religious belief of which he intends to free himself. He will be free of being one of a vast flock of sheep led by ecclestiastics and "ecclesiatics." Free of a bejeweled finger solemnizing his marriage hell, staying the abortionist's hand, removing a contraceptive device, deciding the taste of his food, the length of a dress, the passion of a kiss. Of being perforce content with childishnesses, he an adult palmed off with hocus-pocus and half-digested versions of human reality. Of having thoughts prohibited, of submitting to a ban on ideas, to a punishment for thinking. Of being allowed no uncertainties. Of having a mind swept clear by ukase of all difficulties faced, and denied the delicate pain of doubts stared down. Of ceasing to belong to the Republic of Free Communications. Of having all his future foretold infallibly and all his possible discoveries banalized by a dimissorial "This too shall pass." Of lacking the precision and chrome-bright outlines of a science which can put it all in formulas, which computerizes and explains all with tangible earth, stone, powder, and the microscope. He considers that, if he were not free of all this, he would not be free to be able to experience, to breathe, to live, and to be human.

In the Theater of Longing, to put it briefly and figuratively, man learns to equate belief with painful negatives of life and so cannot look up to any proposed heaven or any god proclaimed by religious institutions to be necessary for his humanness. And the institutions he knows are themselves bound in their own Jesus figures (and he knows these are fallacious), or in other man-made superstitions and figments. His principle, then, is not to look up in religious belief for any such shadowy and deceptive religious ideal.

This principle would at least permit him integrity (perhaps an integrity approaching the unswerving uniformity of a well-run machine), if it was logically applied throughout his life. But instinctively any human being knows at the same time that such a thorough and over-all application of the principle of non-belief would make all human life as we know it impossible. And it is no different in the genuinely human life of man and woman even within the Theater of Longing. Much in the way of proselytism lies under the camouflage of busy-ness; and within the proliferating forest of building and activity and of objective things about him, religion or religious faith is not the only force demanding the indulgence of his belief. Funnily enough but characteristically enough, however, only religious faith is refused that indulgence.

Belief—religious or otherwise—consists essentially of an acceptance, on the word of another, of that which one cannot verify or that others cannot prove or establish by what is called objective means. Belief is, thus, a "looking up" to, an obeisance of the mind and will. Obviously, in his life of knowledge and inquiry as well as in his personal relationships, any man must indulge in belief. He must believe, for instance, that there cannot be a god capable of creating out of nothing; for that negative belief is adduced as the necessary backbone and is the prefabricated presumption of all evolution. If such a god exists, evolution as an explanation of the *origin* of life does not make sense. But it is a belief—on the word of evolutionists and anthropologists. Furthermore, he must believe not merely that *Homo sapiens* can evolve from "lower animals" (implicitly, *Homo sapiens* is just another but "higher" animal, and this, in itself, is another implicit and unquestioned belief), but that man *did* evolve and *must* have evolved from "lower animals." He must believe, further, that someday somehow scientists will prove all these beliefs to be founded on objectively verified facts, "when all the evidence gets in"—this is the usual proviso. But this, whether he realizes it or not, means that science will have to prove non-factual things as realities with merely factual means and instrumentalities; it will mean, in other words, that one will rely on scientific means to prove or disprove realities which do not belong to the scientific order.

In his personal life, one must accept on faith the word of others—no matter how much he should attempt to verify their reliability. Accepting the word of others in personal relationships concerns the most intimate parts of his life as man: love, marriage, loyalty, trust, friendship, hope and confidence, and the web of felt but never proven attitudes which others evoke in us and we in them, and on which is built any social cohesion different from the automated cohesion of well-ordered machines and utterly alien to the inhuman but excellent cohesion of a perfectly normal anthill.

The fact is, then, that within the curious structure of the

Theater of Longing, modern man has been taught to disbelieve in religious faith but to believe in science, and to believe that in so doing he is not "merely believing." But what happens is poignantly simple: insofar as a man or woman has decided to leave aside belief or the possibility of belief in religious matters, but to accept belief in scientific matters as the ultimate ground of living, being, and hoping as a human, so far has he denied his spirit a vital activity. It is tantamount to bidding one's ear to see or one's nose to hear. There follows an incomprehensible frustration, according as what they most desire disappears, leaving an inarticulate agony harassed by insufficient facts and brute data.

Feeling

Badgered by his fear of entrapment in religious belief, committed by the main thrust of his society which carries him to refuse the very possibility of such belief, a modern man cannot look forward feelingly, cannot act intuitively. He cannot entertain that feeling which is typical only of human beings. To feel in a human fashion, to really feel, would mean that he felt aloneness. For, while loneliness is experienced only in relation to our social existence, human aloneness remains as a condition of being human. This is the personal solitude, the impenetrable silence of self with self.

Human aloneness is often confused with loneliness, yet it is quite different. While loneliness is one-sided and monolithic, human aloneness is two-sided and fluid: on one side, there is the consciousness of being an impenetrable self; on the other there is an outward motion to expect, to look forward, to hope, to be buoyed up by an instinctive knowledge of things to come, a conviction that the most exquisitely unpredictable things will happen to the self. Aloneness is built on hope. It is an unproven but, nonetheless, unshakable grasp of a permanence which will come and terminate all transiency, of a perpetual sunrise at the end of an infinitely tiring series of mottled days and stealthy nights. It is not explicitly or necessarily a hope of an "after-life," or a feeling for another order of things where beatitude and happiness will be the lot of beings transfigured with a glory that is more than human. It is, however, a yawning of unshut windows in the self.

Man stands on the open casements of his being and seeks the visit of a god, as it were, who will save him from feeling like the object of a cosmic joke and the fool of crass time. Lord Asquith reportedly said in one of his zanier moments that any adult man who expects a visitant god is a jackass. But Madame Pompadour commented: you lose a man if you make him look like a fool; you destroy a man if you make him feel like one. No one willingly thinks himself into destruction.

Now, a modern man does experience aloneness and at least the danger of loneliness in his social existence. In fact, it is the red eyes of this latter threat which send him running into his febrile activity "to be with it." But he can outlive social loneliness. The aloneness of being human, that human feeling is something he cannot tolerate, much less entertain permanently. Much more decidedly, he cannot adopt the spontaneous human solution—to look forward, to feel in the instinctively intuitive sense. His solution, therefore, is other: he becomes a traveler.

His character as traveler has nothing to do with former religious and philosophical ideas about man as someone traveling on to eternity, to Nirvana, to perfection, or anything as mystical— if sensuous—as Omar Khayyam's picture of man's life as "a battered caravanserai whose open doors are night and day." There is nothing of piety or religion or poetry about it. It is merely that a mobility of knowing and of sensibility has affected all things human since early in the decade of the sixties. Everything in man's world is moving. Men and the societies they compose are moving on a road they do not recognize to a future which has not been announced or planned beforehand. Modern man is the traveler *par excellence.* He must change, transmute, molt one posture of self to take another, and spin a further self from the steely strands of what is effective, of what is expected, of what will do the job. The self must always travel, onward, ever onward.

On that ever-ongoing road, dealing constantly, as he must, with his aloneness and its human tendency to feel for the horizon of final solution and ultimate togetherness, he acts out some of the peculiar situations visible in our modern life. If he reaches for an ideal, his bones creak. If he achieves a genuine beauty (and he sometimes does), it is more a relief hammered in gold than a spontaneous carousal of birds trilling to the light of his glorious day. If he speaks in a gesture of reconciliation, it leaves a queer after-taste in his mouth. If he hears echoes, they are not intimations of any immortality, but the barks of stalking dogs who bay at his back—his nothingness, his poverty of alternatives, his increasing nonentity, his steadily becoming nobody.

He lacks charismatic leaders. He does not have "great ones" in anything: no dean of critics emerges; no genuinely accepted voice of communal hopes is heard in poetry, music, drama; he is battered by self-appointed messiahs and besieged by bards of pain. Everyone is a pygmy humanly, great or small. Elitism is abhorrent; but he fears the anonymity of a human anthill. He has no cyclical celebration ingrained in life: an eating together, a social festival, a national joy. For such celebration ties the present to a past which is melting before his eyes and to a future in which he is little interested; for suddenly today he cannot lean for strength on a feeling conviction that greater things lie ahead.

Self-Control

One of the more tortuous leave-overs of man's era just preceding the Theater of his Longing was the ingrained tendency developed in him to look down. Men were told (not merely by Christianity) never to lose sight of "what was below": their natural weakness, the filth of their moral behavior, the stark mortality of all they were and did, and their persistent condition as beings needing, above all, mercy and forgiveness and salvation, and the ultimate gratuity of a free pardon with a pass into a beatitude they did not merit and they could in no way ensure by their own efforts. "Dust thou art, and unto dust thou shalt return" was the phrase from Judaism which Christianity made its own and Islam adopted wholeheartedly. Eastern religions were built on such an idea of human weakness at the base.

Furthermore, if men of former cultures looked carefully and according to their instructions, other dismal sights presented themselves: avenging angels and punishing devils; surrogates of a god or a demon clambering over their backs demanding allegiance or seducing their attention; there were nether regions of agony or of detention and purification; commands to sustain pain and undertake suffering; to cap it all, there was to be a final cleansing phase full of judicial terror, mass guilt, theocratic decision, and eternal subsistence in absolute good or cohabitation with evil incarnate.

But a modern man cannot afford to "look down" at himself in any such manner. For to do that means one thing: think and act like a creature of a creating god; and since he is constantly exhorted to renounce any belief, this is already difficult and becoming impossible. Alternatively, he could attempt to refuse to contend or to grapple and cope with the mechanisms; he could try to adapt to the influences that paw at him, and somehow to survive amid the rigid structures and systems. But the latter attempt could not last any length of time. For, short of suicide, there is finally no escape from modern life. The Theater of Longing is all-pervasive.

Belief being outlawed because of fear, and feeling being truncated and reduced to that which fits the definitions and does not defy measurement, men and women have a feeling of incompleteness. They have problems "within themselves" arising from the new concept of the container person. Psychologists and psychiatrists have pried open the heavy cover of consciousness and peered down the manhole into the blackness of human motives, human dreams and fantasies, human fears and impulses. It smelled: of prejudices, of hatred, of inverted loves, of crassness, of desires we would never in our sanity allow run free and of decisions we could never in cold reason let reach a practical conclusion.

Sometimes a man will go off the deep end: alcoholism, drug addiction, wholesale lechery, sadism, criminality, mental aberrations of all kinds. He not only looks down; he is hypnotized by what he sees. But this is recognized as aberrant: a golden rule has been broken. He must be recovered for society or permanently put away for the good of all. There is such an instinctive horror of looking down that we do not like any more even the idiosyncrasies of an individual and the usually amusing oddities of the eccentric. We have no tolerance for those forms of private insanity which the British used to take in their stride. A William Blake and or an El Greco would not be understood. Salvador Dali has a difficult time.

Individuals, men and women, turn to psychologists and psychiatrists today when they feel the increasing castration of the inner self to be too much to bear. But these professionals are trained to bring each person "into adjustment" with whatever "reality" is found *around* him. It does not matter one whit whether therapy is directed along lines advocated by Freud or Erikson or Berne or Laing or Janov or Maslow or Adler, except of course as the "adjustment" advocated is colored by each man's view of just what that outer reality is. The implication always is that all within us is quantifiable, observable, and manipulatable in its totality; and the aim is *always* to adjust oneself to the dimensions of what we find around us. Our incompleteness, according to the modern man, arises because either we have never settled upon the right attitude which we can act out, or we spend our lives trying to deceive ourselves and the rest of the world. We suffer from weaknesses attendant on certain deprivations or over-gratifications or maladjustments to the conditions of our lives.

The aim, therefore, is to adjust ourselves to the dimensions of what we find around us. After all, each of us is a container person which must acquire control of self and of one's surroundings. All that our behavior reflects, then, is not content, but, in the most voguish of current jargon, a transaction, a social contract: I will accept you and your actions thus, in order to avoid any unworthy rude shocks or confrontations. Thus, we have polite manners; these express no interior condition but are our part of a social transaction. I will adopt a mask of equanimity (not obeying any inner resolution based on principles) in the face of pain or injustice or death. I will not kill you, even though you have angered me beyond the limit of moderation, only because if all of us acted like that society would surely fall apart; there would be no law and order. In the jargon that Eric Berne has bequeathed his fellow man as his richest legacy, I will include in my "script" a nice mixture of love, hate, guilt, reason, and fear of painful consequences (all defined in terms of structures and never based on the idea of values inner to me). Otherwise, society, as Alan Harrington mirrors it, would be a collection of psychopaths, and human life would be filled with a deathly tension and an all-pervasive madness. Simply: no one of our life styles or human "scripts" could coexist with the other ones.

Somehow or other, all our "scripts" in the Theater of Longing cohere and portray a "successful" human drama, and inevitably mirror as well the longing of all men and women.

Consensus

But this self-control for the individual is not enough for the society of individuals. Society itself as a collectivity must decide upon a script which allows harmony between the scripts of its individual members, and between the society itself and other societies. Collective scripts of a societal kind are found in law. In fact, in the Theater of Longing, a human society is defined as a collectivity of human beings who have made written and codified law the ultimate and only arbiter of how individual members should behave toward each other. In the Theater of Longing, the consensus of a people is publicly defined only by law; and that consensus is viable only insofar as law sets precedents and gives practical rules on which particular judgments can be passed in particular cases.

Most Americans feel instinctively that this country has achieved more in freedom and defense of rights before law than any other country. Great wrongs have been redressed and proud paths have been opened. But one major latter-day conclusion is that law must be able to restore to us as a people that which we feel lacking to us—the dimension of collective and individual self felt as dislocated and increasingly disavowed and disallowed as things are now going.

This seems like a good idea because it is, seemingly, a democratic idea. But law, too, has been stripped of a dimension. Law is always based on some underlying thing, on some prime precedent "platform." In the rush to underscore and reaffirm the intent of the Founding Fathers that freedom of belief prevail, the underlying premise on which such freedom was to be achieved is deemphasized and, whenever possible, ignored. This was the assumption by the Founding Fathers that a general religious belief existed beyond and antecedent to the law. It not only infused the law, in their eyes, with a general meaning which the law itself does not contain, but also gave it its direction and thrust from day to day and decade to decade. The assumption was that a reli-

gious ethic was shared by a generality of the people; and they assumed that this ethic which informed the law was the one contained in the Christian religion. That ethic included and extolled
the concept of the human person and the rights of each. That
concept of person persists; but, clearly, it is increasingly separated
from the ethic that gave it meaning, and in its redefinition today
it is obviously distorted.

This separation of the principles of law from the base which
made those principles natural and inevitable affects law, and all
else in society. Specifically, in law, it represents a separation of
law from an older consensus; and a new one has not yet replaced
it. It nevertheless remains true that, in a free land, law can function only as a reflecter and defender of its underlying consensus;
it cannot re-create that consensus and it cannot and has no right
to form a new one without running the danger, as old as civilization, of the tyranny of law. Law as law and no more—that is,
law as no longer interpretative and reflective of a greater concept
or ethic—has been perhaps man's greatest tool for enslavement
throughout history.

Before this point in time, the religious belief, the moral base of
consensus, that served as the prime precedent or "platform" underlying the intricate system of laws, also underlay the majority
of attitudes and precepts on which societal decisions were made
and maintained by individuals and groups, without any thought
or necessity of recourse to law. As the moral base of consensus
recedes today in favor of system and structure, there are fewer
and fewer established institutions whose authority is recognized
or who are credited with sufficient "authority" to decide moral
questions. At the same time, as the moral consensus recedes, more
and more basic issues are reopened to examination and question
and decision.

In that situation, and even as it is being stripped, like the people it would serve, of a vital dimension that gives it meaning beyond its own competency and "supremacy," law seems to recom-
mend itself especially. For it is the one institution whose systems
and structures appear complex and intricate enough in themselves, without reference to their moral base, to give it the "authority" and the "objectivity" to decide these newly reopened
basic questions.

Increasingly, then, problems which must be re-examined at their deepest levels, problems until recently decided routinely and meaningfully by individuals, are thrust upon law to decide, either in courts or in legislatures or both. Thus, law, which cannot itself replace or invent the underlying ethic of a people, but must be an expression of that ethic, is forced to respond to increasing pressure to do precisely this. Law, which operates daily with the heaviest reliance on precedent, is also asked to entertain issues for which there is no precedent at law: Is the human fetus a person and therefore entitled to its life? Are homosexual acts between consenting males and females "all right"? Must people be employed, even though they are incompetent, merely because of their color?

In such cases, law itself must respond in one of two ways. It must surrender its role as bastion of freedom and defender (not definer) of morality. It must take to itself instead the right to decide on the basis of law alone what is right, good, and moral. But this alternative means that law must declare itself as supreme rather than as servant of man the citizen.

Or, conversely, the law must simply follow the polls. It must follow every pathetically popular whim prevalent at whatever moment an issue arises for decision at law. But this, in effect, means that the law must declare itself useless.

A nation, then, becomes an arena for an ever more complex competition. On one hand, there are the container persons, each one endeavoring to adapt personal scripts for survival and for success. On the other hand, there is society composed more and more of systems and structures designed by container persons to increase the power and pleasure of other container persons. As arbiter there is merely the law and what a majority of container persons can write into it at any given moment, or what any minority of container persons can discover in it as a legal precedent. Without an underlying consensus antecedent to law and producing the bases of law, life in the nation becomes no more than a daily strife and a continuously increasing tension between competing container persons, all fearful of extinction by the system as a whole or suppression by other container persons in particular.

28. The New Self

The Person

A man cannot for endless days sanely tolerate a very peculiar self-awareness that denies him any meaning as an individual except as something upon which a growing battery of influences from the "outside" are operating. In such a state, when he uses the term "person" about himself and others, no matter how he may insist on his "individuality," he finally conveys only the idea of a self-contained entity physically distinct from the "Outside," or, at its most dynamic, a self-contained entity beneath the wash of those influences. Walker Percy's images of conservatives who fall victim to large bowel complaints or liberals apt to contract sexual impotence, morning terrors, and a feeling of abstraction from reality, are far too merciful to express the reality of this optic.

For now we are talking of a state in which the self, the person, escapes or is cut off from each man. It lies beyond the eye. It is not even a mood of being or an atmosphere of doing. At best, it subsists at the tip of a man's mind. It escapes both the majesty of meaning and the namelessness of wishing. It is felt as the teasing promise of a dream and the menace of an unknown, hovering

along the brink of becoming, but never actually being. It holds
and attracts, but when a man tries to realize it, he wakes up to a
cold reality, as from a dream. In the momentary ecstasy of his
loving or the minute-long absorption of horror, when his will is
taken captive and his mind is torn by the roots, self is all that per-
dures. That he knows, even as the self recedes and becomes the
first, great, long-drawn-out syllable of a word he wants all his life
to hear but which is never pronounced in his hearing and is
therefore never known to him.

The influences playing on this now truncated self are not "natural" ones, so to speak: not rain, wind, snow, sunshine, skies, winter, summer, harvests, grass, forests, rivers, oceans, animals, sunrise
and sunset, a twenty-four-hour day, a seven-day week, marital
love and family cohesion. These no longer appreciably mold him;
the new man knows them, not as his mentors and least of all as
his masters or companions. Generally, they are factors largely ignored because ignorable; at most, they are inhibiting factors to be
bypassed.

In exchange, there are rather the mechanistic influences con-
trived and continually refined by other men. Each man has an
image in, and then refined by, law, business, transit, the media,
medical and psychiatric and educational guarantees; social security, insurance, labor unions, credit ratings, bottled water and
frozen food, pre-cooked dinners, standardized cosmetics, and
clothes. These are the warp and woof of the intricate web a man
must weave and into which he must be woven.

Unlike the "natural" influences, these purely mechanistic ones
do not elicit existing qualities in each man; by an iron-clad logic
of their own, they tend not to create a commonality of sentiment
by reaction and of knowledge by experience. To such a commonality each person would contribute. They provide merely,
but imperiously, the exterior environment to which each individual conforms; even as he conforms, he is experienced and "ser-
viced" by others more and more as what he is expected to be in
the reduced optic of self and society, no matter what the self
within him be.

A member of this environment derives no grace from the way
he lives, no character from the place he frequents, and no
strength from what he believes; for all that is based on a negative

imperative. His body, now neither a talent nor a gift, becomes a mortgage to be paid off. His impulses, neither esthetic in origin nor transcendent in aim, draw vibrancy from economic and financial securities. He is a here-and-now, in-and-out thing, strung ever more tautly between the self he is and the influences that constantly paw at that self and would remold it without tapping its depth or admitting even the simplest of its magical possibilities.

In all and through all, a man trapped in such an optic of self is polarized between two extremes: between the thought that is allowed and the meaning he knows is still beyond it and different from it. Only what is feasible within the framework of the truncated self is possible for him. To believe, to "intuit," to be "natural," these three are impossible. For believing is rated as naïve and the "enemy" of "knowledge"; to intuit is unscientific and not "verifiable"; "natural" is by now a portmanteau term pawned to the experts and redeemable only in the coinage of technical examination and verification at a time in the future he hopes as a living being he will not share.

The two main activities allowed him and by which he is supposed to fulfill himself are thinking and doing, reasoning and systematizing that reasoning in mechanical arrangements in the world around him. No other motions are feasible or, indeed, possible to him, no matter if he be educated or refined or subtle or what is called "an ordinary, decent person." If he is educated, the escapes or adaptations a man devises are just that much more subtle, but not less painful or ineffectual. If he is merely informed, he submits to the tyranny of symbols; but their manipulation desiccates his mind. If he is interested in cultural things, he has to employ a cunning that brutalizes, even if it helps somewhat. If he is refined, the tension is merely more acute between what he cannot be and what he must be. If he is simple, his very simplicity is a guarantee that he will surely be swamped and perish before the more sophisticated. If he is sophisticated, the pretense at being an individual is all the more brittle; and if suicide—in any shape or form—is chosen as a way out, the suicide is just all that much more talented and tragic. In fact, no escapes devised by any one individual are more effectual than anybody else's. Education palls, because it becomes essentially either information or technical skill.

The loss of one's self as a person takes place within the Theater of Man's Longing. It would be strange if, caught within the tension of that Longing, and conscious that he is urged onward by irresistible and irreversible forces, man did not evolve an expedient, a temporary concept, a working hypothesis, unique to that Theater and full of its unfulfilled longing and of the tensions that will impel him beyond it. Such an expedient is to be found illustrated in the concepts of the New Class, of Enlightened Sexuality, of Love, and of the Me Empire.

The New Class

For thousands of years, since men lived together in communities and societies, people have been divided into social classes based fundamentally on three categories of elements: property and possessions; heredity, family, blood, and dynasty; and ritual.

From property and heredity there arose "upper" classes, and sometimes intermediate classes such as "upper-middle," "middle-middle," "lower-middle," and then a further set of terms and titles to indicate the pecking order: blue bloods, aristocracy, gentle folk, bourgeoisie (haute and petite), proletariat, Lumpenproletariat, the masses, the people, the Great Unwashed.

Ritual could and did affect everyone and everything in every class. In general, it implied fixity of habits, repeated and periodic events, celebrations, and a whole web of behaviorisms: modes of address, clothes, language; required discipline in the most ordinary actions (eating, hairdos, toilet habits, sleeping, courting, love-making); an accepted set of public norms for personal morality and therefore acceptability. Within the Theater of Longing, the modern self is supposed to fly above these ruts and grooves in which men and women have traveled as bondslaves of "what they did before us, what they said before us, what they thought before us."

The democratization of human society enshrined in the American Declaration of Independence and Constitution and in the Bill of Rights was the first real breach in the class system of sufficient force not only to carry weight for its own people but by the 1960's to have a visible effect in the minds, political actions, and societal institutions of much of the modern world.

The French Revolution actually made very little difference; it merely transferred power. It broke the back of the old order of class and power, but it reached back for an older tradition as its base: it called vocally upon vague concepts of morality.

The Russian Revolution of 1917 was even more pathetically a failure in this context of the human class system. It substituted for an already extremely oppressive class system the most organized tyranny that the world has ever known and furnished it with a centralist authority and unbendable power over the minds and the bodies of millions of people. What had happened touches upon the tragic and the ludicrous. When the United States was in its first century of flower, across the water of the Atlantic a grouchy German scrivened and scribbled in the Reading Rooms of the British Museum, devising a sociopolitical program to free human society altogether from the class system. But Karl Marx suffered from too many carbuncles (the "upper classes had only indispositions, never carbuncles") and he fathered an oppressive system now dominant in the U.S.S.R. and in Mao Tse-tung's China.

Nobody knows really at this stage whether Marx or the American system or a combination of both or some third unknown force gave birth to the new idea of social class. But we do know that today this is the ideal waved in front of the eyes of modern man and woman. And we also know that it is clearly based on that great irreducible quantum in men and women: the self. But its proponents and those who proclaim its benign effects claim that there is here no question of class in the old sense, of a class system for human society. On the contrary, they will claim that this is the emergence point of a truly classless society. It does not matter, it seems, that the individual today still finds himself submerged, except for a personal permissiveness in his behavior that has no reverberations but is only a sublimation of his longing and his directionless condition. In fact, the new class idea is really an exercise of a new tyranny. Classless societies do not result from change, or revolution, or anything else, as human history tells us. In spite of this, the assertive tones of the new class proponents are unmistakable.

The self, we are told, even in its nearly untenable balancing trick, is the source of all human class distinctions. The idea now is that all are equal at the beginning precisely by virtue of being equally empty containers. But the new logic provides that each self cultivate itself and thus fill out the empty container which it is at the beginning. With education, formal or self-acquired; urged on by the innate drive to self-accomplishment (shades of social Darwinism); sustained by the nerve to be alone and self-full; utilizing talents of mind (well, of brain really) and of body; and embossed with a personality that makes all trivia personable —any crudeness is seen as a touch of originality, and any defect as an expression of the "standing on one's legs" attitude so dear to those who cannot really fill any chair. Most importantly, each self is illuminated by an apt set of ideas formulated in the new structuralist creed. The self, or various selves, create the new and the veritable categories of human society. The presupposition is that the self remakes human reality. evokes the new figures which will surround it and all of us. The self is thought to have a creativity and a value completely unrelated to all other men and women and to the human universe. Talents, nerve, personality, drive, and so on, all these are given now by ideas; and all the relevant particular ideas stem from one global idea.

It is this global idea of the new class which matters, and it is simple: since there is no such thing as an inner substance to a human being, and no such thing as a patterned structure to human lives, there are obviously no perennial models for human behavior. There probably are cultural accumulations and accumulated traditions; but individual man and woman can be free of all these, can opt out at a moment's notice; always. For the secret is: empty out the former things, and take new things into the blank receptacle of your humanness.

Property and heredity are just ancient categories used by some people to acquire domination. Ritual is another clever gimmick, like the other two, aimed at freezing and maintaining the status quo in favor of a few. All three are, in fact, elitist stratagems. They make the majority of men and women prisoners, victims of routinization, as free as labor gangs marching in lock step to the tune of repetitiveness and periodicity. Modern men and women can be self-freed from the effect of these gimmicks.

But faced with the iron-clad consequences of its assumption (the past is dead) and of its resultant behavior (which proceeds to kill the past), the new class is forced into an *ad hoc* position which seems to take it by surprise. It seems that if one opts out of one set of rituals, one must opt for another set. Simply enough, others—the new achievers—are going to acquire the property and heredity and hand on new heredities that will become just as entrenched as the old. It is a sad and potentially lethal joke, that those caught up in this self-generated freedom presume that one way or another, the new "successful" ones share at least a touch of genius; the merely talented must have discipline; but genius abides beyond all the rules and norms.

A new class system is in the making by people who, if you ask them or if you don't, will be pleased to give you an iron-clad redefinition of freedom. It happened in Russia and in China (a little more brutally than has generally been thought tasteful, but, as it is past, that can now be ignored). It can happen anywhere. Your humanity may shrivel somewhat in the process; but you can always ignore the new system for a time before it swallows your opposition and insists that you be a "self" in the new system, and that you "do your thing."

The modern correlate to the new global idea of societal structures in which all that went before is nil, comes down to one practical rule: "Do your thing." In everything. Spontaneity is now taken for creativity. Personal taste becomes a universal norm, and personal reactions to an event are more important and normative than the details of the event itself. Manners are good if they make you feel good, bad if they make you feel bad. Art is a form of madness. When conscious control is lost, creativity is born in art, in business, in love, in politics. The transport of rapture is not acquired by the mastery of rules. An achievement is no longer brilliant because the achiever is competent. The new class system, like any class system, finds expression even in its own correlate. Its leaders—changing every day—are the spontaneous achievers who decide ahead what their "thing" is in all sectors, and go ahead and do it.

The newly proposed class, therefore, is the new class of achievers, ego-achievers. The only genuine difficulty in its way is that it cannot work. The individual New Class man or woman supposedly lives in a realm of intimate personal power. But it is of the essence that they live deliberately out of touch with any tradition that could supply a moral base and the means to feel at one with a substantial number of other individuals. A society of intended New Class achievers would explode and fall apart. But there is an even greater obstacle. The New Class individual is supposed to educate himself (this in itself is a painful impossibility), to create his own environment, establish his own norms of good and evil, and seek out and identify his own inspiration. Freedom, supposedly, is the same as total concern for the individual by the same individual and for him alone. To achieve this, one would have to retire to a desert island, a cave beneath the earth, or go to live on the moon. The onrush of life today is too much; no one can escape it. To nourish the illusion of the New Class is just a symptom of the Theater of Longing.

Enlightened Sexuality

Remember the peculiar way we used to speak and think of sexuality? asks modern man in his Theater of Longing. It was exclusively a question of biological characteristics and physiological differences. Well, the byword today is that sexuality, to no one's surprise, has been the means of a huge and cruel hoax in which everyone has been victim and no one has been the perpetrator. In the name of sexuality, male and female have been victimized and abused. Sexuality has only rarely been a means of achieving full human dignity. Instead: it locked men and women and children into leaden systems; it turned people from febrile excitement to absorbing boredom; it did not help them to achieve communication of their selves. Above all, it was completely artificial. *We*, not nature, make little boys little boys and little girls little girls. "Gender identity is the result of programming," Dr. Yachnes concluded for us all. Biology was made into destiny. Sexuality, in fact, was all in the head. Our right to sex was tarnished and obscured.

If you feel that all this is rather heady stuff, you are correct. But you must listen to the voice of men and women caught in the Theater of Longing, not to sit in judgment as to the rightness or wrongness of their attitude, but to understand the significance of what is happening. Longing in itself signifies transition; and the Theater of Longing today is peopled with transitional roles claiming the attention of each and every man and woman. What they declaim in full center stage is quite audible: they condemn the old view of human sexuality as a slavery, excoriate its basic presumption—that male and female are "bad" and have to be "sublimated" and "controlled"; and they propose a new liberation. But the meaning of all this goes beyond the grease paint and the applaudits as well as the boos and the hisses.

The old view was once dominant all over the world and is as long-lived as recorded history. It is the hitherto prevalent view of sexuality propagated by males, pounced upon by religious authorities as a means of enforcing a repressive system of "needed" liberation from "sin" and "moral degradation," and is one of the best examples of what has been deeply wrong in human society, and why that society is undergoing complete bankruptcy today.

In the old view, sexuality was a hard pound-of-flesh obstacle, a subject-in-itself, and not (as the new breed claim it should be) a mere metaphor, a vehicle, for the grand and essential theme of communication between all humans: man and man, woman and woman, man and woman, all together. Because of the old, crass view, there arose the basic operative ideas of man and woman living in a societal system which was, by its essence, class-making, dehumanizing, and therefore repressive. Integral to that societal system was the concept of man as active and of woman as passive. Of male aggression, rape, brutality. Of female frailty, dependence, and fulfillment only by a male. Of patriarch and matriarch. Of "father" and of "mother" ("Mom" and "Dad"). Of "paternal" and "maternal" and "filial." Of father's strength and of mother's wisdom. Of heterosexuality ("normal") and of homosexuality ("unnatural"). Of "lasciviousness," "lust," and "lechery." Of "purity," "modesty," "continence," "virginity," and "chastity." Of training and education as necessary for children. And, finally, of a whole litany of bode-laden concepts exalted by religionists as danger signals, by civil law as parameters of good citizenship, and by common parlance as sure indices of social acceptability: adultery, fornication, buggery, masturbation, the whore figure—male and female—moral goodness and moral badness, the warnings of conscience, flirtation, coquetry, seduction, provocation, exhibitionism, voyeurism, sex play, pornography, obscenity, bestiality, license, moral turpitude, attractiveness and repulsiveness, wifeliness, husbandliness, childlikeness, and so on.

All this development successfully obscured the true value and real destiny of male and female, and, more poignantly, the wrong that had to be (and still has to be) righted in the human order of things on this planet, Earth. Human society, for example, was organized on the presumption that men and women were "good" or "evil." Interpersonal relations of men and women to each other, to life, and to the universe, were developed insensibly as well as consciously on the score that somehow we humans are wrong in the very center and origin of our being. Hence the "salvation" and "curing" proposed by practically all the religions, the "savior" figures, the various Jesus figures before and after Jesus of Nazareth, the various sacrifices and "purification" rituals from Jewish holocausts and multiple washings, Christian Masses and "willing victims," to baptisms and washings, churchings, Confessions and Absolutions.

But all this was spelled out in the alphabet of arrogance. Creature! they said. Dust thou art, and unto dust thou shalt return, they added. Woman, your desire will be for man, they cursed. What God hath put together, let no man put apart, they intoned sententiously. Women, be subject to your husbands, said Paul. I bless Thee, O Lord, the Jew chanted daily in the synagogue, for not having made me a woman. Better marry than burn, cackled Paul. And so it went. The male and female value was obscured. The deep inherent wrong to human liberty was never righted. It was only driven deeper and more painfully in human consciousness.

And thus, men and women grew up absurd. From birth they found themselves thrown into a social system that denied their individuality, into a political way of life which capitalized on what should be their glory. The "reality" forced on them was not reality; for it had outlawed feelings and dreams as just that. Its organizers had laid down a law that maimed by amputation: Be rational and logical. Control your feelings. Seek reason but avoid unreason. Follow thought but exclude feeling. Let mind dominate the body, but with a minimum of feeling. You are earth and earthy, but try to imitate the angels. You may imagine that you feel something. But you really do not.

Well, the bare fact is that male and female do have to be liberated. This is the assertion of today. Sometimes this liberation seems to be going so well that men and women appear likely to liberate themselves past any meaning at all for male and female. We have already, and by an unusually speedy route, arrived at the point where to speak of human sexuality in terms of biological characteristics is, according to today's new man and woman, to trap them in a minor difference. If you insist on building any ramifications on such a minor happenstance, they insist, you will surely entrap us all over again in disastrous consequences. The basic credo of Newsex is repeated and repeated: "You will trap the male again in his clownish, clotish role as aggressor and the female as merely attached to the male and the child as a limitation on the liberty of the male and the personality of the female."

To avoid this tragedy, the current argument goes, we will all simply have to learn that there is no difference of any significance whatsoever between men and woman. Now, we all have prejudices, and this is not an easy step for most people to take. But be fair. The old view of sexuality was not really sexy; it led to a depression of value in humans, and it is completely artificial. Today, liberation is the watchword and the rule of action.

It releases the victims: women from male chauvinism, men from the chains of constricting rationalism, and children from false dependence. All will be freed from the imposed death in their capacity to taste individual experience as the supreme reality to which all else is subservient. No longer will the irrational be outlawed as unhuman or the use of fine language be exalted as a sign of human achievement. The body will not be decried either as the source of temptation or as an outer shell housing a "spirit." Work will not be exalted and play diminished to the status of children's occupation, permitted relaxation, or as a sign of immaturity.

In the new sexual ambit of the container person, as he strides across the stage in the Theater of Longing, sex becomes truly a metaphor: yet another conceptual tool grasped in pursuit of the desperate theme of communication (somehow become so elusive today). In other words (as this view goes), the form of human existence which is just about to replace all previous forms will mean a total transformation. The language of liberation becomes lyrical in describing that transformation.

Work and doing and concrete achievement will cease to be the normal condition of human existence. For that left the playful and the fanciful elements as onetime consolations and periodic sugarplums. Instead, the real structures of human existence will be composed of what is beautiful and sensuous and truly sexual. Men and women will bo longer scrutinize their universe as a vast field of factual knowledge but as a lustrous playground to be sung about, to be laughed in, to be enjoyed with free bodies and minds blown out, out, out.

Of course, for a time many men and women will be confused and will act ambivalently. The Old-Timers will quake with apprehension, build their defenses, and some of them hiding behind dark fortifications will die in their crass security. But you can get an awful lot of music from an old fiddle; and many of them will see the light and emerge to join the throngs of the liberated. The Now-Timers will try to have the best of both worlds, profiting from the Old and stealing from the New; but when death comes, they will scurry off like bonden slaves at evening time, whipped, to their cellars.

The New-Timers, however, will (and actually already do) eschew any last vestiges of subservience in thought, in feeling, in behavior, in association. They will act and be liberated. They will recognize each other automatically by the delicate musk-sweet smell of their liberation, the look in the eyes, the body gesture, the so-called insanity now all sane, the condemned paranoia now all beauty. The reality of life will be a sustained male-female duet in among the amniotic jungles suspended with the animated symbols of a healthy psychology. Back and forth will they swing on the free trapezes of their laughing life, or walk with palms turned upward in pure joy. Phallus will have ceased to be a symbol and vagina will never more be cavern of man's undoing. No love-hate. No prostitution. No Noah's Ark processional of dumb couples plodding. Death will be no miserable ending. Male and female will go sedately like calm beings wrapping their cloaks around them, when the winds of twilight blow, lying down to dream eternally pleasant dreams. The liberation is even assigned to a not too distant day when, as the Beatles so prophetically sang, we will see "we're all one, and life flows on within you and without you." And the exaltation will be so great on the day of final liberation that not even sentiments of reproach or of carping contempt will animate the New Man and the New Woman. Men and women will have but pity for the long dead who never knew the liberation. They will pause now and then for a passing instant in their happiness, gaze backward at the eastern sky, and think together: "Even though they, our forebears, never knew this reality, they were necessary for our enjoyment. May the oblivion of their nothingness be kind to them and to their memory."

But still there is the echoing question, and we have all heard it often of late. What does it all mean? Something has happened: lost is that most intimate, wordless communication of shared fulfillment beyond the self, together with the exquisite, delicate, powerful knowing and intimacy of deepest self with deepest self and with something beyond both. Instead, there is only aggravation and a poorer, paler ideal at the end of a nicely engineered and terribly boring road. We may all be lulled to sleep by it all, before our children can be conceived in love.

Love

Of course, once you liberate human sexuality from its old trappings, human love between man and woman, parent and child, man and man, woman and woman, takes on a totally different dimension. For you can no longer speak with such grained and colored terms as "lover," "beloved," "husband," "wife," "boy," "girl," "male," "female." All such terms are loaded with connotations and significations that reflect the old order which the new sexuality has left behind. Besides, they impinge on the sacrosanct character of the individual.

Love for Newsex is, first of all, not a connotation either of sexual differentiation or of blood or of written contract. Now, the fact that we are man and woman, mother and child (or father and child), brothers and sisters, or wife and husband, has nothing to do with love. These relationships, consecrated in the old oppressive order, have one telltale characteristic: the participants are defined in terms of somebody else. You are a mother *because* of this child. You are a wife *because* of this husband or a husband *because* of this wife. You are a brother *because* of this sister. And so it goes. But, in Newsex, love is not a matter of different gender or of womb. The *petite différence* is much more *petite* than we ever guessed; and the womb is an accident of evolution.

Positively speaking, love according to the new role of man and woman within the Theater of Longing is an expression of the self's freedom. Love is totally the domain of the individual. Even the ancient and beautiful (but quite fascistic) idea that loved and loving one were together absorbed in a third thing, thus searching out and finding ecstasy and life and freedom, this is no more. Definitively. You see the difficulty: The individual was drowned. And to maintain the vibrancy of our "individuality" is paramount, not to say desperate.

Besides, more often than not, one of the two participants in the ancient love yoke somehow or other tried to be that third thing which both were supposed to become. It simply did not work. And, to make it completely unbearable, there were those fanatics who tried to make everyone the victim of their supernatural love. Now in the Theater of Longing there is no explicit role for a victim.

All in all, then, within this new context of human love, it is more advisable to speak of the ever-loving self. For each human being, if left alone and uninterfered with, is just that: an ever-loving self. And, men and women, little boys and little girls, being what they are—completely different and independent beings —assume a series of new roles as expressions of the ever-loving self each one of them is. Each ever-loving self speaks very clearly to what it loves, be it man, woman, poodle, or goat. Each assumes a specific speaking role. Not in terms of "conquest," "getting her man," "possessing his woman," "building a home," or anything so quaint or antiquated. Rather in terms of the particular role the particular ever-loving self has chosen to play. For that is the only dimension of love permissible to that self.

These new speaking roles are conveniently ranged in four categories according to the four main stages through which the ever-loving self of Newsex passes: the Experimentation, the Flowering, the Ecstasy, and the Repose.

In the Experimentation, the self forewarns: "I'm really skittery. How are you? And you're right, of course. We might be barely friends, when this is over. Either the best will merge leaving us as selves, or the worst will slice us both. And I am a botherer. So?

But for goodness' sake, know that this flake of flesh is outside a
core that's very private, very particular, and of necessity luxuri-
ous. An objectifier might say it's some kind of molecular attraction; but be careful. Don't crash-land on me. You have a lot to
learn about. Not about mankind, but about me in particular."

With the Flowering, the self begins to expand: "I say all I say
with foresight. I both know and then will not know where
you're leading me. Pushing and prodding. But you be careful for
yourself. Forget me. I can take care of myself. You know how it
is: living on two levels, it's awfully dangerous. I think that you
started, because something of you noted an iciness crystallizing in
me. And it was a human impulse. And then when things started
to hit the fan, you were there as a friend as well. You gave me
what I needed at the time. A fragment of me burst out as person
under your kneading. But I don't need a father or a mother or
one who husbands my energy now or wifes my nights and days.
Allow yourself me. For your own sake, me or some other."

In the Ecstasy, the language is pithy and definitive and categoric. All is clear: "Things of this earth are good. They evoke celebration. I love you. With you, I'm all of a piece. I am demanding. I taste joy and anger, concern and impatience. I don't dote
on you. I'm not avid for your troubles. Or your time (maybe).
But all the things I have ever loved, I love in you today. And all
the fear I have ever felt, I forget momentarily in you. Trust me.
Please. Think well of me, when it's over."

But it is in the words of the Repose that the full expression of
Newsex love emerges. "In entering my life and feelings, remember you are entering an inner forest. Please take the trees for the
wood. Always. In other words, do not think of me. Feel me. I
wish to explore all forms of sensory information. Feel my heart-
beats. Hear my respiration. Sense my perspiration through the
skin. See my facial expressions in your irises. Ride every wave
that increases my freedom, my enjoyment, my understanding of
myself. The reason I choose you, not an auto-eroticism machine
or the motorized penile contraptions of technicians, is quite simple. I need someone whose eyes will tell me they are as frightened
as I am. Someone to make me aware of myself by hurting me
deeply. Someone to let me know care by caring for me, realize
caress by caressing me. Someone in whom I come alive, alive be-

yond the scavenger of all my beauty and my peace—beyond time, and beyond reason and words and gestures. Others may seek a love that commits severe depredations on their being. You must be volatilized as the mirror of my ever-loving self. A vital part of you must flit away, be dissipated and dispersed, so that my self can roam on wild wings of artistic and human expression too thin and subtle to be netted by the "feelies" of an Aldous Huxley, too substantial and too dominant to be encased in the horror of a pairing off with another ever-loving self."

The Me Empire

The Me Empire is not a dynasty of some obscure time in Japanese or Chinese history, but the new dynasty today within the Theater of Longing. The thrust of all the forces in terms of which we all must operate within that Theater is to indicate that you literally are nobody, or are in terrible danger of becoming nobody, unless you practice a personal imperialism. In an unarticulated desperation, you must think of yourself and make sure that others know that "it's me that matters," precisely against the inevitable realization that increasingly "me" does not matter. Any truly modern man or woman is such a Me Empire.

Of course, first-personalism is as old as men are. Human beings have always spoken of "I," "me," "mine." They have spoken, written, thought, and acted with such concepts and terms as their instruments of expression. Even the papal and the royal "We," "Us," "Our," are merely grandiose forms of "I," "me," "mine." But only today has this first-personalism become a vehicle for the Me Empire. So now these two things must be carefully distinguished: the first-personalism which has always existed and has severely accentuated manifestations today; and the Me Empire which exalts first-personalism into a basically defensive condition of being human.

The Me Empire offers some of its most impressive manifestations in journalism, books, music, theater, and films. When a Greek audience in Athens of 350 B.C. sat out a performance of *Agamemnon* and screamed in horror as Clytemnestra wrapped Agamemnon in a great robe, helped him into a bath, and ran a knife through him some ten times, they were horrified at what

Clytemnestra, the mythical figure, did; they cared little or nothing for the actress carrying the role of Clytemnestra. Today, when Elizabeth Taylor as Cleopatra plots and plans and loses finally to the serpent's bite, the audience is vitally interested in Elizabeth Taylor, only peripherally in Cleopatra, scheming Queen of Egypt and of the Roman world, whose nose should have been longer. Again, in *The Godfather*, it is Marlon Brando as the Godfather, not the Godfather portrayed by Marlon Brando, who gets the comments and analyses. George C. Scott as Patton is unforgettable; but Blood-'n'-Guts Patton is already consigned to the long attic of forgotten Americana. Taylor and Brando and Scott are acknowledged Me Empires, however, in a star system which for some decades has fostered and profited from the Me Empire, for special reasons, within its special tinselized province.

But more and more, the Me Empire becomes a general and distinguishing trait of men and women at large. It is grasped at by those who are increasingly stripped in their culture of every other dimension in which to seek meaning and fulfillment of the self. And the other side of the coin is that many are increasingly pushed toward the Me Empire, as society becomes more and more oriented to the scientific and technological and therefore is, and allows itself to be, run by "qualified experts." Increasingly, he who is not such a "qualified expert" in some field is reduced to speaking only with a "personal" voice. And he who is an acknowledged expert in one field is still disenfranchised in other fields; there, he too can speak only with a "personal" voice.

Subtly transforming examples occur consistently in journalism, in whatever medium we consider. A reporter's first assignment was formerly always to give the news—the hard facts. The Biblical questions for the reporter were the hard-and-fast "who-what-when-where-how-why important." Latterly, "why important" has become the first question. And the importance announced *pro forma* from a totally personal perspective (after all, he is not an "expert" in sociology or penology or astronautics, etc.), which casts its aura over the entire reportage. One must bathe in a reporter's personal political view, if one want the political story, and the devil take the editorial page. One must absorb the reporter's personal feelings on Blacks or on Puerto Ricans or on landlords, if one wants the story on the slum problem. One must increasingly know what does and does not produce a greening in his being. And as the same reporters are writing day after day in the same papers we all read, we come to know much more intimately the individual attitudes of a reporter, rather than the attitudes and views of the people about whom he might some years ago have given us valuable information on which to form a less fettered view of our own.

It is not, of course, as any long-time newspaper reader knows well, that journalism and journalists have always been factually pristine; but the *standard* was for reportage to be so; and criticism was considered fairly leveled on that issue. Today, any such criticism is considered an abridgment of the reporter as a Me Empire; and his use of public media is *de facto* subservient to the new role of Me primacy.

The compensation derived from this ploy makes it attractive to many. It is behind the rising tendency of book reviewers, who are supposed to be literary experts, but who seem voluntarily to disenfranchise themselves of the right to such a title, and who prefer to tell you how they spent their summers, how the weather is the night they are writing the review, the effect of the weather on morale and appetite, how the family is taking the heat; in a throw-away paragraph or two, something about the book announced for review is given, but nearly always subjectively and in terms which eschew as far as possible any comparison over against more objective standards of accomplishment.

The Me Empire is behind many other manifestations in personal life styles. Behind the diversified and highly personalized rationales for marriages and affairs, for childless unions which have substitutes in pet dogs, in the choice of automobiles and churches and clothes and presidents, there is a single world of ideas which have latterly been grasped as the due furniture of the human being. There is, first of all, a delight in self: in my body I carry about with me all or most of what is significant for other men, whether they like it or know it or not. Wordsworth could say, of his Tinker: A primrose by the river's bank, a yellow primrose was for him, and nothing more. Not so for the modern Me Empire: See the twitching of my eyes as I perceive the primrose! Feel the slavery and mire of my ecological soul, at the very sight!

But this concept, this working hypothesis of Me Empire, meant to aid the New Self of the West through its unique trials, is no more effective than the New Class concept, or the New Sexuality or Love; there is a peculiar twist along the path; there remains, at the base, a feeling of powerlessness which lends to all the Me Empire expression an edgy quality; and this turns quickly to anger, intolerance, desperation, and an allowance of very little freedom. Thus is justified the radical revolutionary who says: "I believe in no system," and who usurps power without the consent of the governed. And thus industry and media flaunt liberty by eschewing the responsibilities they have recognized as theirs in the past, viewing them now as constrictions.

On the individual plane, we find a poignant, almost tearful plea expressed in "I" terms. "I am a walking empire of feeling, understanding, compassion, achievement, and general excellence. My mind is thoughtful. My concerns are liberal. My knowledge is informed on local, national, and international affairs. I am an excellent lover. Given my head, I can lead people. I eschew human meanness, writhe at human misery, believe in beauty and honesty, and taste the deep, deep pathos of the individual. But this 'I' that I am, with its thought, belief, knowledge, understanding, capacity for leadership, this 'I' is without power to make people understand how well I know, how deeply I understand, how feelingly I pity, how magnanimously I can lead. This empire that I am is impotent. How can I undo or counteract this impotency?"

Now this has been the plea and the plaint of many men in many ages; but in an age when the societal slogans are boastful and are of the people ("Knowledge has made us masters; knowledge has made us free"), the inner eye must turn to the chasm between what was the aim, what was effected, and the reality that has come instead.

The problem becomes more acute every day, according as the value and the position of the individual diminish within the bowels of ever more complex and ever more mechanical living systems. Thus, the Me Empire, which was to be the personal solution, becomes the societal problem: it is the chosen and the most vulnerable target of our modern depersonalization. My ethnic color, my job situation, my age bracket, my sex, my family ties, any one or all of these create an aching desire to be rid of the integuments which hold down the Me Empire. Its role is impossible in my normal life situation? Then, let me seek out a shattering release. For all the objects and subjects around me make me feel other, make me an object and/or a subject. My ego must be released from them, from their otherness, from the horrible coldness of their rationalities, and the grinning mockery of their separatednesses.

The release must raise my soul to the more than merely cognitive, gather in its energies in a private, highly concentrated spotlight of exuberance, freedom, feeling, color of individuality, and mystical union—but only with the self, and reduced to a lonely and very secret inner tryst. In the hard-edged, gravelly field of humanscape around me, locations, people, objects, all lose their frozen otherness, melt their stiffnesses, begin to flow and merge and move. Human mentalism and logic cease to be my pathways. Words cease, not merely as well-minted metallic tokens of human commerce. They cease. Within that mind-blown spotlight, my ego slithers and slides free, free at last.

Carried to its logical extreme, the problem of Me Empire as lonely combatant against "I" impotency is solved only on a plane beyond all common sense—beyond all meaning: in a flowing oneness which engulfs the ego and enables the modern person to persist into a new glory untouchable by the prosaic ones who categorize and label and discern and critique every action. For all the stiffened substances of entities and classes will be dissolved within and around the Me Empire.

I will be sophisticated with a sophistication that is inaccessible to bourgeois minds. I will cease to be a mere onlooker of restless and strident details. I will not be the target body of other bodies, the open box into which other onlooking selves crowd like sticky raisins in a jar. Nor will they jeopardize my glory. Nor will any single thing exist non-merged and not transcended by me. I will be supremest. Adam Haqadmon. Ayin Sof. Alpha and Omega. Beyond my past and present, beyond all my possible futures. Only the supremest self of me—imperial, self-contained, but leaping every barrier. Only conscious. Nothing more. Because there is nothing more. Is nothing. Nothing.

29. The New Mime of Destiny

The Mime of Destiny

No matter what society of men we study in past history, we find that the men and women of that society had formed some general idea of what used to be called their "destiny," as individuals and as a group. For the ancient Jews, it was the destiny of the Messianic age, when Israel headed by the Messiah would peacefully rule the world. For the Romans, it was a grandiose and glorious scheme: a Roman peace would embrace all men living beneath the rule of Caesar. For Christians it was the rule of Christ through his Church and a sociopolitical arrangement which subserved that reign. For Russian Marxists, it is a world of socialist brother-and-sister states tied to the U.S.S.R. as parent and guardian. For the Founding Fathers of the United States, it was a world in which each man was free under God to pursue life and happiness.

This concept of destiny never remained at the conceptual stage. It was always incarnated in the concrete ways of doing things: the way people judged and assessed situations, the way in which they interpreted events, the roles they attributed to themselves, the decisions they took in disputes and discussions, the way in which they treated themselves and others. These concrete ways of expressing the generally accepted concept of destiny of a people or an age constitute the Mime of that people, of that age: the expression of whatever meaning man reads into his simple actions, and into his life taken as a totality of continuing actions.

Within the Theater of Longing, the Mime is of a particular kind. Strung along the tension between his felt self and the influences of his world, the dimensions of the Mime, like everything else for modern man, are severely reduced. He lives for this time on the razor-thin edge between reason and system. Thought is reduced to reason tied to the pragmatic here and now; an idea has valency if it serves as a cog in the system; "why" searches no farther than "because it works." Man's own humanness has been reduced to pygmy dimensions which deny him any link upward with the transcendent and thwart his inward gaze with terms of measurement that at best reduce, but finally deride, all that is felt beyond the measurable.

Every assertion of self is a query: I am? I really am? Continued success becomes a deathless pragmatic tedium; every start in exultation leads to the futility of sameness serving only itself. Amusement is defiance. A joke, as Woody Allen remarked, is an emotion or an epitaph. If there is wit, it is caustic. If there is humor, it is at somebody's expense or a substitute for tears; or it is what W. C. Fields called lewd-lavatory rather than the lewd-bawdy, which the Elizabethans loved and almost perfected but which we moderns seem to have forgotten.

Obviously, no one can survive by balancing on the razor edge between heartless extremes. Nothing is more compassionless than thought and reason in themselves. And there is no more effective way of killing all a man is than by reducing him to an activated being, a doer; the mechanisms of his contrivance finally control him.

How, then, does modern man do it? He enacts his modern Mime, and throws it like a veil over all he thinks and does. Rather than express a commonality by it, he seeks to become by it what he is not in any natural way: a willing and inwardly functioning part of society which denies his unmeasured innerliness. His thought and action become ridden with the modern Mime and are significant because of it alone. To adapt a phrase of

John Berryman's, when what we hope for has not come again for the last time, only two choices are open: suicide or the Mime. For the Mime entices him away from unreachables with the vicarious taste of sweet power and a redefined transcendence of his mortality. It is a sometime sop to man's ancient dream: to be like the gods, to share their perpetuity, their creativity, and their sovereign independence and freedom from confining littleness. The Jesus figures originally carried a similar promise.

Essentially, then, in the modern Mime, two views of self are possible. A man views himself as at the end of a line: he is a faltering vestige; a last exemplar of an anciently developed type; an archeological assemblage of living fossil remains—bits of cultures and wisdoms developed at points along evolution's road; a walking flea market of wares from all cultures, arts, techniques, civilizations, religions; merely an organism chock-full of the trash and leavings of the ages.

Or, he goes beyond all that, sees himself as the messenger of universal unity, the announcer of the human mystery, the forerunner of cosmic energy. Part of the promise of this view of the Mime is of the perpetuity which the Mime evokes and reflects. All hopes and energies are concentrated now on the final solution of human problems by an applied science. But each problem solved, man has found, introduces another unimagined at the outset. Each invention created to solve a problem creates another problem for which a new invention is created. With the same results. He applies himself in perpetuity to this problem-invention sequence, and he calls the result unprecedented progress. He feels in control. He needs speed in traveling—an obvious boon. He makes the airplane. He needs more room in the plane for greater numbers: he builds a jumbo-jet. But then he needs a greater runway for the jumbo-jet, more fuel, a solution to the air and noise pollution, more land for runways. So it goes.

The perpetuity sequence he follows in things, he also follows in ideas. He forms an idea of himself at variance with conventions and habits hitherto entertained. This idea generates fresh habits and conventions which in turn give rise to yet another perception of himself, and so on in proposed perpetuity without an end in sight. A Female Liberationist should get job parity and salary parity. But then she should not be burdened with the children.

Others should take care of the children. But if the children are to be cared for by others, then we will need social engineering both for the children and for the child specialists who will be replacing, after all, the natural mother. And so it goes.

For a while, this process will be seen as a perfectly legitimate problem-solving sequence. But when not only man's "progress" but man's human identity is tied to a perpetuity sequence, when man is told, "You are nothing till we know what you are . . . but, hold on, we're making progress," when human identity must be sought but never arrived at, the boredom and aimlessness of "being on the way to it," of being a problem like any other problem to be solved, affects a vital part of us. For our meaning as human beings is at one and the same time reduced to nothing more than the answer to a structural puzzle, and (even so drastically reduced as that) is laid up as an achievement we never achieve, and a status (however meager) we never acquire.

But the modern Mime is not only a promissory note of dubious worth. It also must concern itself with those processes originally and mythically attributed to vague deities and supposedly invisible powers. Take creation and creativity of living beings. As a neurobiologist, I can separate individual cells from the forebrain of mouse embryos, suspend them in a solution, and then, using as glue a material called cerebrum cell-ligand, "stick" them back together again in exactly the same way as they were before the separation. Of course, I took the "glue" and the cells from mouse embryo brains. I have in one sense created or fabricated living brain tissue. Even if I am not a neurobiologist, but just a student in college, a high-school teacher, an avid enthusiast for science, or merely a modern man, I still feel that I participate in the creativity of the neurobiologists who feel they participate in the creativity of "nature" itself.

Or I can take brain cells from a mouse embryo and place them in laboratory culture, and, lo and behold! they reaggregate themselves and even develop synapses. Now, synaptic points are vital for transmitting impulses from one neuron to another. Without that, we have not got a living brain. I have therefore "fabricated" the all-important synaptic brain function. I am thus on my way to creating the brain.

I am a creator.

The modern Mime can often also be a social condition of being in which no particular relationships confine one. This is mime of the godlet or hero figure: cut off from any roots and without any ties he cannot sever, he is able to function flexibly; paradoxically he can enter any relationship, because he is incapable of any commitment; he is thus unburdened, is free, open, and "on top" of things. All of this makes sense because it is intelligence, not instinct, which drives him. (It finally defeats him.) He derives his motive power largely from the sight of little men—the family man, the one-wife husband, the successfully obscure and the obscurely successful, the petit bourgeois of man's commonwealth. These are the powerless in whose lives everything can occur but to no effect. They want to live on earth; but he wants simply to live. Their status, therefore, he shuns like the death, because maturity for him consists in being careful; and these people stand like frail reeds up a deserted creek in Nowhere Land. Carefulness is a habit of being in this Mime.

Thus, as a consequence, enthusiasm is always channeled, spontaneity is a weakness, and compassion is a refuge. A person enters the lives of others as a matter of fact, never a form of meaning. His two major instruments are his brain and his mind. And, most impressively, he is bound for a mysterious destiny for which the imitative perpetuity and creativity of his independent way of acting have prepared him.

His mime of perpetuity, creativity, and independence makes him a symbol and a sign proclaiming: "Seek for yourself, man, within yourself, man! Man himself is the only measuring rod of all that man can be." If any transcendence is possible to such a man, it is this: Being a zero, a poorly built and progressively self-corrupting and self-disintegrating animal, man can leap out of his own skin, over his own head, by thinking it and systematizing himself in view of this feat; the more he is zero, the more he becomes the cosmos; incarnated at conception, dehumanized at death, personalized only by his brain, depersonalized by his mind, invented by diligent technicians of his organism, obliterated by the super-production lines he installs, man the Mimer only finds meaning by his Mime, when he assumes the empire of all men to be within himself, and then claims that he is progressing to a mystery by means only of his brain and his mind.

Mind over Brain

Within the scope of the modern Mime, man finds a very cohesive, intellectually satisfying, rather smug, but on the whole an ennobling concept of himself, as long as he excludes any element which he cannot measure and quantify. Once he avows this sanction, modern man can indulge even in language and concepts which he cannot explain immediately. He argues, however, that his vagueness is obviously different from the vagueness of philosophers and religionists of former influence. For, in the modern Mime, he is covered by the underlying premise, the principle on which all unanswered questions and all vagueness now depend for redemption in the meantime: "Eventually, it will all become clear." Why, therefore, restrict his marvelous aspirations—even though he cannot yet measure them? It is thus that I, a modern man, having taken the structuralist vows, can come to a placid and prideful contemplation of myself.

So. I originated billions of years ago in some formless assemblage of chemical compounds, and I am the end product of thousands of evolving animals, insects, and plants, I am told. Who cares? The process is irreversible, they tell us. Very well. It is not, mind you, that I am content with that. Some of the myths are much more satisfying. Chinese. Hebrew. Samoan. Greek. Germanic. But the scientists tell me this: The ape will always be in my heart, and I accept it. In my nightmares: when I am angered to the point of desiring to kill; or when on a trip, perhaps. At moments of weakness, he will stir, mumble, fear, recall. I hear resonances of deep-buried memories: ancient bellowings from the iron throats of long-fossilized cousins; see furnaces belching fire from volcanoes of my dead past; dodge reptiles' wings rushing past me in primeval forests; and, then, breathlessly free-fall some quicksilver distances screaming for Mom and Dad during infancy and youth; and I am fascinated at moments of evening quiet by phantoms, will-o'-the-wisps, faery lights, and shapes within the buried caverns of departed eons which will never return, to my living room, my office, the passenger lounge of the jet plane, the pub on Broadway and Forty-second. It was all so long ago. The scientists are quite right. And my head-shrink is right: all must be integrated by brain and mind. He's the man to do it. . . .

The difference between my brain and my mind is much the same as between an electric battery and the hand that guides its energy. Brain handles single cases; mind handles generalizations. Like my brain says: this is a koala bear; and my mind says: this koala bear is the end of the marsupial line of evolution, but his monkey cousin went on as a link in the chain of primate to man. Mind tells me the innards of my story and the yawning stretch of its future. Brain receives, stores, retrieves, compares, selects, interchanges, single events, facts, cases. As quick as mercury, but not as quick as a computer. Mind guides these operations and discoveries. Brain feeds on all my trial-and-error experiences, but mind traces the weightless patterns of my thinking. Mind rearranges the constituents of my world and tells me: I live in an omniself-regenerative and omni-expanding physical universe throughout an evolutionary scenario. It says further: there is an order and a harmony in the universe's totality; all your little disorders are relative to this ordered harmony: wars, death, pain, effort, disease, beauty, ugliness, bigness, littleness; the disorderliness is the debris and trash of our continually exploding effort to ensure, not merely that biological life survives, but that the universe is regenerated eternally in the eternal design complex.

My brain, being as totally physical as the rest of my body, is always going out, expanding its restless horizons of facts, expending energy. Just like every merely physical thing in the universe. Expanding, spewing out a never-ending radiance of facts, items, figures, diagrams, relations, weights, colors, distances. And thus the explosive disorderliness.

My mind does not contribute to this radiant disorder, this dazzling forest of details, this unharmonious disorder. It walks with metaphysical steps tracing the insubstantial reality of the eternal omni-regenerative universe.

Thus, in the middle of the ever-expanding universe, my mind is bent on discovering the eternal complex. As when Euclid the Brain draws a triangle with chalk on a Greek paving stone: "This is an isosceles triangle; equal angles, equal sides," and Euclid the Mind says: "All triangles with equal sides have equal base angles totaling 180 degrees." This is eternal, immutable, a priori. This is creation: it never began, always existed, will never end, will always be. Mind finds this phase of the universe while brain expands. Creation always was: the scientist's mind delineates its forms when that mind works at its purest. It may refer to images and start from inches, pounds, smells; but its bent is to create. The inventor and technologist do not create; they assemble a dishwasher, a heart pump, with the measurements and forces and weights born of their brains. The scientist participates in that creation, thus unifying all things. The others use creation to generate further expansion.

With my brain, I identify by fragmenting it sensorially. Thus, I marry, have children, design a synthetic cloth. Thus, I am aware of myself. I am an I. Without my brain, I would not be aware of myself. I would not be alive or human.

But without my mind, even though self-aware, I will not have a meaning. Only mind gives meaning and tells significance. Mind extolls the dream concepts of my paleolithic grandfathers into reality, translates the animal images of my distant swamp cousins, the marsupials, into eternal frames. I have come to where I am, in order that I reach still further, I and all men. For the ultimate point.

That ultimate point is reached by a leapfrogging to and fro of mind and brain. We will by our brains increase our experiences universally; we will expand our brains until the entire universe of matter becomes our kitchen midden, the city dump of our brains. And then mind will combine all the scattered bits, fragments, numbers, weights, atoms, combined memories and recorded totalities of millions of experiences belonging to billions of men over thousands of years. Metaphysical schematics will draw in the physical fragments. The weightless integrities of eternity will radiate inwardly over the confusion of the material proliferation. All woven and unified within a single line of a horizontal concept; the eternal design complex. For ever since the first pair of eyes caught its image in a natural mirror—looking in the still face of a lake, gazing at its shadow on a rock—the eternal weightless design became apparent to mind in the ever-growing diversity.

If you snicker at me and my expressions, do not forget that I am permitted to use such expressions precisely because I started from science and its data, not from some religious belief. Of course, these expressions are not verified scientifically, but they will be. In the sense in which I use them, that is to say. Not in the sense in which religionists have used them. In the meantime, you cannot use them for religious purposes, because in that case a scientific verification will become complicated or even impossible. There must be a scientific verification—at least in the offing and in the assertions of scientists. That is the latter-day replacement for the old *nihil obstat.* It is our *imprimatur scientificum.*

As long as I and the humans of my generation have lived, we have been conscious of self, self-aware. That consciousness is a luminous clearing in the scattered restlessness of detail we find as our physical world. I and my consciousness of my self as an "I" stand facing each other as two, but as two united in one while remaining separate; as two balanced on a horizontal line which is the razor's edge of my sanity. One complementing the other; never one without the other—except in sickness; always one accompanying the other. And at times, mind opens a window vertically, so that the luminous I and the self fuse upward, I loosing and losing into self, self loosing and losing into I. At that point, I know that while my feelings are earthy, warm, bubbling, I have a lot to learn about sculpturing and shading what my brain works. But there is a conversation between me and the eternal. It is not about the contours of the physical world or the contents of my brain or of all our brains. Not about a puzzle or conundrum to be solved by brains, but about a mystery to be achieved by my mind as a thin Gothic spire of sheer luminosity thrusting past all the hooded domes and basilicas, and streaking weight-free, color-free, sense-free, height-free, depth-free, free of I and free of self, streaking, not downward, not upward, not slantward, but to the fullness of the creative, eternal universe within the unfolded and silent completion of the Lotus Flower: the ultimate mystery in which man is crowned as man.

When we have listened fully and untiringly to such an expression of modern man in the Theater of Longing, it is clear that we are listening to the saddest of human expressions. For this is the most distorted formulation of the Mime—itself a pathetic attempt to put clothes on the naked emperor. On the very unhuman basis of chemical states and organized matter, it proposes that man lift himself beyond all chemical states and out of reach of all concrete matter.

When the archeologists lifted the gold mask off the face of Tut-ankhamen's mummy, they found themselves looking at a misera-ble, desiccated, wrinkled, dead human face lined with the mute throes of chemically preserved dead matter. The mask was the Pharaoh's claim to a golden destiny; the sunken wasted face was the reality of the human bondage and its dreadful incapacity in helplessness in the face of ultimate decay.

The Mystery

We will always know that a man or woman is a full-fledged member in the Theater of Longing by one infallible sign. It is the unbreakable tension that is set up within human spirits when they are completely and exclusively servile to, and dependent upon, the benefits and potentialities of science, on the one hand, and when, simultaneously with or directly succeeding that point, they think of, and wish for—even openly strive and campaign to attain—a mystery of which human life by itself, even when bolstered by science, is incapable.

On the one hand, they deny anything that factual knowledge or experimental verification cannot assess and attain. On the other hand, they wish for a completeness and a satiety that factual knowledge cannot supply factually and science cannot ensure sci-entifically. The contradiction and clash of these two tendencies go a long way to produce the tension of the Theater of Longing. Men shook off what they thought were the trammels of a vicious deceit: the claim, for instance, of organized religion, and the pre-eminence claimed by spirit informed by morality and ethics. They now find that their desire for ultimate and all-satisfying mystery ends as a cruel hoax. They have a longing. But there is no means of satisfying that longing.

Men and women can undertake the fruitless task of grasping the mystery merely on the basis of their psycho-physical state conditioned and sharpened by all the glories of man's achieve-ments. Their language in this case is typical.

To arrive at the mystery, however short my stay (death is al-ways the end), however I describe it, is the ultimate reach. It is mystery now, not because it puzzles but because it fulfills with completeness; and not because it must be analyzed, but because it provokes no further questioning. It is the Lotus of the mind. It is not a communication but a communing. The image-laden and the myth-makers will try and encapsulate the Lotus in their little prefabricated boxes, each with a worn label: religious experience, mystical life, revelation, natural piety. Some, because they have clothed all images in abstract clothing, will use so-called metaphysical labels: Gestalt therapy, intuition, movement dynamics, hallucination, astral projection, trances, extra-sensory perception. Some others, bitten by the mordant loneliness of their selves, will dress it all up as group encounter, solidarity of man, social behavior, consciousness-raising, group ceramics. All in vain.

For all this is careful brain work. Even when their minds are operating on the multiplicity of their brain products, even then, the eternal design is lost, and it ends always in a flame-wreathed landscape where dog eats dog and all the gods die fast. The luminous thrust of the self never rises above the dreadful complementarity of I and self. Across that threshold, the scientific twilight and the shadow of technology cast long, cloaking fingers.

It need not end like this. The mind can come to the mystery. Like a Lazarus emergent from a tomb of darksome facts and doings, called by the voice of our Lord Universe, my head too dead to sound, my arms as useless branches lashed to my body, my throat parched peppery, stumbling and falling forth in a shroud, wailing with a cry to the rediscovered light and the birds of the living air, having my eyes uncovered by my sisters, and looking on my cosmic Christ force, as a quiet spring in all the dryness. But, like all miracles of my new being as a modern man, its purpose is to bend me beyond only bones and break my heart to some new and permanent hope, the substance of being human.

Mind thus becomes otherwise than mere brain. The mystery can unfold. The mind then plunges into uncharted regions, is now out of touch with outer physical realities and alone with the spaceless stretches of the inner reality, as a spaceship hurtling silently beyond the edges of our earth's galaxy. It is not so much an examination of states of consciousness as a living of some one dimension which includes the conscious me as part of all that ever was, is, and ever can be. It comes, perhaps, after a good meal, a satisfactory bowel movement, or a needed orgasm; with a first long pull on a favored cigar after dining on filet mignon and a fine Beaujolais; at the bottom of an isolation tank soundless, sight-less, smell-less, feeling-less; during an LSD trip. It is the afterglow of a searing beauty seen in flowers, within a woman's eyes, or just before the dawn twilight.

If it happens in a city, all is changed. One moment, streets are covered corridors; high stories are terraces above the head hous-ing hidden threats; pavements only offer steps and strides; lamp-posts and street signals are deceptive eyes winking green, saffron, and red warnings to maintain me in the false perspective of a cosmic ballet which ends in the cosmic joke on us; skylines gri-mace; vehicles are formalized nightmares and daymares; crowds are choruses of ayes and noes.

The next moment: all becomes absorbed in a future that has been hovering in the air with shrouded wings long before man arose along the ladder of evolution. All suspense is gone. Intolera-ble waiting is ended. There is no more endless rising and falling of waves in my mortality. Now I can feverishly lick the anus of the deepest Hell conceivable, or I can gaze rapturously into the innards of the eternal godhead. I am not in inner space. I am not caught within the web of interpersonal-relations experience, or balancing on seesaw surfaces with dyadic partners or moving in lock step with triadic helpmates. I am not merely related to the natural universe. For given instants I am that universe up above the rotating cyclone of my self, beyond the egotistical clawing of the I forever crying: "I am an I." No low pressure. No high pres-sure. No pressure. Not going with a flow. Not static. Not partic-ular. Without nihilism. Without absolutism.

Thus, the full expression of the mystery to which the modern container person can strive is a strange admixture. It uses the vaguest of concepts, appropriates formulas once consecrated by the tradition of great religious bodies of men and tried in the cru-cible of daily religious living. It assumes that, though distant and difficult to achieve, the mystery is achievable by the Me Empire, that the mystery is the due fate of the man perfected by systems and structures, rarefied in intellect and life habits, and acted upon chemically by "uppers" and "downers."

It may be that this mirage of mystery and ultimate satiety, ac-companied by the continual frustration of that mirage's fulfill-ment in modern life, is what produces in so many modern con-

tainer persons the pyschopathic behavior increasingly evident in
our society: the suddenly berserk, the senseless assassinations, the
mounting criminality, the imitative draw of skyjacking, the wan-
derlust of youth, the vogue of drug addiction, the polarization of
minorities, the internationalization of terror and revolt. For at its
most developed stage the typical container person is separated
from the razor-edge consciousness of psychopathy in daily life
only by screens of the flimsiest of stuff.

Genuine mystery is unreachable, because it is excluded by the
very terms on which the container person is constructed and conceived. The container person, Me Empire and all, relies on his
own efforts. An insurmountable barrier separates him from any
genuine mystery, because the image-laden, image-making imagi-
ners and inventors and thinkers and doers will insist on physical
continuities, trying to amplify neural transmissions by physical
chemistry, slicing up synapses to be scrutinized between laboratory plates, tacking cybernetic appliances on to brain areas. They
can ever dally on the vast shores of the universe, play with the
ready-made seeds of dying and living worlds they find at hand.
They will hurry from stone to stone, invention to invention,
clever structure to clever structure.

But, finally, they will look inside themselves, because that is
where they pain and pine, where they laugh betimes, and where
on the final day they wither and die long before their bodies fail
and die. They may sustain beauty for a while, feel compassion for
a day, live an ecstasy of moments. But like all their man-made ar-
tifacts, they return them to the solid compact earth and dissipate
their memory and images and desires in the wild movements of
the air blown by the storms that come from nowhere and are
going no place. Such men had a longing. They acted out the sad,
clown roles of those who not only yearned but planned to be
their own lovers.

THE
JESUS
SELF

30. The Self

The greatest contribution to the self today is jargon consolation: men and women can pretend—rather successfully to others, sometimes with partial success to themselves—that they *know* what they are, or at least what is *going on* inside them. Knowledge, in effect, is confused with words; and words are identified with reality. Breathe the *word* for it, you *have* it. It is an ancient Semitic persuasion that the word is the thing.

Here and now, this fashion has been resurrected and made the source of reasonable man's consolation. The conscious. The subconscious. The unconscious. The reality of the unmanifest. Archaic emotional strivings. Objectified expression of unconscious mental states. Symbolism of primary processes. Identification. Primary narcissism. Differentiation of the archaic ego. The Id. Identity of womb and tomb in the subliminal consciousness of mankind. And so on and so forth. Many an ancient error is compounded in the modern jargon consolation of the self: it is the witch doctor fooling himself (partially) and his victims (totally); and it is the religious propagator providing pap, now in the name of science (and, often, pseudo-science), for unknowing subjects.

A further extension of jargon consolation and a more dangerous one comes from some anthropologists, paleontologists, and ethologists, together with a most energetically publicized version from popularizers in these fields. From these sources, there pours a veritable stream of explanations not merely of each self but of all mankind: all we are and do and think is paralleled by samples drawn from the animal kingdom, by what "higher" and "lower" animals do and think. From ants to water hens, to chimpanzees, gorillas, foxes, rabbits, wolves, and even elephants come innumerable illustrations and explanations of why we do what we do and the *meaning* of what we do. The argument is not simply: "The animals do this, therefore . . ." Rather it is: "The animals do this and they do it because . . ." In that "because" and its subsequent reason is encompassed the marvelous jargon consolation. The Descent of Man and the Descent of Woman become as fixed landmarks in the mind. Marriage becomes the mating of gibbons, geese, and painted shrimp. The act of human love between a man and woman becomes the "missionary position for sexual intercourse." We are "weeping primates" (the only ones).

In the rush to objectify and define at last our true identity and function as mankind, generations of experts set out to lead telling and informative lives with the lions, with the monkeys, with the frogs, with the hamsters, with the chimps. The purpose seems to have been to have "experience" which then is codified, and by its very codification is seen as miraculously transformed into a most precious form of "knowledge."

And, finally, this "knowing," this jargon consolation does not satisfy. A man lies down at night, alone. He walks away from his friends, solitary. After years of getting up, washing, dressing, eating, working, amusing himself, tiring, sleeping, he has—of himself—only two alternatives. Either he is driven outward into total immersion in things outside him, into the wild-eyed dizziness and the restlessness of all the herding details and galloping differences that trample across his vision, and he takes the sting out of his lone privacy by allowing himself no time to think or feel too deeply. Or he is eventually cowed back into the "me" he fears he is and ultimately will turn out to be: one, alone, lonely, at bay, in a blind alley of life with his back to an unyielding brick wall of the inevitable. The human bondage remains for him a stark bondage; and its meaning is taken as being this:

human life is meaningless. In the end, the jargon is barren and cannot make him free.

In the Jesus Self, there is all that man ever hated and loved, all that he ever feared and hoped, all that he seeks and shuns. For in the Jesus Self the human self is not denied; the Jesus Self is not a funny formula or a mysterious alchemy that wipes all tears away, negates our misery, grants immortality here and now, enables man to infuse his work with godliness and create his own relevance in a totally irrelevant world. The Jesus Self does not confirm the good in us forever, banishing the evil for aye. What the Jesus Self becomes was made possible by Jesus and is based on a response by the human self. The self faced with others who are alien is not asked to make these alien people and things and animals his own, to make them him and himself them, sweetening all the bitterness offered him, intellectualizing dumb pain, explaining the enmity and blind hate he receives as part of "nature's way." The self, caught in the million-fold boredom of daily living, is not expected to transform that boredom into heaven-on-earth by self-injection into boring situations, or to hear the same universal melody through the galaxies of chaos and integrate all the galaxies as sections of that melody. The self confronted by alien and powerful fatalities is not expected to keep a stiff upper lip, go down fighting, and enter the womb of nature's nothingness unprotestingly and bravely. This would not be human. The self is not asked, in sum, to establish a guarded empire of its own wherein it will walk intact until the stronger one, death, takes it by storm.

The invitation of the Jesus Self is to overleap oneself, to transcend the petty and insufficient independence of the human self. There is no request for patience with the human bondage; merely an invitation to exit from it by identifying with the self and the being of Jesus. Capitulation is demanded peremptorily. Capitulation of all protective thinking, of every self-perpetuating mental explanation. But the capitulation is to love rather than to an unknown conqueror of unfathomable intent. When the human self cries: "I am a human being," the Jesus Self echoes and completes that cry: "You are a human being who is loved." When the human self would state its needs, hammer out demands, formulate its rights, the Jesus Self answers: "All these—your dignity as a human self—are only possible because you are loved, and loved before you ever thought of any dignity for yourself."

When the human self would seek to find absorption in factual observations, or to discover the certainties yearned for in the dead-sure measurements and quantifications and conventional weights of human ingenuity and logical syllogisms, the Jesus Self refuses this search any success. It says: "I will break the circular motion of your human thought. I will liberate you from the everlasting treadmill of human banality. With me you will escape the ever-turning wheel of unreturning novelty."

The request to identify with Jesus and thus to accept one's identity as a Jesus Self does not imply a set of concepts, a mystical marriage, a secret knowledge, or any esoteric happening or consummation. It is made possible by a god who is a loving god, and who belongs to human history, not as an idea, as the conclusion of a reasoning process, as a principle of thought, or as a derivative from any known human capacity. A living god such as this is found only in the Jesus "fact": that Jesus lived and died and lived again humanly. But the meeting of the human self and the living Jesus is not a fact as all other facts—a phenomenon capable of being explained scientifically and by human historical means. The voice of that Jesus in each self is unmistakable but in no way coercive and self-imposing.

"What you are asked to accept is not that I, Jesus, am alive with all my bodily characteristics, but that I Jesus am the same self as I was from my human conception and before it. For I am God. It is not important that my human body was once dead and now is alive again. Many have claimed this anciently and today. What is significant for you is that I overcame death by dying and made it your doorway to perpetual life by living again among men and as God.

"There is no value in blood-letting, any blood-letting, as such, and no telling human significance in human death—of itself. Just pain, waste, and the immobility of lifelessness. Nothing is bettered by such waste and lifelessness. No sacrifice of itself is humanly valuable or objectively beautiful. The stench of death hangs over all. I did not merely shed my blood and die. I made all shedding of blood and any dying holy. For I am holiness itself. Henceforth, all human dying is holy, because of me.

"All this you can reject, but your human self will thereby be bereft of meaning. And your human bondage will persist, because you have not identified with me, God, who as man identified with you, within human history.

"The meaning of your human bondage is the danger that your self will entertain only its own sufficiency. For every perception you have of truth will be partial, your analyses will be deficient, your judgments irresponsible, and your hopes irredeemably fictitious, your vision of beauty always bent.

"You have some alternatives, but none free you from the ultimate inanity. You can, for instance, judge that I, God, seek out man and that therefore I become a man. But this is vanity, and its result is that then you are joined in the isolation of the merely human and in the aimlessness of mere potentiality by one who need not have been so restricted. Nor does this help you: you will never escape from your prejudices; you will not be able to renew your mind, nor create in beauty, nor be re-created in love; you and I, as all human beings, will be locked in the repetitive cycle of the ever-recurring.

"Or, alternatively, you could aim at being God. But this would rid your human self of the little you possess for yourself—your own identity. There would be no nobleness in your pain, no regnancy in your mortality, no basis for your human courage in raw and naked fear. And that surrender would mean personal obliteration. Calling that self-transcendence is merely dressing up destruction and annihilation with another polysyllabic and faintly pleasant-sounding name. Sanctity would be as impersonal and somnolent as the turning of a Buddhist prayer wheel. Love would be the desired sleep of the fabled Lotus-Eaters. And Heaven would be, certainly, pie-in-the-sky-when-you-die, but roughly equivalent in human value to being disintegrated atop the fifteen-hundred-foot lethal mushroom cloud of an atomic explosion.

"No, it is not useful that God become man merely for that. Nor is it practical that man become God. But, for your self to be intact as a human self, it is necessary that human being in its living and its dying be sanctified. Necessary that human mortality be clothed in that immortality which I have achieved. Necessary that you should be able and be invited, but not forced, to accept as a trust of faith and not as a factually proven event, that throughout the universe of human being I have effected a change so that whether you will it or not, you will live forever, not merely as a living soul, but as a life-giving spirit. That, forever, each human being's self is substantiated with quiddity and freed of all constricting circumstances."

When a man or woman responds to this invitation of Jesus, it is only then that the Jesus Self in each of them flourishes and develops. For that response implies identity with Jesus in order to find the self we all wish to be. To be in touch with non-time existence while within the time span of our human lives. To assure a future for the self, so that the present can be regarded without flinching and so that we can undergo present renunciations and adaptations because of what the future certainly holds for us. There is no postponement of gratifications and no ethical behavior possible, unless the future is guaranteed. And the response enables us to achieve more. To make the self's mortality a ransom for a mercy the self craves above all other goods. Hence an ennoblement of human love made in a bed. Hence the inner resonance of an esthetic perception composed of smelling, touching, seeing, hearing, and tasting. Hence the dignity of dying and the dark daring of death entered with firmity of knowing that where all human living ends, all the granted worth of a human self begins.

With a human response to the invitation of the Jesus Self, all is transformed. The self is not strung out on the struts of concepts, but is transmuted by an accepted present transparent to spirit but opaque and unintelligible to the senses. There is no factual knowing, because it is believed; no firm possession, because all the present is lodged in a hope against all hopes as wild and as high-flying as migrating birds; no hardship of lonely perseverance, because love has been the beginning, will be the bridge, and will subsist when what is hoped for is possessed and when faith in permanence melts in the light of confirmed subsistence. "There now remain these three," wrote Paul, "faith, hope, and love. But the greatest of these is love."

But in spite of this love and this inviting presence, a man's response can always be negative. No love, even subsistent love, can force acceptance. But any negative response, any cosmic "no," is enveloped in love's plan, and in the end it will be judged, the

man and his refusal, by love itself. A man can close off his spirit
because of an accepted poverty and because of a mysterious am-
bivalence in his make-up. He can take refuge in jargon consolation, and can interpret his own life as a psycho-biography and
other men's lives as psycho-histories. He thus allows the stream of
his consciousness to figure as his substance; its fleeting images in
daydreams and nightmares provide him with formulations of reality filling the awkward silences which threaten and pall on his
existence. He takes all departures from life by the innocent and
the good as meaningless tragedy, for were they not, by definition,
too young or too good to have offended a Father in Heaven or a
loving Earth Mother? He takes the wood for the trees: he feels a
hunger for life and immortality, but he takes that hunger to be
the constitutive element in life.

If he mythologizes, as only modern intellectuals and pseudo-
intellectuals can do, he describes this hunger as some ancient deep-
seated yearning, stronger than every other instinct in us, which
orients us urgently and irresistibly back to where we sink into the
"primordial undifferentiated unity of a benignly indifferent universe." And that is the finest example of pure jargon consolation
—words that mystify, entrance, convince, but express nothing in
reality—which the modern mind has devised. Even in this
dead, closed-spirit ego-world, in which all happenings are painted
as leaden fatalities and the earthly condition of men as a total ab-
surdity, each one awaiting the consuming jaws of an imagined
and wholly supposititious earth progenetrix, even then love includes this wan outlook and forlorn heart as a part of the whole
of human life.

Man's last consciousness may be filled with the same rickety
furniture he has desperately created during his lifetime. But his
spirit must end in the clear light of the hope to which he refused
response and of the love he never acknowledged.

31. The Identity

The Jesus Self is the identity, the singular quality which constitutes the individual oneness of each man or woman. It is the
quiddity of "I" and of "me." It is the possessor denoted by
"mine." It is not merely feelings, or merely thoughts, or merely
memories, or merely hopes, or merely loves, or all these in a
weave of time and space. It is that which feels and thinks and re-
members and hopes and loves. It is no inert substratum out of
which pop initiatives and motions. Nor is it merely a set of biological circumstances or organic compounds. But it is that which
establishes certain biologisms and sets of organic compounds as
human beings, as selves.

But each of these selves is not merely a human being, a self.
Each is a Jesus Self, because it was made possible only by Jesus of
Nazareth. The human identity of any man or woman is the first
great effect of Jesus in the universe of man. All men and women
who ever lived, live, and will live, were and are and will be
human only because of Jesus. Each one is a Jesus Self. For Jesus
of Nazareth, who once lived and died within human time and
space, is of this universe of human being forever. But he is not
subject to the time and space of that universe. Our identity as in-

dividual human selves depends immutably on Jesus. Nor did this human identity due to Jesus begin merely when he was conceived and born some nineteen hundred years ago. That occasion of his life, teaching, and death provided man with *explicit* knowledge of what it means to be human: that each one is a Jesus Self.

The Jesus Self was such a complete innovation on the human scene, in reality, in human thought and in human language, that Christians found no word for it in the languages they spoke at their beginnings (Aramaic, Greek, and Latin, mainly). They finally took a known word, "person," and used it to mean the Jesus Self. What the word meant originally need not hold us up here. What is important is the meaning Christian primitives gave it or, rather, the truth they expressed by that word. For the early Christians were not directly concerned with reality such as we moderns conceive it. That reality can be understood and taken in many ways: there is only one truth about that reality. And, unfortunately, Christians gave their idea of "person" a philosophical and cultural coloring which we today cannot quite accept.

For, today, any use of the word "person" brings on innumerable difficulties, and merely to explain these difficulties is to enter into them and not necessarily to gain any light for their solution. In its original usage, when we analyze it today, the term "person" expressed two elements which are distinct for our minds, but which were seen as one by the Christian primitives of the first four centuries. One element was that of *human being* as distinct from any other form of life known. The other was that of *human self* as distinct in one human being from the human self in any other human being. Both elements were simultaneously connoted by the term "person" originally.

It was the first time in any language that a word was coined and appropriated to express this duplex reality: a human being as a person. It was, in its origins, exclusively a Christian term. The other versions of the human self we can find in history (they are discussed further on) appear inadequate under this heading; for they were partial, distorted, and incomplete. They did, however, manifest an apparently more viable and durable character. The Jewish Self and the China Self have infinite possibilities of adaptation to practical circumstances. The Muslim Self, the Hindu Self, the Japan Self, and the Christian Self can undergo rather extensive variations and transmute their consecrated mythologies, just as the Greek Self and the Roman Self. The Buddha Self essentially implies that what is human and what is self are finally nothing; and this viewpoint feeds all our modern masochism and self-hate. The Impossible Self is merely a nice idea and neither partakes of truth nor figures in reality.

Their capacity for survival is only apparent. For, as history and modern times amply demonstrate, one after another of these versions of the human self is liquidated by slow dilution. Their very adaptability helps in their dissolution. Their masochism or their dilettantism indicates their perishable nature.

At first sight, the Jesus Self seems to be bound for a like fate. Nowadays, in their verbal and conceptual structures, men are not allowed by the prevalent mind to accept any idea of reality which we cannot measure and quantify. And how can one quantify the Jesus Self?

This primary emphasis on quantifiability is partly due to a very curious event. Somewhere between the 18th and 19th centuries, a series of scholarly and serious-minded men seized on the activity of all men up to that point, their religious activity included, and insisted that it be measured and quantified, just as their intellectual contemporaries then and later were measuring and quantifying the material universe with a fine frenzy. In the observation, in the quantifying and measuring itself, was the meaning for them. This, whether we like it or not, has been handed on to us as our intellectual heritage today. "How did it come about," they asked, "that men have always believed in a god and always engaged in religious belief and practice?" It was a fair question. However, it was asked in the same mental framework as: "Why does an apple fall?" or "Why does water boil?" or "When did *Homo sapiens* first appear on the planet Earth?" To ask this question about religion in that fashion was not merely to presuppose infinite ability on their part to understand everything by the same means and with the same tools; it was, as the other side of the same coin, to begin to define out of existence all that could not be so understood. To ask the question about religion as about some physical phenomena was to prestructure the answer. For the a priori conclusion, the presupposition of such a question is that no answer is acceptable which is not as palpable as the answers to the other puzzles of a different nature. Regrettably, the fact was (and continues to be) ignored that such a priori conclusions and presuppositions themselves violate the new rules at the outset: What proof was there that the cause of man's religion and religious instinct was measurable and quantifiable?

But the prevalence of this 18th and 19th century intellectual prejudice is only one of the causes for the waning understanding of the Jesus Self and why men find the idea of the Jesus Self seemingly incompatible with the mainstream of human thought and word today, or why they are inclined to make febrile use of "scientific" legerdemain in order to reinforce and "prove" that incompatibility. The second and more telling cause lies precisely in the action of Jesus through the complex events of human history.

Long before there arose among the fresh-minded men of the 1700's and 1800's the mental attitude and the rejection described above, it was Christian institutions, the churches and their formularies of the Christian Self, which made the rejection inevitable. They obfuscated Jesus, the Jesus Self, and the identity of a human being with cultural accretions, racial bias, socio-political outlooks, and folkloric traditions. As long as that Christian Self is the prevalent view of reality and put forward as the truth about that reality, men's view of Jesus and the Jesus Self will be obstructed.

Jesus, who works *through* events in human history, has the most effective way of strangulating that distorted picture of the truth presented by the Christian Self: under his guidance, human events simply leave the offending elements behind. Human life moves on.

In fact, the modern mental attitude of rejection to which we have referred was directed, not at the Jesus Self, but at the Christian Self—as, indeed, at *all* artificial and culturally dependent versions of the human self. In Christian terms, one must say that the power to believe has been to a large extent withdrawn by God, at least the power to believe in the authority, and leadership, and the authenticity of religious institutions. "Whom do men say I am?" Jesus once asked his followers. Within the tem-

LIBRARY ST. MARY'S COLLEGE

per of the non-religious 1970's men answer: "Nothing we can know in the quantitative orders of culture, science, and psychology."

The simple fact today is that the majority of Christians do not believe in their religious institutions as such. In their human condition, they are drawing nearer and nearer to the mass of mankind, sharing with them the same anguish in man's Theater of Longing; and, of course, they are subject like all other men to the non-human change effected by Jesus in their natures.

But with all rejection of the Jesus Self by modern intellectuals in the aura of embarrassment at the very mention of the name of Jesus, and despite all inability of present religious leaders and institutions to free themselves of cultural attachments, the problem for men and women today is a problem of self-identity. Particular efforts at solution are legion. Millions, for example, seek their identity by vicarious sharing in the lives of the televised few. They become, they figure, what they see. Others are more concrete-minded. "Everybody should have something to point to," stated steel worker Mike Fitzgerald, recommending that the names of all who worked in a skyscraper be inscribed on its outer walls. ("See! That's me over on the forty-fifth floor.")

The artificial alternative sought by many others in this anguish and paucity of spirit is really a self-cannibalism. Today, under the force of circumstances, we find no pleasure even in evoking atavistic images, ancient memories, or obsessional states. We get fascinated by the very process of ourselves because it is identity we lack. We associate sensation and thoughts freely in a hot rush of imagery, endeavoring now and then to snatch from that stream some item and give it a form which will tell us how we are, how we think, how we think that we think and feel, and thus formulate some coherent geography of the selves we think we wish to be.

All this takes place in a world of men and women who love and hate, live and die; where one man mercifully clothes the naked, while another tendentiously disrobes in front of a child; where one woman sacrifices all her years washing window curtains, fifty cents apiece, to nourish seven children, while another strangles her first-born with picture wire; where some people bury their dead in sorrow, and others urinate on the graves of their masters; where one baby is born screaming and healthy, while another baby dies of incurable bone disease; where one man operates and saves, while another stabs to death for a contract; where some men die for the truth they hold, and others lie that they may live. Some still shake their heads, but for most it all has no meaning, because there is no forgiveness for the one and no perpetuity for the other. Only the equality of death evens all out. But even the graves are irregular humps or uneven hollows in the ground. Without the identity of the Jesus Self, the affairs of human beings compose a Grand Guignol of farcical hopes and of meaningless pain. And, in a world reft of the Spirit and inhabited by merely highly evolved animals, its title should be written as *les très riches heures* of man's pointless existence.

If, on the other hand, men and women have more than factual knowing and knowledge at their disposal; if their human being is capable of more than being merely human; if there is a salvation within time and space but independent of time and space; then the Jesus Self subsists, and human existence will always be worth the time, the space, the living, and the dying to which all men and women are heirs.

32. Knowing Factually

Understanding of the Jesus Self is based on a simple first principle: we as human beings have two fundamental ways of knowing and of knowledge. Both are necessary for human living. Each one has a delight and a discomfort all its own. One is factual knowing and knowledge. The other is knowing and knowledge of the spirit.

A major problem in modern times for the Jesus Self is that we are increasingly urged by the facts and exigencies of practical life to cut ourselves almost completely off from knowing and knowledge of the spirit. We are more and more unwilling to admit that *both* kinds of knowing and knowledge are built on presuppositions which can in *neither* case be factually proven or disproven.

The most obvious way of knowing and of knowledge is the factual. We are quite comfortable with that. It is effective and eminently useful; it transforms our material world daily before our own eyes. Within twenty-odd years, a person can be given sufficient factual knowledge to fly to the moon, build revolutionary machines, revitalize agriculture, build cities to replace wilderness. This kind of knowledge, we are told, will give us control of all around us and of our very destiny.

Meanwhile, it is becoming apparent at an accelerating rate that factual knowledge is humanly injurious, unless coupled with its less obvious partner, knowledge and knowing of the spirit. But this gets a little difficult for our modern mind. The urgings of such spirit knowledge are felt dimly to be dangerous. "Irrational," "a-rational," "blind," are some of the suspicion-laden adjectives affixed to it. Indulging in anything but the facts means a severely dangerous deflection of our attention.

Factual knowing, factual knowledge, is at once our greatest pride and the means on which we moderns increasingly are urged to rely, in order to remain human and to progress as human beings. No matter what use is made of this knowledge, or how this knowing is adapted for good or for ill, some degree of such knowing and knowledge obviously is necessary for us. Just recently, as world history goes, we have made its fine exercise a prime condition of our civilization and the source of all our life-supportive systems. It is at its most refined in the "hard sciences," and at its most demonstrably "real" in the applications of technology in thousands of ways all around us, affecting every moment of our modern lives in a cacophony of persuasion. It is always a knowing of what is and a knowledge of what was and what could be, in the visible, measurable, and expanding world of dimensions.

In that world, it is all a question of probability; where to place your bets; the choice of the pragmatically reliable on the basis of the mathematically satisfied formula. Just look all around you! It *works*. It is, *in fact*, reliable. It does, *in fact*, give us the sense of feel and control of the world around us. But, by some alchemy of inner human working, we go further than the fact. *We take this sense of control as proof and reality;* and then our aim is to feel and control *everything*, known and unknown. This might be acceptable, if a major problem did not keep cropping up like a Puck's head peering with a wink of malice at all those measuring rods.

To come within the legitimate sphere of this brand of scrutiny and knowledge, a subject must by its own nature be quantifiable —or at least be able to be made so, without any loss or distortion of its nature and its wholeness. Otherwise, you are just not measuring what you set out to measure; and if what you predict depends on what you measure, and if what you do depends on what you predict, you are up a scientific creek. It is no use trying to paddle down from that creek on the argument that what is not quantifiable is simply not fit for inquiry—or even that it does not exist. That is too self-serving a charade of an argument to hold any water. And it is a sorry ruse that leads to sorry states of man.

Factual knowing and knowledge possess a quality of delight and a quality of discomfort that are everyday matters for all of us; and where the one is, the other cannot long remain. Delight in our sense of factual knowing comes with the clinched argument, the achieved demonstration, the established objective fact, the completed survey, the known and controlled system or system of systems. Discomfort is the negation, the absence of this, or, at least, the realization that we are not quite there yet: the experiment was not conclusive or all-inclusive; we have not proved a point beyond a shadow of factual doubt; the objective reality has not been demonstrated; we have covered only one small field adequately but not completely; and many more fields—infinite, it seems, in number—lie beyond. Control lies beyond all that. How can we wait? (At times, the truth is, some cannot wait; they begin to proclaim what they cannot prove.)

Insofar as single things escape our feeling of their being factually known to us, thus far we undergo a sense of being incomplete. We must labor to complete that incompleteness. For we take that incompleteness as a reproach, as a sign that we are less than what we should be, and a warning that the only "other" confronting us is negation, absence, nothingness. Ignorance it is called; it is a yawning chasm of all we never want to be, for it appears to us that to be thus, or insofar as we are thus, we are not. In whatever part of our universe we walk, we are aliens until we make it ours by this busy process of measuring and quantifying and predicting which feeds our *sense* of factual knowing and knowledge which we have come to take as full knowledge. Yet the more we fill our deficiency, the more we find ourselves ignorant. The more facts we know, the more we find to know, the less we seem in control, and are thus incomplete all over again.

In the pursuit of factual knowledge and our dependence on it, there are regularly times when the most purposeful of such pursuits tastes aimless, precisely because it delves into life as life emerges, develops, divides, disappears, re-emerges, and renews the ever-ever cycle. The suspicion dawns and then nags that the control we seek is minuscule. A door opens, not in the brain, but somewhere else in us, showing us the endless boredom of ever progressing horizontally and vertically in a world space whose limits expand to accommodate our every move forward.

At such times, the bizarre idea hits us that it is not facts and factual knowledge which of themselves give us reality, but that it is *we* who have *decided* that what we know by such factual knowledge is reality. And we mean total reality. Or, to be redundant, genuine reality. The "real" world, we presume, is exclusively a world of facts. But, by that very stroke, we are trapped and foiled. For this can only be a presumption, and that alone is enough to shake a believer in facts.

Still, by now it is built in all around us. So we go on; and we begin to find that words mean less and less, because we have more to say than words can say, or because the only words worth saying are so inextricably deep in us that we cannot bring them forth. They are echoes simmering and shimmering in some secret inner ear of ours. When we want to express ourselves, we find that outward expression is like a surface very far above our heads, and we are buried at a very deep level. Or we find that we must stop looking at things we see, in order to be able to look clearly, to see beyond facts to where we still know meaning lies.

But thus to stop looking in order to see, means we go beyond factual knowing and knowledge. A pool of panic begins to form: "they" are going to feed us fairy stories; we will be fooled with fictions and pampered with the pernicious pap of simpletons; we will not be able to choose our thoughts; we will cease to labor for complete control of our environment; we humans will retrogress and lose ourselves; we will not enjoy that stage of ease which our neighbors possess. Sometimes, rather than risk all that, we ridicule those deep words; we bite and chew on the aimlessness of the ever-ever cycle. The fever of measuring more to give ourselves the sense of knowing more, the fever of accumulating more facts, becomes our normal temperature. We label its aimlessness with pleasing terms, "infinite possibility," "man's quest for the All." We carefully choose epithets transferred from the other field of knowing but totally transmuted in the process: "man's mystical union with his universe" (as if we could go to bed with it); "our brotherhood with bones and boulders" (as if any of us wished these as our blood relatives); "the comfort of being one with all things" (as if all things will dry our tears); "our marvelous home within the galaxies" (as if our heartsickness will be stilled by arid moonscapes and the gas-filled lethal atmosphere of dead planets); "our human control over our destiny" (as if, looking down from the puny summit of genetic manipulation and computer medicine, we were unaware of our confusion and sadness); "the building of a world without pain or disease or want or inequality" (as if all pain, want, inequality, and disease are of the purely physical order of man's existence).

In that very optic and within a long-term outlook, we can foresee the end of all need for human beings to know factually. For we can build machines that know more, retain more, judge more accurately, analyze more thoroughly, understand problems more dispassionately, solve them more efficiently, and—within the realm of practical possibility—repair themselves, generate their own kind, and do all the factual knowing human beings can do, only much better and much more. If factual knowing and knowledge is man's only hope, and if the reality defined and attainable by factual knowledge is the only kind of reality, then human beings are indeed very imperfect and primitive stages in a long haul up to a plateau where the factually existent is all that matters.

Human love then becomes retrogressively imperfect. Human freedom really amounts to uncontrolled actions. Human kindness is a fiction. Human aspirations are writs of illusion. What is good is what works, what performs, according to fixed norms. The spontaneous and the wild belong to another and earlier era of reality. Black is ugly, because it has not been factually successful. The striving for equality is meaningless, if genocide removes the need for it in fact. Morality, as we have hitherto known it disappears; for morality does not derive from any condition such as is encompassed by the seeable, measurable, factual reality. And it is only morality which dictates the choice we make among the facts—and even these are incomplete as yet—at our disposal.

If one feels embattled and threatened enough by the existence or even the possibility of another manner of knowledge and knowing to want to destroy belief in it, one can only engage in a massive tautology: "A non-factual order of reality cannot exist, if I cannot know it factually."

And, so, one may go into eternity biting one's tail in a self-defeating hurdy-gurdy of woeful repetitiveness. And in the world of full human knowledge, one has been a fool.

33. Knowing Spiritually

The second mode of knowing and of knowledge is by now almost unfit for modern language, because almost all the words and concepts at our disposal have by now been appropriated by subtle transformation to express exclusively factual knowing and knowledge. Thus appropriated have been, not only "knowing" and "knowledge," but "rational," "logical," "education," "information," "history," "realization," "reality," and any word or concept that expresses the relation and activity of our conscious selves to all other beings, objects, and things. Thus we speak of "mind," but the only respectable usage today implies the geography of brain areas, electrical circuits, and synaptic joinings. Any other use of such terms is called to account at the bar of factual reality; and inevitably it is thrown out of court for want of factual evidence, and it is presumed guilty of non-existence.

With the words and terms of reference appropriated and defined, on the one hand, by the disciplines of factual knowledge, the difficulty of talking about this spiritual knowing is furthered and heightened by the fact that any expression of it is confused with the thought and speech habits of men and women who lived at an earlier, less sophisticated and less developed period of history.

Human beings who regard themselves as progressive have categorized that thought and those speech habits as myth-making, mythological, mythic. They admire the beauty in them and are struck by their quaintness—but always with the knowing patience of an adult at the child's questioning daydreams and with a modern man's askance look at the ancients' agile and aery answers. Why does a star fall but a bird does not? Why does the moon change shape? Where does the wind come from? Because the star is a fallen angel. Because Reahou, the Sky Monster and evil brother of the Sun, devours the Moon. To the far north, a young god sleeps in a quiet cave and dreams of a beautiful girl. In his sleep, he breathes love to her, and Night kisses the sighs from his lips. Thus, the wind. There is not one humanism or religious system which, at least in its past, does not suffer from the admitted presence of such elements.

Yet a third difficulty arises from the cheapening, the vilification, and the disuse of words and terms formerly in vogue to express spiritual knowing. It is not that terms such as "spirit," "mind," "intuition," "soul," "essence," are not in use, but that in practical life we are embarrassed to concede to them any reality other than factual. Nevertheless, there is no other verbal means of talking about this second mode of knowing except by calling it spirit knowing and spirit knowledge. For thus we can conventionally express the fundamental presupposition of this mode of knowing. The presupposition is that there is an order of reality other than the factual. While the factual order is the order of all that is measurable or dimensional or quantifiable, this other is the order of what simply is and of what should be. To say that this latter order is "as real as" the order of factual reality is as impractical and as foolish as comparing apples and pears and as ridiculous as describing a circle as a square with its corners rounded off. But to say it is and that it should be, in order that the factual order of reality be human—rather than be an order of mere "things" and "objects"—this is to state the essence and the relationship of *both* the factual and the spiritual presuppositions.

It is thus that we judge an act of heroism or love or kindness.

And it is because of this presumed order that we sanction esthetic beauty as valid. Even if the factual searcher and knower arrives with exact measurements and descriptions to describe factually what happened at a specific moment in place, in time, in body, and in brain, we still spontaneously presume that, apart from any concrete result of an act of heroism (say, the saving of a drowning child), the heroic act has a certain value and a certain beauty; that we as humans have a faculty or an "inner eye" with which to recognize automatically that value and beauty; and that these belong to an order of reality that is and should be, in order that we humans be truly human. It is the same with esthetic beauty —shape, color, form, sound. Whatever grace and symmetry and winsomeness we perceive (and we do), these are again ranged in that same order of reality that is and should be. Again, human traits such as dignity, freedom, rights—regarded as innately human—are allocated to that same order of reality.

As there is no proof that the factual order is the only order, so there is no possible proof of this other order of reality. Yet we are firm in our presupposition that we can and we do know all these things, and that this knowledge is both knowledge of reality and human knowledge. We build our marriages, our associations, our political systems, and our sense of humanness on that knowledge. For what we commonly call human feeling is always accompanied by knowing. And all human knowing is accompanied by feeling. Both are an exercise of the spirit: whether we perceive the patterns traced in space by the feet of the dancer, or see the colors, location, and shape of mountains and landscapes, or hear the volume and rhythm and melody of music.

In each case, every element of what takes place before us is quantifiable; but its human meaning and its human effect lie beyond the pragmatic facts. We are not composed of two watertight compartments, one ticking with sensation wheels, the other ticking with thought cogs; each with connecting shutters and circuits. We are psycho-physical, but not after a washer-drier or mower-reaper model. We are one center or unit of knowing. It is I, myself, who know and feel; and the same self knows while it feels and feels while it knows. I am one. Nothing is in my feelings and not in my spirit. Nothing is in my spirit and not in my feelings. And what I know and feel gives me a spirit knowing of values, realities, and aims that have no dimensional representation.

Behind all these is the unacknowledged ground of all such values. Without that invisible ground of spirit reality in which all my human experiences are rooted, the most beautiful and attractive aspects of human life dissolve into gray clouds of nothingness, and factual reality becomes a jumbled graveyard of drabness resembling Irving Peltin's *Rubbings from a Calcium Garden*. That alternative is grim beyond our imagining and our desire; some take their lives rather than suffer its futility. And this is logical, if by some aberration I judge my life to be merely factual.

Delight in spirit knowing and knowledge is the delight at a presence which, we feel, completes us while remaining distinct from us. The discomfort in this mode of knowing is in the nature of being overawed. We have the definite sense of being completed in some deep and valuable part of ourselves, while we by definition remain incomplete when or if left to ourselves. Our balance, our sanity, our sense of ourselves, and our sense of factual reality are seen to hang by a simple thread—and to that extent to lie forever and by their nature under a real threat of extinction. This knowledge thus buffets us; and facts do not shield us from the buffeting. Life becomes a confirmed incompleteness. And death or extinction passes from the stage of possibility (factually, the direct human possibility) to that of accompanying actuality. Anciently, people described this discomfort as "humility." But the word no longer has much validity or vogue.

Once we experience spirit knowing and knowledge, we realize that factual knowing and knowledge, according to which the practical things of life are arranged, has not been and can never be the prime nourishment of our humanness. We only thought or imagined it could be. Nevertheless, the sense of incompleteness that accompanies this insight is not of the foreboding kind: it summons no monsters, does not suggest suicide as a way out (one does not desire a way out), and does not let us go into wayward fancies. It generates a small pool of awe. That pool is ever unruffled. It lies deep in the selves which more and more we daily become with this knowledge. Over the ever-present waters of that accepted awe there always hover our own unspoken whisperings of the human statement and question: "All that is, will never be again. And there go I, but for . . .?"

The pool of awe seems quite congenial to us. It is calm but liq-uid, ever-moving. Hence we are not stilled to inaction. It is not dark but luminous. Hence we are not bound up in darkness. It throws back a reflected light, but this does not explode, blinding us; for its exquisite reflections whirl inward not outward, and they convey lovely and delicate realizations. And sometime, somewhere, in our pursuit, we realize that the delicacy is from our loving dependence on a great love, and that the loveliness is really our state of being loved by unceasing love without which we would fall back into a nothingness we dread, and cease to be ourselves forever.

In comparison and in contrast, therefore, the two modes of knowledge and of reality complement each other in our human-ness. Factual knowledge and knowing leads us forever to human-ize all the things and objects we find in the real order of the di-mensional world. We presume that we are aliens until we make those things and objects ours; but, that accomplished, we then become alone with ourselves until confronted with the next alien object. And so it goes.

Spirit knowing and knowledge leads us to acknowledge, not that we are aliens until we make the alien objects and things our own, but that we are in an eternal duality which guarantees us to be ourselves both with and in spite of the alien objects and things of our universe of man. We, together with all men and women and things, are in a firm duality: we and the love that makes us and all things possible. Further, that there is no removing of that duality, except at the cost of undoing our humanness—something we are really incapable of doing or desiring. And, further still, that the "other" in this eternal duality in which we are bound has a continuing character, whereas we appear as the ones loved continually. As human beings, we are in the order of what is, what was, what will be; and all such beings go from the harmony of physicial existence to the disharmony of physical non-existence. This love, however, remains harmoniously. It is, we feel, and it should be. So that we be.

This harmony of what is and what should be in the order of the spirit is the essence of love. And all else: expectation, hope, embrace, enjoyment, recollection, are pendants of that harmony. There is, however, no immediate idea of obligation, ethical com-

mand, or moral structure in that "should be." It is an order of
reality and only secondarily an order of action.

This spirit knowing and knowledge is the first basic principle
of the Jesus Self. Without it, the Jesus Self cannot be. And with
the impossibility of the Jesus Self is born the despair of humans
and eventually the worse than useless character of mere factual
knowledge. Christians have translated both knowing and knowledge into a complete scheme of inner faculties and laws: soul,
mind, will, nature, virtues, vices, laws, commandments, precepts,
and so on. So have other men in other religions and systems.
Many others have mythologized and fabled in this area. But the
Christian translation, whatever be its errors and fables and myths,
is ultimately based on the change wrought in human affairs by
the Jesus Self. And this is the only guarantee Christians have that,
with all their myth-making and fabling, they have the truth.
Christians, in their right senses and apart from the self-indulgent
somersaults of philosophers and thinkers, have never claimed to
have a lien on reality. But they did claim to have the truth about
man and his universe of existence. For that truth does not concern what is in the factual order but what should be in the
human order and what is and should be in the order of the spirit,
so that the factual order in which we as humans live, be human.

34. The Universe

The second basic principle for the understanding of the Jesus Self concerns man's universe. Modern man's attitude to this second principle is tied to the heels of the dilemma that foils him in the question of the two kinds of knowing and of knowledge. According to the second principle, man's universe is not merely and exclusively one of material things. As a consequence, we as human beings do not and can never know what such a universe composed merely of material things would be like, or what the male and female human beings of such a universe would be like.

This second principle, tied as it is to the modern misconception concerning the nature of knowledge and knowing, is currently seen as being somehow in collision with a whole new venture of man whose parameters are defined now by his interplanetary exploration, his analysis of the material universe, his probing of man's genetics, and his formulary concept of man's place in the hierarchy of being in that universe.

But there is here no question of "angels," of "spirits," of "souls," of "underworlds," of preternatural forces, or of supernatural presences. It is rather that in this universe, each man and woman embodies a non-human element, and that the presence of this non-human element has changed the nature and the role of man in that universe and of his relations and interactions with all the material universe. This non-human element is not here in the way in which we speak of the addition of an artificial limb, and not as Christians and others have spoken about the "soul" or the "spirit" or "supernatural grace" in men. It is non-human compared to the "soul" or the "spirit" of which people speak; and it is in no way supernatural or preternatural. It is not as removable as that artificial limb. In the idea of the Jesus Self, each man and woman is, by the fact of existing, a living soul, as are, indeed, all insects and animals living souls. As in Judaism, and in the explicit doctrine of the Jewish Bible, between man and animals, in this respect, there is only a difference of gradation. It is, after all, more "advanced" or in a "higher order of life," as both modern anthropologist and ancient Jewish writer would agree, to be a chimpanzee than a crab. "We are highly developed biologisms," states the evolutionary biologist. Men and women have, besides the difference in gradation between themselves and animals, something else specific only to them. This is the non-human element of men.

The non-human element is more difficult to describe than, say, the "emptiness" of a cup. If the cup is really empty of liquid, this means two things: the cup contains no liquid; and the walls of the cup are so made and disposed as to be able to contain liquid. Nobody is going to pretend that we can take the emptiness and balance it in our hand separately from the cup. But where the cup is, there you have an empty space ready to receive liquid. That empty space constitutes the capacity of the cup. It is the cupness of the cup. But at this early point in the comparison, the image of the cup ceases to be useful as an image of the non-human element in man. For the emptiness of the cup is formed by the material walls of the cup; whereas the non-human element, a *capacity* of man, is not formed by any material walls or by any material constituent of man.

The Jesus Self is the result of a disposing action affecting the very constituents of man. As a living being, man now has an inherent disposition to receive what is non-human. It is non-human because it makes us capable of what is not human: eternal, undying, and infinite love. It is also non-human because no human agency or force could develop it. Only an infinite love could produce it and, on its basis, the Jesus Self of each man. For the Jesus Self is a direct result of an intrusion and an intervention in human things by an order of reality that has no necessary connection with this universe and no automatic place within the habitat of man. It is because of this disposition of man himself, that he can never be equated on all points with any form of animal life known to us.

Our difficulty in understanding and expressing this non-human element is multiple. *First*, we cannot know the constituent parts of the soul after a factual manner, for they are not part of factual reality. In fact, to call them constituent parts is to speak in a factual way of what is non-factual, of what is spiritual. But we have no other way of speaking or, rather, of indicating a reality which forever eludes all phenomenal description. *Second*, in the present historical order of things, human beings are not born without that non-human element; we have never known man or woman without this non-human element. Hence we have nothing to compare with it—except animals. And in the case of animals, no matter what their similarity to man, there is always a mysterious breakpoint, a point of no return where animal ceases and man begins. *Third*, just as spirit knowing and knowledge is unmeasurable and unquantifiable, so is this non-human element. And it could not be otherwise. For, as far as we can judge, spirit knowing and knowledge is possible precisely and only because of this non-human element in us as men and women.

On account of this capacity, men and women can move in the two intertwined orders of reality: factual existence and spirit existence; the two orders of what is in a factual manner and of what is and should be spiritually. And it is on account of that capacity that any prolonged attempt to reduce man to the ability to move merely in the factual order ignites within him a severe sense of dislocation and disharmony.

It has been fashionable among Christians for many centuries to divide a man or a woman into animal parts and man (or woman) parts. Man, as a general term to cover both males and females, was defined for us as "rational animal." This, it was stated, was his nature. An entire theology and philosophy of "natural" man was built up, without any human being ever having a shred of objective thought as to what man in this "natural" state would be

like. The god of Christians was then pictured as making an offering, a "deal," to "natural" man: "You do this, okay? And I'll do
that, okay? You don't eat those apples, and I'll make you tremen-
dously happy forever." The Deal. Naughty man, "Adam and
Eve," that miserable primal couple, would go and eat that apple.
Original Sin! God's plans were in fragments. What to do? God
decides to tack on something to man: supernature, the supernatural. Hence Jesus, God's son, jumps into human time and space
from "eternity," dies on a cross, thus satisfying God's anger and
offended honor, and "winning" the supernature for "natural"
man. Jesus then jumps out of human time and space back into
"eternity." Hence the Church, the Churches, the Sacraments, the
Commandments, Hell and Heaven.

Teilhard de Chardin saw the difficulty vitiating this long pre-
Semitic rigmarole; so he took off on another line of thought
based on his paleontological and biological studies. Actually, he
said, we have been mistaken about the function that Jesus exercised: repairer of fragments, putter-together of an originally beautiful plan. Jesus, de Chardin said, evolves to his supreme cosmic
role through successive stages of human evolution starting from
the very unconscious consciousness (sic!) of an amoeba in the bi-
osphere, right up past the conscious glories of *Homo sapiens*, on
to the noosphere, up, up, up, to the Omega Point, the culmination where Jesus, fully garbed as the crowning of the human universe, appears as the final pitch, the summary incarnation of its
naturally ordained evolution.

Chardin said all this with love of Jesus of Nazareth, but to the
terrible detriment of that same Jesus and of the Jesus Self. For in
rightly criticizing the idea of the "supernature" tacked on to the
"nature" of man, he unwittingly but nonetheless successfully in
terms of logic made Jesus only man; and, worse still, but logically
once he took that first step, he assumed that spirit knowing and
knowledge would belong to man and woman whether or no
there was a Jesus, a salvation, or a Jesus Self. He turned all history into a process of phenomena. He made the human reality we
see and touch and measure and use throughout our universe into
the truth of all our being and into the truth of all that universe.

For the Jesus Self, however, *that* reality is not the truth, but
the material and physical setting of the truth. For Chardin, Jesus

Omega Point became as necessary as the moss on stones, the boiling of water at 100 degrees centigrade, the stream of blood in a bullet wound, and the rising and falling of winter tides. Chardin guessed, as through a glass darkly, that this human universe was not merely human. But he confused the setting of that not-merely-human universe with the truth of the unceasing love which originally disposed the stones and earth and bones and flesh and spirit of that universe to be the setting for the Jesus Self. In that fatal confusion, he tied man again to the bondage of which the Jesus Self is uniquely freed.

A similar but more strident reproach has to be laid against the proselytizing proponents of the evolutionary theory, beginning with Charles Darwin, who gave it the first systematic formulation. Evolutionists presume that all we see and can find in the universe of being, including man and woman, is a product of innate evolutionary laws within the environment of the universe of matter. In the case of man, the theory is so precarious that it must rely on a completely theological, not a scientific, process for its anchor, while at the same time claiming validity in scientific terms.

True enough, we find within species a certain progress in forms from one to the other. But at that early and inconclusive stage, the evidence as such for evolution ends. We have no scientific evidence that any forms evolved from one species or family to another species or family. We have, in other words, no transitional forms, no definite links, no evidence that the human frame as we know it came from animal forms we know by transitioning through still other forms we know. There is merely a belief ardently held by some scientists and a plea that we too believe at a crucial point where we have a right, by requirement of science itself, to ask for visible, measurable evidence.

However, the alternative for Darwin and for evolutionists is to admit that a god created man specially. And, because of a poverty of mind which provided no other alternatives, their "anti-theology" forbade them to admit this in any shape or form—even as equal to the possibility of the "missing link" theory. The "anti-theology" presupposed that there is no god to do such creating. As more than one eminent scientist of the time recognized (D. M. S. Watson, Alister Hardy, Albert Seward, for example) with equal parts of candor and satifaction, evolution was the right theory (and theory it remains) at the right time in order to give a much-sought foundation to this theological principle of negative value.

The insistence and one-sided decision in this matter was understandable within the Christian climate of the 19th century. For the alternative of a god specially creating man came garbed in the ridiculous and childish myths of the Jewish Bible: six days of creation, one day of rest for a tired god, bodies rising from the slime, serpents talking, and the fate of the universe hanging on the appetite of a proto-female for fresh apples. It was already too much, when, into the bargain, the idea of a special creation of man was proposed by a dogmatic Church, together with a whole farrago of unbearable nonsense concerning human life and laminated over with civilizational veneers and cultural prejudices and bias. It was the breaking point; evolution, with its mask of reason, stooped to pick up the pieces and deposit them in its bag of tricks.

The whole climate of discussion has changed since that day. One would have to be blind not to recognize that the very fear of falling beneath the control of error-ridden minds and age-old myths leaves us prey to errors just as deep and myths that are merely newer: interpreting all that is human in this universe in the light of a supposed evolution and by analogy with animals which we are to regard as our forebears and in whose hunting, eating, and mating habits, we are to search for the keys of the human heart.

The Jesus Self, an old and constituent factor in the universe, can have none of all this. That universe has been adapted from its beginnings for the Jesus Self, the ground and basis of its humanness.

35. Human Being

The third basic principle of the Jesus Self concerns the meaning of human living and of life. The word "life" is used today either as a general term (as in "All life ceases on the planet") or as a visible characteristic of some organism (as in "The signs of life still appear in the mugger's victim who lies comatose in the hospital"). In both cases, life is assessed by means of actions and by physically continuous and pulsating states.

To say that a human being is a Jesus Self implies that the human being, as distinct from all other beings, has an invisible, intangible, non-quantifiable life which is a continuous state; that there are signs and actions appropriate and proper to that life; that, as in physical life, there are outside influences, good and bad; that the continuous state, the actions, and the influences of this life are all as invisible, intangible, and unquantifiable as this life itself.

Furthermore, individual man is not conscious of his inner life in the same way that he is conscious of his bodily sensations and mental states; but just as for physical life, there are visible signs, results, and effects of this inner life, both for the individual in his own consciousness and exteriorly for those around him. This inner life has a history all its own, from the birth of each individual onward. The inner life does not cease with his physical dissolution and death. Human beings, as a collectivity, have also got a history of interconnection, influence, interpenetration, diminution, augmentation, homogenization, and differentiation, which began with the first human individuals and will last beyond the physical disappearance from the universe of the last group of human individuals.

Now, all this can be too much, definitely too much, for our modern mind. It can be too much because it could be both too good and too bad. Too good: because, if true, it means that we are loved by a love which will never desert us and never let us cease to be. Men and women yearn for such a love, but find it very difficult to believe it possible. Too bad: because, if it is not true, to propose it is to propose a hoax more cruel than the South Sea Bubble and more inhuman than the Nazi trick of promising their intended victims cleansing and purifying showers in order to herd them to their death in gas chambers. Too bad, also: because, if it is not true, those who have been "good" have been "good" in vain; those in human history who have been cruel and selfish and murderous and grasping and domineering and robbing and victimizing, those were the wise, the successful ones, the praiseworthy ones, the enviable ones. "If there is a God," said Pope Urban VIII in December 1642 on hearing of Cardinal Richelieu's death, "the Cardinal has a lot to answer for. But if there is no God, why, the Cardinal has had a very successful life." Everyone who would control men for their own good, from Pharaoh Akhenaton in the 14th century B.C. to Adolf Hitler in the 20th century, would then be as "right" as any of the rest of us. The very basis of the concepts of dignity and equality evaporate.

Modern paleontology and anthropology, which are charged with the study of certain factual elements of man's history, are often used to turn the Jesus configuration of the human being into unintelligible nonsense. According to that configuration, a change has been operated in the species of man: a non-human element differentiates it from all other species possible or actual in the past, present, or future of this universe; and by its very nature, this element will not be found in the fossil record. Now, in the proper parlance of anthropologists and paleontologists, that

species is described as *Homo sapiens*. The reality to which we
refer by that proper parlance (not to be outdone by any old
Church Latin tag) is imagined to be of an order whose origins,
development, and essence can and will be revealed in the factual
order; and that being the case, we are told that we can reliably
suppose a priori the full scope of those origins, of that development, of that essence. An open and shut case, then. A sanctioned
tautology.

In the Jesus configuration, the truth of the reality is hidden
from us as anthropologists and paleontologists. The real traits
which we label anthropologically and paleontologically as those
of *Homo sapiens* are exterior ones in the observable order of
physical phenomena. They are merely the results of the deep
change operated in a physical species by the introduction of the
non-human element, in order to produce a new dimension in the
human being. In other words, all men alive, and all men who
ever lived, and all who shall ever live, were, are, and will be men
in virtue of Jesus. For according to Christians, Jesus, who once
lived in time and space, is not of time and space as human beings
are. But the humanness of all beings in the universe is a direct result of Jesus having once entered that universe, thus shattering
forever the bondage to which all other things, living and non-
living, are constrained.

This means that the human race is more than a mere collection
of individual men, but that this term "more" does not imply that
they all compose one big, invisible, and mystical blob; or, much
less, that the "human race" as such is gripped by a communal instinct, or that a tribal unity binds them together much as tribes of
monkeys and chimpanzees, herds of elephants, flocks of geese,
schools of whales, or colonies of ants are bound by a specific
unity in the physical order. It thus means that the humanness of
men reposes primarily in an order of what spiritually is and what
spiritually should be, and that this order of existence is as humanly essential as the order of what is visibly and factually.

It means that a member of the human race is not a cipher
among many other ciphers, not one of the millions of waves that
rise and fall on the human shore, and not just one of an indistin-
guishable series stretching on without end and without particu-
larity, a reproduction with due variations of its fellows, one of a

series of red pennies stamped with the same year, or an ant like any other ant. It means that he is not the product of a blind, impersonal, unconscious, and automatic force or thrust in physical nature, nor, like the animals, is he confined and limited in potential, in taste, in hope, in aspiration, in outlook.

All of this remains true even in the midst of unprecedented efforts to shatter man's sense of his dignity. Our modern research has begun to dance some very colorful steps on the fringes of science in the effort to homogenize man with matter and with matter only. A professor of physics, Philip Morrison at the Massachusetts Institute of Technology, has proposed that in the future we should recognize five forms of life: human life; animal life; plant life; life in the test tube created by biologists using off-the-shelf chemicals, living organisms on other planets; and a form of machine life which will be the outgrowth of today's computer science.

The fact is that today the essentials of life are held to be physical functions and not physical forms. If wires, magnets, and transistors can be induced by scientific technology to function in ways analogous to the function of protoplasm and nerve fibers, are they not just as much alive as human beings who reproduce the same functions? The question, of course, presupposes its answer by presupposing that human life (as well as all life) consists of functions. Once we start with that self-serving definition of life, the conclusion is inevitable.

As the experts go on to point out, the beauty of machine life is that it has no need for the complications, the weaknesses, and the mortality of proteins, fats, and carbohydrates. Dr. Morrison, of course, assumes that the attainment of such life has been the object of all ancient traditions. "I think it is fair to say," he commented, "that there is no theme in intellectual life so persistent as the theme of the mechanical reproduction of life and the effort to reflect the cosmic motions." This sounds fair enough for those who know nothing about the intellectual tradition of man. But it is about as accurate as stating that Leonardo da Vinci really planned to become a bird or that Galileo really wished to become one of the moons orbiting around Saturn. It is unbelievable ignorance.

The erroneous view of man inculcated by such total and unprecedented ignorance on the part of an "intellectual" is the "cruelest cut of all." In such an opinion, a human being is always a version of a puppet show: wandering in the cobwebbed rooms of individual meaninglessness, straining up the stepladder of his memory to retain or attain echoes of value and hints of meaning, or stock-still in the storeroom of the mind fascinated by fresh-gilt mental formulas and infatuated with the symbols, the signs, and the labels he places on reality around him. In none of the above does the title human being possess an innate attribute of dignity, nor is a human being proclaimed to be of value in its individual humanness, except for the elite, the chosen ones, those human beings specially marked. But an elite only emphasizes the degradation of all others, the Lumpenproletariat of human society. There is always a bitter note, the tone of regret: that human spells mortal; that mortal spells weakness; that this weakness spells out the inconsequential character of the human being caught in the toils of billions and lost in the teeming flow of never-ending life and death and life.

36. Time and Space

The fourth basic principle of the Jesus Self concerns time and space. It is in time and in space that modern man's most ambitious achievements have taken successful form. He has telescoped both of them for traveling and for communication. In a certain definite and true sense, we have merely begun to conquer time and space and to begin the long road of redefining them in the terms of man. For hitherto time and space, like so many other dimensions of man's environment in the universe, have imposed their limits and their rule on man. Disease once did the same on a universal scale. Hunger once did the same. The waters of the oceans once did the same. Time and space still limit man but much less than ever before. The prospect is that man will eventually subjugate time and space, too, thus expanding his horizons and his possibilities.

All these new conquests are not only compatible with the spirit; in the Jesus configuration of the human self, they are results of the spirit's activity. Nevertheless, the activity and life of the spirit is frequently confused with merely physical domination, partial or whole, of physical conditions. This is particularly the danger as regards time and space; and the danger reposes ultimately on confused ideas about the spirit in relation to time and space.

There is nothing in the life of the spirit that corresponds to the point-by-point process of time, nor is there anything in the spirit that reproduces the sweep and stretch and endless extent of space. Time and space are coordinates of material things. While the time process shuffles or races onward, the spirit merely becomes. And while space extends onward wherever we turn our face and direct our steps, the spirit subsists in its becoming.

While what is spirit becomes and subsists in total independence of time and space, it can enter into a relationship with time and space. But such a relationship does not make the spirit dependent on time and space. And our language here must be carefully chosen. Only a human and convenient mode of speech allows us to state that the spirit is *in* time and space. For, thus, men have said that the "soul" or "spirit" is *in* the body or *in* man, or that "Jesus is *in* the Eucharist," or that "God is *in* this world." Strictly speaking, of course, this is impossible. An object is in a physical location or place when its physical dimensions are applied to the material dimensions of the location. But the spirit has no material dimensions. In fact, it cannot be somewhere or anywhere, for "somewhere" and "anywhere" imply a physical location and relationship to material things. And, by the same token, spirit is not nowhere. For if anything is said to be nowhere, this implies both that it does not exist and that, if it did exist, it would be somewhere. *Where* is not an essential coordinate of the spirit. Spirit becomes and subsists, not in function of material coordinates, but wholly and solely in itself.

Jesus in time and space was not, therefore, an expert jumper from the spaceship of eternity onto the vehicle of time, and back again to eternity. Crudely put, he could not, because "eternity" is not a spaceship cruising through space parallel to the planet Earth and within the coordinates of a time parallel to the time process of Earth. Anyway, there was no need to do such jumping. Nor will there ever be a need to do so. His relationship to time and space was always of one order: that of spirit to matter which it dominates.

For the years of his human life within time and space, his relationship was of a particular kind: that of a human being born, living, and dying. But there never will be a point in time and space when he renews or must renew that particular relationship. We can state all this in factual terms of conception, birth from a human mother, and death and disappearance—all three are historically attested as solidly as the conception, birth, and death of any ancient figure before or after him.

But having said only that, we have not, in the Christian configuration, said anything of what is central and essential to Jesus. For, in this recitation of solely factual reality, we mirror him as just another man. And, as such, he supplies nothing to other men. He merely swells the ranks of mortals.

The point about the birth, life, and death of Jesus *in* time and space is far more revolutionary. As a human being, he had the same non-human element in his make-up as all other human beings ever born. In all the latter, the non-human element established the peculiar characteristic of the human bondage. For, because of the non-human element, every human being who is by *his* nature inescapably locked into material dimensions and into a destiny within a material universe, is *capable* of the spirit and of a destiny which exceeds the material universe.

From this human bondage there is no other escape. And this is the poignancy of the human situation. To desire the infinite but not to be capable of attaining it. To aspire to live forever but to have no hope of living forever. To drink in every drop of beauty in form and sound and taste and touch and sight, and, simultaneously, at each sip to know it was only a sip and that the whole draught of beauty could never be drunk. To be capable of doing ill but to know it always as the negation of what one acknowledges. To be capable of doing good, but in the doing to see it as a reflection of a total good not attained by merely doing good. To be one in dizzying diversity, and singly to be completely diverse in a felt unity. To be aware that the most differing expressions of human excellence all belong to one excellence, but to find all efforts at attaining that one excellence frustrated, vain, futile, and marked by human evil. To be able only transitionally to taste the ecstasy of being united while remaining distinct and not to have even an afterglow of that ecstasy but only a memory. All these are the traits of human behavior and human experience made possible and inevitable by the non-human ele-

ment, the spirit of man. It is a bondage, because humans know instinctively that they have no exit from it.

The achievement of Jesus in time and space was to make that
exit possible. Jesus effected this by entry into the human dimension of time and space, but not as any other man or woman enters it. Before that entry he subsisted in an order of being which
by the same token is an order of truth, of beauty, and of power.
But that beauty and truth and power are subsistent in a being
which knows no change and undergoes no evolution. Humanly,
we have neither words nor concepts to express all this. And we
would not have any surety that it existed and subsisted, unless
Jesus had provided us with the necessary guarantees. His entry
into human existence and his actions within it were neither symbolic nor meant merely as examples nor intended merely as moral
pointers. Entry, human existence, and actions right up to his passing from that existence were effective, had concrete effects, in the
universe of human beings. It is this complex of concrete effects
Jesus caused which we call the Jesus Self. They are to be found
within the human dimension of each human individual.

Still, the listing of the effects of Jesus' achievements is only
part of the description of the Jesus Self. There is a further refinement of Jesus' presence in time and space which must be noted.
Again, it is not perceptible for the merely factually knowing
mind of today. While within time and space, Jesus acted as any
normal man: he ate, drank, slept, walked, worked, sweated,
pained, talked, listened, looked, lived days and nights and months
and years; finally, he died and was buried. All these are the factually determinable actions and the effects of his actions. As such,
these actions and effects were limited by time and space: he spoke
once to a woman in Samaria, near a well. It was, and it is done,
over, and finished with forever. Once and only once, he drew a
last breath, his blood ceased to circulate, his brain cleared of all
oxygen, his heart stopped, he was dead. It was, and is done, over,
and finished with forever. For, whatever else Jesus was, he was
also just like any other man. His life as man was in every detail
lived and concluded within a time span and within various locations in human space.

The refinement in Jesus' case of this human condition was that
only certain of his actions and the effects of those actions belong

to the above class. All his processes of digestion, secretion, elimination, and the automatic reflexes of his psycho-physical structure—these were just the same as in any other man or woman.

Side by side with these were voluntary actions which, though performed in time and space, had, as products of his thought and will, the force, the quality, and the significance which were not of time and space. The same was true of the effects of such actions. If he decided to walk to the well at Samaria, to go up to Jerusalem, to help a diseased man or woman, to preach, to do what in human calculation would surely bring on suffering and death, these voluntary actions and their effects were simultaneously of and not of the order of reality within time and space.

We cannot say that this non-time and non-space character of his actions and their effects was "outside space" or "beyond" (or "before" or "after") any time span. All these terms imply a relation to time and space. And there was no such relationship. The refinement gets still more intangible and volatilized for our minds when we remind ourselves that we cannot describe the force, quality, and significance of these actions by any word implying a time span. Strictly speaking, "was," "is," "will be," "did," "done," "will do," "had," "has," "will have," are not applicable. His actions are not trans-time or trans-space, or supra-time or supra-space. The only relation to time and space could be that of cause and effect: they produced effects in time and space. His actions in their force, quality, and significance are the non-time and non-space causes of certain willed effects which are located in time and within space.

In much of Christian thought and language, Jesus is pictured as having been born once and having died once (both of which are true); and he is represented as a sort of marvelous spiritual lighthouse with beams of healing, saving grace flashing in two directions simultaneously: backward to all the dead generations of men and forward to all the as-yet-unborn generations. The already dead were to be judged by their expectation of a redeemer. All the future about-to-be-born generations were to be judged by their reactions to that complex past event: Jesus of Nazareth. But this is a traditional Jewish concept and way of language which has no place in accurate and correct descriptions and expressions of Jesus and his accomplishments. Such a concept of Jesus depends on a concept of time, of man's world, and the universe of human being, and it springs from cultural presuppositions which are not valid or objective. It is a fatal borrowing that has helped to obscure the full truth. The salvation Jesus effected and the Jesus Self he made possible for men cannot be described in any such framework.

37. Salvation

It is commonly said by Christians that Jesus achieved all men's salvation by dying on Calvary, that he set up a special memorial service of that salvation during the last meal he took with his followers the night before Calvary, and that to clinch it all, he was buried as truly dead, rose again from the dead three days afterward, and was seen and touched by his followers. Death on the Cross. The Last Supper. Resurrection. The three "moments" of Christian salvation.

This salvation can be thought about and verbalized only within a time-and-space framework. It is true to say that the marriage ceremony of two people, their act of love, and the conception and birth of their child are several "moments" of their love. But even within the time-and-space framework of their lives, they look on their love as one thing and on those "moments" as explications of that love. Thus one must think of the salvation effected by Jesus. In itself, it was one act with one effect. Jesus did perform certain actions in time and space: eating, blessing, suffering, dying, rising. Yet all these actions were material expressions of a salvation which in its essence does not and cannot depend on either time or space. The significance and value of that salvation lie only in the non-time and non-space character of these actions and their effects. How this salvation is related to humans living in time and space cannot be explained logically and factually. But we can say what that relationship is not.

Jesus is not miniaturized (as, roughly speaking, we miniaturize radio circuits) in the Bread or in the Wine of the Eucharist; nor are Bread and Wine mere symbols like the Lincoln Memorial in Washington or the Sphinx of Egypt. "If I believed they were mere symbols, I'd say the hell with it," said Flannery O'Connor.

Jesus was not the object of God's anger and punishment on Calvary; but he truly suffered and died; and in themselves his pain and death were just as ugly and depressing as any man's pain and death. When he lived again, this did not take place because his heart started once more to beat, the cold blood was warm again, his brain received oxygen, the whole cadaveric chemistry of his body was reversed back to that of a breathing organism, his eyes opened, his vision focused, his ears heard, his limbs moved, and he stood up. This is not what happened, because all that is mythic, makes no biological or medical sense, and is what happens to Frankenstein's monster and Count Dracula at midnight in eerie Transylvanian castles beneath the whispering of the devil bat's wings.

Briefly, Jesus performed no disappearing and reappearing Indian rope trick, nor did he leave behind institutions for "sacred bread patties" or for ritual drinking of the "cup of fellowship." Whenever the "rite of his sacrifice," as Christians have called it, is performed duly and authentically, Jesus is not crucified again and does not die again; the priest is neither Jesus nor Jesus' ritual executioner. When Christians partake of the Bread and Wine, they are obeying the injunction of Jesus to do so. But they are not engaged in a mime of the Last Supper or perpetuating a marvelous Miracle Play, or celebrating the fellowship of man, or engaged in any cannibalistic or anthropophagic act such as we find to have been in vogue among the Huron Indians or the head-hunters of Borneo. And in no part of Christianity, since its beginnings, do we find any logical explanation or verbal formulas which will in any way cohere with the factual way in which our modern minds think and the way we conceive reality to be exclusively of the physically factual order.

The act of partaking in the Christian communion rite unites

the participant with Jesus. But this union and Jesus' act of salvation and each person's identity as a Jesus Self are not intelligible in the terms of factual knowledge. Apart from the ambit of factual knowing and knowledge, the spirit in any man and woman can know and accept Jesus, his salvation, and the Jesus Self. That salvation contains all that the human spirit needs but of itself cannot have. Under two headings we can describe this need.

First, since that salvation was effected, the human condition of conception, birth, living, breathing, growing, and dying have received a value and significance which would be otherwise inaccessible and impossible. This value and significance cannot be measured or quantified. We have only analogies to indicate them, much as in human hero-worship men and women adopt the wearing of clothes or the use of accents which the hero wears and uses. "Because Jesus was in our human condition, we are like him." For by merely being human and living even for a brief period of time in human space, Jesus introduced into the universe of human being some power and quality and significance for which we have neither words nor concepts. The specific effect of this power and quality and significance lies in the area of man's moral and ethical being, his attitude and reaction to the order of what should be.

Christians have traditionally expressed all this in terms of "original sin," presence or absence of "grace" in the "soul," "morally bad" and "morally good" actions, and "winning" of "eternal salvation" and of "Heaven," the "forgiveness of sins" because of the supreme sacrifice of Jesus, the "damnation" of those who die with "sins" on their "souls." In our factual-minded world of today, most of these and similar terms are either ignored or explained away. Yet, in man's knowing and knowledge of the spirit, there is no diminution of their force insofar as they are labels and tags invented and used to express realities in the order of the spirit which are inaccessible to factual knowledge and knowing.

The second heading under which man's need can be told concerns what we call nowadays the personalism of Jesus. The effects of Jesus' actions in the universe of human being are of the spirit. But this is not an impersonal and unconscious thing; it was based by Jesus on himself, and in a way that could not have been more personal.

That personalism made all the difference between appeals to be "good" because it is "good" to be "good," on the one hand, and direct commendations from one being to another, commendations based on the age-old and humanly irreducible appeal: "because I ask you to do so." It is this supreme first-personalism which characterized the Jesus interpretation of human behavior.

"The treatment which you do not like for yourself, you must not hand out to others," admonishes Confucius in the *Chung Yung*. But a man can always ask: Why not? If I am strong enough and the others are weaker, what do I lose? "Do to others as you would have them do to you," Jesus said. Why? "Whatever you do to them, you do to me"

In the Buddhist *Agni Purana*, we are told: "Even a small cup of water presented to the parched lips of man out of a heartfelt sympathy, brings immortal merit to the offerer." Supposing I do not feel heartfelt sympathy? Why should I feel sympathy to that point? "Whoever gives a cup of cold water even in the name of a disciple of mine, will not lose his reward," Jesus affirmed.

"Promote general welfare and remove evil," Confucianist Mo Tzu advised, because all men are good. "In my name," adds Jesus firmly.

The aging Diotima in Plato's *Symposium* says that lovers of the "good" will cut off their own hands and feet and cast them away if these are "evil." Why? she asks rhetorically. Because they love the "good." Jesus personalizes: If your foot or your hand or your eye is evil, cut it off or pluck it out and cast it away. Why? because it is better for you one-footed, one-handed, or one-eyed, to enjoy me, Jesus, in the Heaven I have won for you, than to rot in Hell for eternity without me, Jesus, but with your feet, hands, and two eyes.

The emphasis throughout is personalistic. Jesus himself is the only motive sufficient and necessary. Other motives can help but are not necessary or required. Thus Jesus confirms our own personal salvation, not a vague and general attainment of eternal safety.

This is the complex of salvation in Jesus with all its factual unintelligibility and in all its irreducible starkness. That unintelligibility is patent. But its irreducibility is the more striking of the two. For all men and women, past, present, and future, the value and significance of being merely human (apart from any "salvation") and the possibility of being "saved" depend exclusively on Jesus. To state this irreducibility is to state the specific vulnerability particular to Christianity in our modern world. For it lies there as a hard lump indigestible by human logic and unassimilable by human factual knowing.

This is the tough kernel of the "Jesus thing," the hard, unbreakable core of the "fact" of Jesus. The unchangeable. The unmalleable. The consummate stumbling block for Jews. The summary cause of folly for all others. The property of no man. The appropriate mark of all men. The only thing no man can get rid of. It sticks in the mind like an object which cannot be dissected, like something we cannot digest, secrete, or assimilate to our natural beings. It is unassimilable to anything human because it is non-human, as we configure the human order of things. But it cannot thereby be dismissed and forgotten or even momentarily ignored in man's history, because it is not inhuman; it wards off what is inhuman, rejects all efforts to attain a trans-human state as superstitious and all ambition of being super-human as fictional pride. It sticks there and refuses to budge. Whether we like it or not, it will not be expelled, can be neglected but not repulsed, and will not pass from the human scene.

It cannot be gainsaid, parleyed with, segregated, colored, explained, or explained away. It suffers no discussion, hears no protest, listens to no argument, eschews human logic—but it completes human desire, converts human lust to blessed passion, makes a kiss more than incitement, gives meaning to physical fever, and prolongs our momentary ecstasy into an abiding silence of quiet glory. It cannot be mitigated or mollified or softened. It is irredentist and intractable. It demands to be taken on its own terms, has no ambassadors, mediators, messengers, surrogates, or substitutes. It will not allow compromises. It will not diminish its color or bend its strength or curry favor, or phase into a third thing or suffer decline, or allow entombment within sacred memory or be clothed in the garments of another. It will bear no masks or disguises or make-up. It brooks no rivals. It admits no equals. It will not take half. Will share man with no one else, with no idea, ideal, ideology, or ism. It suffers no cavil, no finessing, no raffeening of its meaning, no nice balancing between a this and a that, between perhaps so and perhaps not, between probably plus but perhaps minus, between some positive and some negative. There is no equilibrium in it, no seesawing between pleasant and neutral alternatives, no subtle shifting of emphasis to suit the moment, no catering to a mood. It looks askance at fashion, regards vogue as transitory and fad as a habit which might be possible in another order of being but not in the actual order of human being in our universe.

It can choke all man's efforts. It can be choked in its own efforts. It can kill simply by being neglected. It gives life merely by being accepted. But in that accepting, it underwrites man and woman and child and fetus and old and young and sick and diseased and black and white and red and yellow and the live and the dead, all as children of love and destined denizens of one eternal house of happiness. It is man's writ of destiny in function of which he was, is, and shall be. It suffers his hate, even when he brooks no sufferance. It is the proof that he will die in time. It is the guarantee that he will live forever. It is the cause of the Nietzschean nightmare, because it means that man can never be a god; and it is the reason why all suicide is futile, because it means that any effort to destroy one's humanness is an assertion of it. It makes any human death more than death, and any single human life something pathetically less than life itself.

It is the deeply engraven letter on the rock of our individual existence, and it cannot be effaced. It is not debatable, will not be caged by dialogues and councils and agreements and understandings. It cannot be confined by formulas or comprised in conventions or cabined in carefully constructed contracts. It makes a man possible as man because of a woman; and makes the impossible in a woman possible because, although God created man, woman is of the earth, of creation, and of human hope. It enables a man to love a woman today more tenderly than he did yesterday but less deeply than he can hope to love her tomorrow. And when he loses his love in death, it makes his memory not a scented tomb but a living flower fragrancing his days and lulling his nights. It makes one man companion to another as brother, as sister, as fellow. It ennobles his loneliness, elevating it with a substance of hope for future togetherness. And if he is alone, it shines so luminously in the darkness that he is never less alone than when alone. It demands his full attention, but will not allow him to fragment its unity in his weakness; because, when all has been separated in his logic and thought, it reappears to his heart and inner vision as a marvelous coherence of one in all and all in one.

It tortures man by never allowing him to forget he could be better. It consoles him by continually showing that he would be less but for it. It remains there as his sign of life and his warranty of humanness. It reminds his murderers that it was a man they killed. It tells the rapist that it was a woman he soiled, the child corrupter that he hurt human innocence itself, the liar that he deceived another man. It does not allow a man to pass by the sick or the wounded or the maimed without averting his eyes. It will not permit him to pass by a dead body without seeing his own mortality. It leaves him no excuse to be indifferent, tells him that his supposed neutrality is cowardice, his retreat from taking positions is in itself the taking of a very definite position. It allows him to be cold at another's suffering but only by paying a price, and to do injustice only on condition of being harshly judged and condemned in himself by himself. It allows him to think of death as nothingness and the ending of his life as the entry into complete negation, provided he conceives that nothingness as something and thinks of that negation as a positive absence. For he cannot even imagine nothing, but always sees it as something like nothing he ever saw or knew or heard. It does not indulge man in this way, as animals are indulged. It does not favor him with insensibility as the stones and stars. It does not allow him to die, as all other living things, without the knowledge of mercy and without the flutter of human hope. This is the "fact" of Jesus and the human assertion of his salvation for all men and women.

About the Author

Malachi Martin, a former Jesuit professor at the Pontifical Biblical Institute in Rome, was trained in theology at Louvain, specializing in the Dead Sea Scrolls and intertestamentary studies. He received his doctorate in Semitic languages, archeology, and Oriental history. He subsequently studied at Oxford and at the Hebrew University, concentrating on knowledge of Jesus as transmitted in Jewish and Islamic sources. He maintained personal scholarly contact with several of the men whose thought has profoundly influenced the direction of modern life dealt with so intimately in these pages: men such as Chardin, Piaget, and others. Now an American citizen and a New Yorker, Dr. Martin is the author of *Three Popes and the Cardinal, The Encounter, The Scribal Character of the Dead Sea Scrolls* and *The Pilgrim,* and numerous articles for magazines and journals.